THE MEMOIRS
OF HENRY HETH

Edited by James L. Morrison, Jr.

Contributions in Military History, Number 6

Greenwood Press
Westport, Connecticut   •   London, England

Library of Congress Cataloging in Publication Data

Heth, Henry, 1825-1899.
    The memoirs of Henry Heth.

    (Contributions in military history, no. 6)
    Bibliography: p.
    1. Heth, Henry, 1825-1899. 2. United States—
History—Civil War—Personal narratives—Confederate
side. 1. Morrison, James L., 1923-   ed.
II. Title. III. Series.
E181.H47A35   973.7'42'0924 [B]   72-820
ISBN 0-8371-6389-7

Library of Congress Catalog Card Number: 72-820
ISBN: 0-8371-6389-7

First published in 1974

Greenwood Press, a division of Williamhouse-Regency Inc.
51 Riverside Avenue, Westport, Connecticut 06880

Manufactured in the United States of America

This book is dedicated to George S. Morrison, First Sergeant, Co. A, 12th Virginia Infantry; Edward A. Wyatt, Captain, Dinwiddie Cavalry, and Lieutenant Colonel, 83rd Virginia Regiment; John R. Barner, Private, Co. I, 3rd Virginia Cavalry (Dinwiddie Troop); Edward L. Perkins, First Sergeant, Co. I, 3rd Virginia Cavalry (Dinwiddie Troop); Emmett M. Morrison, (VMI '61), Colonel, 15th Virginia Infantry; to my parents; to my wife; and to our children.

Contents

Illustrations

Map

Preface

When Henry Heth began his memoirs in the fall of 1897, he was in his seventy-second year, and some of the sharp detail already had faded from the events, names, and places which had constituted segments of his life. This is readily understandable considering the multitude of experiences which had filled those seventy-two years. Moreover, Heth had to cope simultaneously with the problems of ill health and poverty while writing the memoirs. Indeed, under the circumstances it is surprising that he accurately remembered as much as he did. A strongly opinionated man, Heth was not always objective in his appraisals of others, but in fairness it should also be pointed out that, unlike most soldier-memoirists, he candidly admitted his own weaknesses and manfully resisted the temptation to take himself too seriously. Measured against present-day standards of judgment, Heth may stand guilty of failing to sift the significant from the unimportant in his memoirs. Although he lived through, and participated in, some of the most momentous events in American history, these seem to have impressed him little more than other matters which the modern reader perhaps will find trivial. We should not be too quick to judge him on that score, however; Henry Heth was, after all, a nineteenth century soldier, not a twentieth century historian.

For several reasons I have decided to present Heth's memoirs intact, making minor grammatical corrections and adding words in brackets only when necessary to maintain coherence. Heth reveals much of his own personality by his choice of items to record. Similarly, some of the material he includes, though of little intrinsic consequence, provides intimate glimpses of several major historical figures—Winfield Scott, Ulysses S. Grant, Robert E. Lee, and Ambrose E. Burnside, to name but a few. In their entirety the memoirs represent a view of nineteenth century America as seen by a man of the times, and any attempt at excision would inevitably risk adulterating this authenticity.

To bring the author's work into focus historically, I have added explanatory notes to the body of his text. I also found it necessary to introduce the memoirs with a short, biographical sketch, for Heth left so much unsaid that the annotated memoirs could not stand alone. This sketch is based primarily on external sources and does not contain material from the memoirs except where omission would disrupt continuity.

Heth wrote the memoirs in the hope that he could publish them commercially. He failed in this endeavor, and the manuscript remained in the possession of his family until Mrs. Emlyn Marsteller deposited it in the Alderman Library of the University of Virginia in 1955. The original is still on file there. I thank Emlyn H. Marsteller, Jr., for permission to publish the memoirs. Those sections of the memoirs which dealt with the Civil War appeared in the March and September 1962 issues of *Civil War History*; the editor of that journal has graciously consented to their reproduction in this book.

I am indebted to many people for assisting me. Professor Edward Younger of the University of Virginia unfailingly provided the inspiration, guidance, and encouragement so necessary to bring the project to fruition. Archivists in the Library of Congress, the National Archives, the University of Virginia and Virginia State libraries, the Virginia Historical Society, the Confederate Museum in Richmond, and the United States Military Academy Library, gave their indispensible services freely and cheerfully. Mr. Edward J. Krasnoborski of the Department of History at West Point applied his unique touch to the cartography. Mrs. Leslie J. (Sally) French of the same office typed the manuscript with the skill, and efficiency, that are the hallmarks of her work. I am also grateful to my colleagues in the Department of History, United States Military Academy, and at York College of Pennsylvania, who lightened the burden in many ways.

Introduction

Genesis

Life in antebellum Virginia was good, particularly for folk of wealth and breeding. The Heths met both these qualifications. The first Henry Heth of Virginia had been almost, but not quite, an FFV (First Family of Virginia). He had migrated from Northern Ireland to Pennsylvania and then to Frederick County, sometime before 1750. He married Agnes McMachan after his arrival in Virginia, and they had three sons, each an officer in the American Revolution: William, a colonel in the Continental Line; Andrew, who later migrated to Kentucky; and Henry, the first owner of Blackheath, the family estate in Chesterfield County.

Henry of Blackheath married Nancy Hare of Richmond in November 1787. They had eight children, the fourth of whom was John, father of the memoirist. John once had planned on a naval career but had given it up in 1822 to return to Black-heath and Margaret Pickett, whom he married in the same year. Theirs was a fruitful union, producing eleven children, Henry being the fourth eldest.[1]

In addition to the family plantation, John Heth had interests in the Heth Manufacturing Company, incorporated in 1836,[2] which produced textiles and paper, and the Blackheath and Huguenot Coal and Iron Company, founded in 1837.[3] But business interests, varied and successful though they were, did not occupy all his time. As his son points out, he was an ardent devotee of horseflesh, and took an active part in militia affairs. He also ensured that Henry received the education appropriate for a planter scion.

At about the age of six, Henry Heth enrolled at the Amelia Academy, a small private school limited to twenty students annually.[4] Later he attended a school in Chase City County operated by Hugh Nelson, the first holder of a Master's Degree from the University of Virginia to teach in the elementary schools of the state.[5] After several years in these two schools Heth entered William N. Page's School in Cumberland County.[6]

According to his memoirs the young Heth went to George-town College in the District of Columbia at about the age of twelve. This institution was at that time a boy's preparatory school operated by the Jesuits, but open to all denominations.[7] From Georgetown he went to William A. Muhlenburg's school on Long Island, New York. This too was a preparatory school for young men who intended to enter colleges and universities.[8]

The next way station in Heth's preparatory education was the Peugnet Frères School for Boys, sometimes called the "French School," which was also located in New York. Entering this institution in 1841, Heth pursued a curriculum which stressed mathematics, rhetoric, geography, and other subjects needed by candidates for the Military Academy at West Point.[9] The Peugnets, former Napoleonic captains, frequently livened their lectures with tales of Jena and Austerlitz and strove to inculcate the "Little Corporal's" standards of discipline upon their charges. Heth's memoirs show that he enjoyed his stay at this semi-military school. Apparently he made a favorable impression on his instructors, for in their efforts to help him win an appointment to West Point they testified to his "amiable disposition, moral habits, fine talents, good application to his studies and more than ordinary proficiency for his age."[10]

Testimonials from teachers were not enough, however. There were a few presidential appointments available annually for sons of War of 1812 and Revolutionary veterans, but competition was keen, and political influence was a *sine qua non*. This was not a serious obstacle for John Heth's son. Gouverneur Kemble,[11] onetime consul to Cádiz, and owner of the West Point Foundry which manufactured cannons for the army, wrote President Tyler a letter of recommendation. William G. McNeill,[12] a West Pointer and former engineer officer, now president of the Chesapeake and Ohio Canal Company, also assisted, as did Henry A. Wise,[13] the Virginia congressman, who was later to be chastised by Heth for military ineptitude. Their efforts were successful. Henry won his appointment in March 1843.[14]

West Point

In the memoirs Heth mentions that in April 1843, a month after he had received the appointment to West Point, his father died. He does not report, however, that John Heth's death quickly brought a reversal in the family's fortunes. In fact, this reversal was so drastic that by the time Henry entered the Military Academy on 13 June 1843 he had to list the condition of his family as "Badly off," in "Reduced Circumstances."[15] For Heth this was but the beginning of a long and close association with want.

Heth's own account of his experiences at the Military
Academy is amusing and accurate, but too fragmentary to qual-
ify as a comprehensive picture of his life there. Immediately
after reporting for duty he turned over all the cash in his possession to the treasurer, then went to the quartermaster's where
he drew the minimal furniture and equipment he would need
for his stay in barracks prior to taking the entrance examinations. This consisted of a pair of blankets, a chair, a bucket,
a broom, a tin or cocoanut dipper, a tin washbasin, a lump
of soap, a candlestick, some tallow candles, a slate, and an
arithmetic text,[16] all of which he had to haul up to his room
and stow according to the regulations. Not even Southern aris-
tocrats were permitted body servants at West Point.

In the interval between his arrival and the entrance examinations Heth divided his time between the classroom, where for
four hours daily cadet instructors tutored him in arithmetic, writing, and grammar; and the parade ground where cadet drillmas-
ters taught him the basic military skills. These educational and
training processes began even before Heth and his classmates
had been fitted for uniforms. The first formation of a group
of new cadets still in civilian clothes made a curious spectacle.
Heth's memoirs do not record his impressions of that fateful
occasion, but John Tidball, who entered the Academy a year
later, described a sight which must have resembled closely what
Heth had seen a year earlier. As Tidball portrayed his classmates,

There were about sixty of us . . . and as we marched,
or tried to march, there was a constant losing of step, occa-
sioning the most ludicrous and to us the most vexatious,
shuffling, stumbling and kicking of heels. A motly [sic]
gang we were. . . . Coming from every quarter of the
country they necessarily represent[ed] every degree of pro-

vincialism. . . . Some were arrayed in straw hats while others sweltered in fur caps; some—the great majority—were painfully rustic in homemade clothes, while a few were foppish with city fashions.[17]

The program of military indoctrination was temporarily interrupted on 27 June when Heth and his classmates were required to demonstrate their proficiency in reading, arithmetic, spelling and penmanship before a board consisting of the superintendent and several professors.[18] Neither these tests nor the accompanying physical examination were difficult; nonetheless, twelve of the seventy-two candidates for the Class of 1847 failed to negotiate these initial obstacles and returned to civilian life.[19] Heth, of course, after his years with the Puegnets got by without difficulty.[20]

Passing the mental and physical examinations did not mean that Heth and his classmates had become full-fledged cadets, however. In those days Fourth Classmen (Freshmen) remained on probation until they successfully had passed the January examinations. Only then did they take the oath of allegiance and receive their cadet warrants.[21] But such things as midyear examinations and warrants must have seemed centuries away to Heth, Burnside, Gus Seward, Orlando Wilcox and the rest as they marched off to the cadet summer encampment on the "Plain." Here the new Fourth Classmen, (colloquially called "Plebes," "Animals," or "Beasts") together with the Third (Sophomore) and First (Senior) Classes, lived under canvas until the end of August. The upper classmen engaged in advanced tactical training while the Plebes concentrated on learning the rudiments of the manual of arms, the duties of the private soldier, infantry drill, and interior guard. In the toils of a strange routine and subjected to "deviling" by the upper classmen Heth and his mates may have found it difficult to understand why the corps so eagerly anticipated and so thoroughly enjoyed this temporary escape from the section room,[22] but they were soon to learn.

Early in September the Corps of Cadets returned to barracks and resumed academic work. For the Class of 1847 this marked the beginning of a ruthless weeding out process which was to last until graduation day; of the sixty admitted in the summer of 1843 only thirty-eight were to receive their diplomas in June 1847.[23]

West Point cadets in the antebellum era attended class in sections divided according to academic merit. Initially, the new Fourth Class was sectioned alphabetically, but at the end of the first six weeks of the fall term and periodically thereafter, new sections were formed on the basis of academic performance. The dozen or so men standing highest in a given subject comprised the first section for that subject, the next twelve the second, and so on down the line to the group at the bottom, the "Immortals" of the last section.[24]

Heth does not exaggerate his poor academic performance at the Military Academy—it was "abominable," considering his preparatory education. He did manage to maintain a respectable standing in French for the two years he took that subject, due no doubt to the Puegnets. With this lone exception, however, he marched among the "Immortals" for the entire four years. In fact, he narrowly escaped being sent home for deficiency in mathematics at the January examinations in 1844.[25] Heth's conduct record was equally notorious. Most of the official sins he committed—"laughing in ranks," "absent from quarters," "smoking and cooking in quarters," "visiting during unauthorized hours," "making improper use of vicinity of coal pile," "having a nail in the heel of his boot for the purpose of pricking his horse," and "neglect of duty as sentinel"—were minor ones and typical of cadets at the time. Heth certainly exceeded the norm quantitatively, however, coming within a hair's breadth of deficiency in conduct each year, and amassing a grand total of 683 demerits for the four years, which ranked him next to last in conduct at graduation.[26] One offense, committed early in his cadet career, earned young Henry a public rebuke in special orders. On 4 December 1843, he was reported for using "vulgar and offensive language." Richard Delafield, the superintendent, took occasion to remind the corps of Washington's general order against swearing, which had been published at West Point, then added for Heth's special edification

> that an indulgence in language so pointedly rebuked by General Washington is a stain upon his [Heth's] character that requires the most sincere and determined efforts from him to correct.
>
> It is with regret the Superintendent learns that a young gentleman of Cadet Heth's education should have so far forgotten what was due to his character as to have been guilty of the offensive and vulgar language used by him.[27]

Heth alludes to a far graver offense in the memoirs but does not mention that it almost resulted in his dismissal, possibly because he never knew how seriously the authorities considered taking such action. In the summer of 1846, while confined to the hospital, Henry sneaked out one night and called on a young lady at the hotel. The couple went for a walk and remained absent for several hours. The mother, becoming frantic, asked two officers to search for the pair. They did so but failed to find them. Finally, about 11:00 P.M. Heth returned the girl to the hotel. The superintendent, on learning of the incident, considered remanding him to a general court martial, which could have resulted in his dismissal, but fortunately for the cadet the authorities decided not to take formal action in order to avoid embarrassing the young lady.[28]

Dabney Maury once maintained that had the course lasted one more year his classmate Thomas J. Jackson would probably have graduated first in the class.[29] Heth, on the other hand, would undoubtedly have been sent home had he remained at West Point another year, for at the end of each examination period his class standing dropped to a lower level as those beneath him were cut away. Finally, he stood at the foot of the class.

With a few notable exceptions, such as Robert E. and Custis (but not Fitzhugh) Lee, J. E. B. Stuart, P. G. T. Beauregard, E. P. Alexander, and R. K. Meade, Southern cadets generally fell lower on the academic scale at antebellum West Point than those from the New England and Middle Atlantic states.[30] Richard Ewell of Virginia, who graduated in 1840, blamed this on poor preparation: "A person who comes here without a knowledge [sic] has to contend against those who have been preparing themselves for years under the best teachers and who have used the same class books. The yankees generally take the lead in every class."[31] George Strong, a Vermonter of the Class of 1857, gave a different explanation: "There is a remarkable difference between cadets of the Northern and Southern States; the former are generally studious and industrious; the latter, brought up among slaves, are idle and inattentive."[32] Heth, to his eternal credit, did not ascribe his poor showing to lack of preparation, slavery, or the bad influence of his roommate Burnside. Consequently, we can accept at face value his own explanation. He enjoyed life too much to take it seriously.

Although Heth's *joie de vivre* and sense of humor—rare commodities among West Pointers of any vintage—did not elevate him in the eyes of the authorities, there can be no doubt that they endeared him to his fellow cadets. The citadel on the Hudson was a grim place in the 1840s, as several future Civil War generals have written.[33] There was no such thing as organized athletics and precious little in the way of authorized entertainment to relieve the tension and boredom of the spartan regimen. Because of this the corps relished buffoonery, and in that field Heth and Burnside excelled.

Several of their antics are described in the memoirs. Burnside's biographer has added another. On one accasion, after the two had become Third Classmen, they camouflaged their quarters, Room 8, North Barracks, to resemble a barber shop. Heth then went out, found a brand-new Plebe, and ordered him to report for a haircut. The novice cadet, Thomas F. McLean of Missouri, nicknamed the "Bison" because of his long beard and shaggy locks, took a seat and Burnside went to work on him with clippers and razor. By timing his movements precisely, the "barber" managed to have shorn half of McLean's head and shaved off half his beard just as the drum beat the warning call for evening parade. At this signal Heth and Burnside dashed out to ranks leaving McLean to explain his bizarre appearance to the superintendent as best he could.[34]

Traditionally, graduating West Point cadets choose their branches of service based on their overall standing, or general order of merit, for the four years of the course. This practice was in vogue in the spring of 1847 when Heth applied for a commission in the artillery, either of the two regiments of dragoons, or the mounted rifles; but standing at the foot of the class, as he did, these elite units were beyond his reach. Like many other low-ranking cadets, before and since, Heth was destined for the infantry.[35]

Finally, on 19 June 1847, Henry Heth and his classmates "kicked their hats" at the last parade.[36] Heth, like the others, must have felt both joy and relief, tinged, perhaps, with a touch of nostalgia, as he stood in ranks for the last time. Fortunately, he had no way of knowing then how portentous the motto, *"Nous Nous Soutenons,"* and the stacked muskets engraved on his class ring were to be.[37]

The Old Army

The actual strength of the regular army in the summer of 1847 when Heth joined it as a brevet second lieutenant, First Infantry, was 1,353 commissioned officers and 29,512 enlisted men. In the demobilization following the Mexican War, however, this figure dropped to a level of approximately 945 officers and 9,640 men where it remained until 1855 when four additional regiments were activated,[38] an event of some consequence to the memoirist.

Had Heth hoped to recoup his family's lost fortune, he could scarcely have chosen a worse career. As an infantry subaltern he drew $64.50 monthly, a figure which included his basic pay and all allowances. In 1853, when he became a first lieutenant, the sum increased to $69.50, and on reaching the grade of captain, two years later, he received $93.50 a month.[39] This salary scale put Heth on the same footing, roughly, as a professor at a small college or a construction foreman. In short, it may have been adequate but hardly munificent. Perhaps even more discouraging was the rule that promotions in the antebellum regular army went according to seniority, with rare exceptions; furthermore, there were no provisions for retirement. An officer remained on active duty until he died unless, of course, resignation or dismissal cut short his career.[40]

Hostilities had ended in Mexico before Heth arrived there in January, 1848.[41] He had graduated from West Point a year too late to earn brevets for valor, lead desperate charges, or storm battlements at bayonet point. All that remained was the ever-present danger of tropical disease, and the monotony of occupation duty. To be sure, there were occasional breaks in the official routine—mountain climbing expeditions, visits to points of interest, bullfights to attend and pretty girls to court—but otherwise Heth and his brother officers devoted their time to patrolling, marching on and off guard, administering summary justice, and the other dull but necessary tasks incident to military housekeeping in a foreign country.

Duty in Mexico also provided an excellent opportunity for an observant junior officer to learn things about his trade which had not been taught at West Point. He could see, for instance, that the regular army, stripped of synthetic glamour, was something quite different from the pictures "Old Fuss and Feathers" (Winfield Scott) used to paint for cadets during his summer sojourns on the Hudson. A new lieutenant might also learn, from gossip if not from firsthand observation, that politics and politicians frequently played as important a role in military affairs as did generals and tactical operations. Moreover, a sensitive subaltern, if he made the effort, might discern something of the difference in leadership techniques required to handle the regular and the volunteer. Undoubtedly, the postwar tour of duty in Mexico could have been a profitable learning experience even though it did not afford a chance to lead troops in combat.

Probably, Heth did not make the most of this opportunity for professional betterment. He was still a youngster, and there were too many interesting things to see and do. Furthermore, Heth was not by nature a reflective man. But while he may have been derelict with respect to professional self-improvement, the gregarious Virginian did not neglect the social aspects of occupation life. As the memoirs reflect, the tour in Mexico provided an opportunity to renew old acquaintances and make new ones with such men as Lewis Armistead, "Cousin George" Pickett, Winfield Scott Hancock, the ubiquitous Burnside, and a quiet captain named Grant. These officers would loom large in Heth's life in future years.

The next stage in the military career of Henry Heth was a

long and critical one, stretching from 1848 to 1861. During this period he saw extensive service on the Kansas frontier, held several independent commands, led a company in combat, made a reputation as an expert in rifle marksmanship, and certainly not least important, took a wife. Heth devotes a large portion of the memoirs to these years between the Mexican and Civil Wars, and rightfully so, for they marked his final transition from boyhood to maturity.

In the memoirs Heth relates, accurately enough, his early frontier experiences and the events leading up to the recuperative leave he spent in Virginia in the winter and early spring of 1850, but the impression he conveys of a visit unmarred by difficulty is somewhat fanciful. Perhaps by 1897 the old man had forgotten that it was on this visit he had wooed and lost a young lady known only to posterity as Miss Julia. Although the rebuff did not permanently dampen Heth's ebullient spirit, it caused him grave concern at the time. Highly sensitive to the possibility of ridicule, he worried lest the matter become public.[42]

More unfortunate for the military historian is Heth's omission of much of the background information concerning army life prior to the Civil War. He tells little about the enlisted men—their ethnic and social origins, their style of living, and morale problems. Perhaps the memoirist considered such matters too mundane to be recorded, but less explicable is his failure to mention the return trip he made to the Plains following the expiration of his ill-starred leave. On reporting for duty at Governor's Island in May 1850, Heth was detailed to escort a draft of 136 recruits and seven laundresses from New York, via Tampa Bay, to their various posts in Florida. After completing this chore he returned to Fort Leavenworth where he awaited assignment to his new post. The only account of this journey, which should have been an interesting and exciting one, is the terse and fragmentary official report.[43]

At Leavenworth Heth, with a column of First Dragoons under the command of First Lieutenant Abraham ("Abe") Buford, made a trek to the "Great Bend" of the Arkansas. There Heth joined a detachment of 6th Infantry soldiers who were constructing a small sod fort, one of many such one-company garrisons scattered along the Santa Fe Trail. At first the site was known simply as "new Post," but subsequently it was officially designated Fort Atkinson (near present-day Dodge City Kansas). To the irreverent soldiers, however, it remained "Fort Soddy" or "Fort Sodom."[44] The total strength of this outpost of "Manifest Destiny" never exceeded six officers, one of whom was an assistant surgeon, and eighty-three enlisted men. Usually, detached service and leaves reduced the number of men present for duty to an even smaller figure.[45]

Fortunately for this lilliputian force the Cheyenne, Kiowa, and Arapaho who lived in the area, as well as the other tribes who occasionally interloped in their quest for buffalo, were relatively peaceful in the antebellum era. To be sure, there were frequent thefts and minor forays against isolated whites, but nothing remotely comparable to the savage warfare which wracked the Plains in the years following the Civil War. All the same, serious trouble almost occurred in May of 1851 when Captain Philip Thompson of the First Dragoons horsewhipped a Cheyenne. Heth presents one version of this incident in the memoirs. Another one, more accurate if less dramatic, is that members of the expedition to which Thompson belonged had become overly friendly with the Cheyennes while stopping at Fort Atkinson. Thomas Fitzpatrick, an Indian agent, had warned the white visitors against permitting the Cheyennes to have the freedom of their camp, but they ignored his advice. Fitzpatrick's warning came home to roost one morning when a warrior, spying a ring on Mrs. Thompson's hand, reached for it in order to take a closer look. The lady screamed, and her husband, misunderstanding the Indian's intent, struck him with the whip.

Also, according to the less dramatic account, trader William Bent and agent Fitzpatrick, not Colonels Hoffman of the 6th Infantry and Sumner of the Dragoons, calmed the Indians and averted what might have been a catastrophe.[46]

Generally, life at Fort Atkinson was less exciting. Aside from the occasional visits of immigrant trains, buffalo hunts, and amateur theatricals, the routine consisted of patrolling; mounting guard; drilling; convoying the mail; parleying with Indians about raids, tribal feuds, white captives and stolen horses; administering military justice; trying to preserve the health of the garrison; and, of course, filing reports. Nor were Heth and his fellows exempt from that bane of every line officer's existence, the bureaucrat, who, comfortably situated in a higher headquarters miles away, refuses to acknowledge, much less understand, the problems of the field soldier.[47] This, however, was a minor hardship compared to the one which accompanied the first heavy snowfall each year—complete isolation from the outside world. As Heth once wrote his sister from the fort,

> With winter we are cut off from everything, even the monthly mail. We do not know who the new president is and are now in a great state of suspense. Some, not me, wishing success to General Scott as it will create a vacancy.[48]

Neither the tedium of garrison life nor the awesome silence of the Great Plains in winter seems to have depressed Heth. To the contrary, the same features of army life on the frontier which drove other men to alcohol or resignation apparently appealed to him. Certainly, the memoirs reflect a genuine affection for Fort Atkinson and a corresponding sorrow at having to leave it for more comfortable surroundings. Solitude and adversity held no terror for this tough-souled Virginian.

An economy drive, together with the difficulty of maintaining communications, and the tactical logic of consolidating forces, led to the abandonment of Fort Atkinson in the summer of 1853. Heth, along with the other members of Company D, moved to a new site at the junction of the Republican and Smoky Hill Rivers. Here, approximately 250 miles northeast of their former station and 120 miles west of Fort Leavenworth, they constructed Fort Riley.[49] This fort, like its predecessor, became a 6th Infantry outpost.

In February 1854, while Heth was at Fort Riley, he was promoted to first lieutenant.[50] Then, in the following month came another indication that his service up to that point, if not brilliant, had at least been satisfactory. At the time Heth, was seeking command of a surveying expedition which was to complete the work of Captain Gunnison, who had been killed by Indians in Utah the year before. Colonel William Hoffman, the regimental commander, took this occasion to commend the young Virginian:

> I take great pleasure in recommending him as peculiarly fitted for the position. He has great energy and decision of character, is very devoted to his duties, and his three years on the Plains . . . have well prepared him to have a command. . . . I am well assured that if this service is entrusted to him, he will be found equal to any emergency.[51]

Heth did not win the coveted position, but in June he took command of Fort Kearny, Nebraska Territory.[52] This post on the Platte, about 150 miles west of present-day Omaha, guarded the Oregon Trail.[53] Although the terrain and the Indians were somewhat different, duty at Kearny remained essentially what it had been at Atkinson and Riley. The Ponca and Sioux who ranged this area, however, were more brazen and violent than the Indians in Kansas had been; thus, the demands on Heth and his troops were heavier than had been the case at their old posts.[54]

Heth's tour at Fort Kearny did not last long. In November 1854, less than a year after assuming command, he was appointed regimental quartermaster. But soon after Heth turned over the post and reported for his new duty, he was designated as an aide to General Harney for the forthcoming punitive expedition against the Brule Sioux; however, a surprising event overtook this assignment. In March 1855 Heth was promoted to captain ahead of all his classmates and transferred to the 10th Infantry, one of the regiments which had just been organized.[55]

In the absence of evidence to the contrary, we must accept Heth's own explanation that the Secretary of War selected him for a captaincy in the new regiment on the basis of merit. For what it is worth, this claim is substantiated by the writer of Heth's obituary and the historian of the West Point Class of 1847.[56] It does seem strange that a man who only two years before had been one of the last members of his class to make first lieutenant should suddenly emerge ahead of his contemporaries. To be sure, Heth's service had been exemplary, and he had demonstrated his capacity to command under rigorous conditions, but the same could as easily be said of many other young officers. Speculation is futile, however; if family connections, Southern birth, or political influence played a part, the evidence was successfully hidden.

The new captain and his new command, Company E, 10th Infantry, were soon to see action with the selfsame Harney expedition which Heth had almost joined as an aide. Assembling at Fort Leavenworth, Harney's command left that post on 5 August 1855 and marched to Fort Kearny, Heth's old station, where the expedition halted temporarily to make final preparations for the campaign. Here, five companies of the 6th Infantry joined the column.[57]

On 24 August, Harney, with blood in his eye, led a mixed

force of about 600 infantry, cavalry, and artillery out from Fort
Kearny in search of the Sioux. Warriors from the Brule band
of this tribe had massacred the Grattan party a year earlier, and
Harney's mission was to take revenge in such a manner that
the Indians would be discouraged from further depredations
against whites.[58] Marching northwest along the Platte, the
expedition reached Ash Hollow in the late afternoon of 2 September; here the troops made camp and prepared to go into battle, for Harney had learned that the band of Brules he sought
were encamped on Blue Water Creek about six miles away.

The general decided to envelop the Indians from the rear and
cut their line of retreat with cavalry while simultaneously
marching another force to their front. Lieutenant Colonel Philip
St. George Cooke, with Companies E and K of the Second
Dragoons, Light Company G of the 4th Artillery and Heth's
Company E of the 10th Infantry, left camp at 3:00 A.M. 3 September, and by dawn had taken position in rear of the Indians.
Heth's unit, incidentally, had been issued horses so that it could
keep up with the cavalry. At 4:30 A.M. Harney, with Companies A. E. H, I, and K of the 6th Infantry, began the march
to the front of the Indian village.[59]

Heth adequately describes the military aspects of the action
which ensued; however, he does not mention that the almost
flawless tactical operation resulted in the ruthless, and probably
unnecessary, slaughter of more than eighty Sioux, including
women and children. Although he was by no means a professional Indian hater and, in fact enjoyed something of a reputation in the army for his understanding of and sympathy for the
western tribes,[60] he was too much a man of the times and too
much the typical regular to brood on the morality of killing
"savages."

For his part, the young Virginian performed satisfactorily in
his first sizable combat action as a commander. Initially, Heth
had failed to cover an escape route when deploying his unit;

as a result some of the Indians got away, but he quickly corrected this deficiency and made no other mistakes. Harney did not see fit to single him out for individual distinction but did mention "Captain Heth, 10th Infantry," as one of the officers "whose position either in the engagement or pursuit, brought them in closest contact with the enemy."[61]

There was an element of fine historical irony in the action at Blue Water. John Buford, then a First Lieutenant in the Second Dragoons, commanded troops in Cooke's maneuver force along with Heth. Eight years later Buford was to employ his cavalrymen dismounted at Gettysburg just as Heth had at Blue Water. Only this time the enemy was not the Sioux but Heth himself.[62]

The records do not reveal exactly when Henry Heth decided to marry Harriett "Teny" Selden, a first cousin nine years his junior. They had been writing to each other since the spring of 1853,[63] but the chances are they had not become sweethearts by that early date. It can definitely be established, however, that soon after he arrived in Richmond in January 1857, Heth proposed, and she accepted. They were wed a few months later on 7 April at Norwood, the family home in Powhatan County, Virginia.[64] In the course of this forty year marriage "Teny" Selden would come to know loneliness, fear, grief, and suffering. And in the end she, who had started life as the daughter of a wealthy planter, would die in poverty.[65] Yet, true to the ethic of her breed, she never flinched. Perhaps, life with the dashing Heth was worth it after all. Certainly it was if the devotion which the memoirs reflect was genuine, and if he took to heart the advice he once gave a sister:

I think in the great majority of marriages both parties are apt to expect too much; the main spring of human action is selfishness; keep that in mind, and remember no perfect man or woman exists.[66]

Heth remained on leave throughout the remainder of the summer and then secured a temporary assignment in Washington to work on the system of rifle marksmanship he mentions in the memoirs. He started work on the project in October 1857 and completed it the following February.[67] The account of the evolution of Heth's system, as set forth in the memoirs, is confusing and not altogether accurate. Prior to leaving the West for his nuptial leave in Virginia, he had experimented with a method of rifle practice which had been devised by Sir Henry Hardinge of the British Army. Contrary to the statement in the memoirs, however, the report of this experiment, duly credited to Heth, did reach Washington where it was read by the Chief of Ordnance and referred to the headquarters of the army in July 1856.[68]

The system Heth developed and wrote up in Washington was not an original one, but a synthesis of a French pamphlet and reports by American officers, including the one Heth had submitted earlier. In short, his task was to translate a French manual and modify it to fit the needs of the United States army. Heth says as much in the preface to his work: "The undersigned [Heth] does not claim the credit of presenting the army anything new, but only a digest of what has already been practised."[69]

Heth's treatise may not have been original, but it was thoroughgoing. His manual covered all phases of marksmanship instruction: aiming, positions, trigger pull, simulated firing exercises, and practice with ball ammunition. Lesson I covered preliminary training; Lessons II, III, and IV embraced firing practice, starting with the individual soldier and proceeding through the company. In addition, Heth illustrated the text with sketches showing the various firing positions and included a section on range operation and target construction. John B. Floyd, then Secretary of War, was quick to appreciate the merit of the work. Less than a month after Heth submitted the manuscript, Floyd approved it and ordered that the system be adopted throughout the army.[70] A few years later both men would have cause to regret this contribution they had made to Federal marksmanship.

In March 1858, Heth returned to his unit in the West and in June of the same year led it on the Mormon pacification expedition commanded by Albert Sidney Johnston.[71] Heth remained in Utah until October 1860, and his experiences in that unhappy territory, together with the preexisting prejudices which he probably carried with him, left the memoirist with an undying hatred for the Mormons. This bias not only stands out in the memoirs but in articles he wrote in later years—vitriolic accounts titled "Mountain Meadows Massacre" and "The Utah Flour Contract."[72] The reasons for Heth's point of view are not difficult to unravel. Like most American Protestants of his day, he thought the tenets of Mormonism weird and shocking; moreover, the sight of the skeletons which the army had unearthed in 1859, evincing, as it did, that the Mormons had massacred their fellow white Americans, increased hostility toward the sect. Then, too, the Mormons' harassment of the occupation troops in Utah certainly did little to improve matters. Heth, in particular, had to endure great vexation and frustration in his attempts to enforce federal law.[73] Probably, it was fortunate for the Mormons as well as the young Virginian that fate intervened and cut short his tour.

On 9 October 1860, Henry Heth left Camp Floyd, for Virginia. Ann Randolph, the two year old daughter whom he had never seen, was ill, and he had obtained a leave of absence in order to visit her.[74] As he journeyed eastward, Heth could not have foreseen that one phase of his life was ending and another beginning, or that his next tour of duty in the Indian country would be as a civilian.

The Civil War

Probably, the war talk he heard enroute to Virginia disturbed

Heth. Few Virginians serving in the regular army at the time were enthusiastic about secession and the prospects of civil war. And there can be little doubt that when the South Carolinians fired on the "Old Flag" at Fort Sumter, Heth, who had served proudly under that banner for fourteen years, felt bitter pangs. When Virginia seceded, however, he could postpone the hard choice no longer. On 17 April 1861 Henry Heth wrote the Adjutant General, U.S. Army, "I have the honor to resign my commission as a Captain in the 10th Regiment, United States Infantry."[75] On the same day he volunteered for the Confederate army, stating in his letter of application to Jefferson Davis,

> I have the honor to offer you my services in the defense of our common country. To you I owe more than any other man living; to the common cause you now represent, I offer my services in whatever capacity or position you may see proper to place me.

Across the top of the letter Davis pencilled, "Secty. of War—special attention, this is a first rate soldier and of the cast of man most needed."[76]

Heth entered the Confederate service as a captain, but almost immediately thereafter became a lieutenant colonel. From April until the end of May he was on temporary duty with the Quartermaster Department in Richmond.[77] While assigned to that office he accompanied the comic-opera Taliaferro expedition which left Richmond on 18 April and made a two day march to Norfolk only to find that the Federals had scuttled the fleet and set fire to the navy yard. On his return to Richmond, Heth became Acting Quartermaster General, Virginia State Forces, a position he held until 31 May.[78]

After his experiences in the Norfolk fiasco, Heth may have hoped that he had seen the last of rashly planned and poorly executed operations; if so, he was doomed to disappointment.

John B. Floyd who, as Buchanan's Secretary of War, had endorsed Heth's system of target practice, had followed the current fad among politicians, and turned military commander. Davis wisely dispatched the former captain of United States Infantry to help him.

Heth rendered Floyd valuable service; it is safe to say that without his professional advice, the former secretary of war together with Henry Wise, another politician-turned-general, would have wrought even more havoc in western Virginia than they did. While serving under Floyd, Heth not only had to raise and train his own regiment which, by the end of July, had reached a strength of 842, he also had to serve as Floyd's inspector general and subsequently to command a brigade on occasion.[79]

Floyd's Army of the Kanawha first saw action on 26 August 1861 when it crossed the Gauley River at Carnifix Ferry and routed the 7th Ohio Regiment which McClellan had sent there. Immediately after this victory Floyd threw a wire-rope bridge across the gorge and established a protective strongpoint in the immediate vicinity. On 10 September, Rosecrans, with a Union division, reached Cross Lanes about two miles from Floyd's position and immediately launched an attack. The Confederate fortifications were too strong, however, and the assault failed. Despite their inability to carry the position, the Federals were able to site a field piece so that it enfiladed the Confederate entrenchments; a shell fragment from this piece wounded Floyd slightly, but sufficiently to cool his fighting ardor. During the night he ordered the Army of the Kanawha to fall back across the river.[80]

Earlier, Jefferson Davis had dispatched Lee to western Virginia for the purpose of improving relations between Floyd and Wise and establishing order; but by the time Lee arrived on 21 September the situation was beyond salvation. The best the

Confederates could hope for was a withdrawal without further disaster; this they managed to accomplish. Whether the rebel success was more attributable to Heth's skill in handling the rear guard or to the ineptitude of the Federal commander, at least John B. Floyd escaped having to tour the North in a cage.

In November, Heth sought Lee's aid in obtaining an assignment elsewhere. On the 23rd, that officer wrote to the Secretary of War:

> Colonel Henry Heth, now with General Floyd, will, I think from what I learn, apply to you for further service, and I would be very glad to have him in any capacity. He is the only officer of any experience that I know could be spared without detriment.[81]

President Davis had other plans for Heth, however; trouble was brewing in the Trans-Mississippi. At the time, fighting Yankees was of secondary importance in that disputed area. The critical battle was between the partisans of Sterling Price and Ben McCulloch, each group attempting to secure control of all Confederate troops in the theatre. Davis hoped to solve the dilemma by appointing Heth to command. This proposal immediately provoked a storm of protest.[82]—Neither side relished serving under a West Pointer.—Davis held to his decision as long as he could, arguing that

> To bring these different forces into harmonious cooperation is a necessity. I have sought to effect it by selecting General Heth to command them in combination. If it is designed, by calling Heth a West Point cadet, merely to object to his education in the science of war, it may pass for what it is worth; but if it is intended to assert that he is without experience, his years of active service on the

frontier of Missouri and the territory to the west of it will,
to those who examine before they censure, be a sufficient
answer.[83]

In the end, however, the Missouri politicians had their way,
and on 18 January 1862, Heth became commander of the Lewisburg Military District in Virginia. Previously, on 6 January, he
had been appointed a brigadier general; this occurred three
weeks after his thirty-sixth birthday.[84] Had he known what the
Lewisburg assignment held in store for him, Heth might have
turned it down, for he had merely extricated himself from one
undesirable situation and narrowly avoided another, only to end
up in a third which turned out to be no better, and perhaps
worse than the other two.

Troubles began immediately after he assumed command on
6 February.[85] Heth faced an almost insoluble problem in communications. There were few roads in the area, and these were
impassable in bad weather; furthermore, the Virginia Central
Railroad, already overtaxed by demands elsewhere, could not
support the Lewisburg command adequately. In addition, Heth
had great difficulty in organizing and equipping his troops: the
8th Virginia Cavalry, the 22th Virginia Infantry, and his old
regiment, the 45th Virginia Infantry, together with a battery of
four six-pounders (one of which was unserviceable). In Heth's
view, the cavalry could not operate effectively in the mountain-
ous terrain; moreover, forage for the horses constituted a serious
logistical problem. He decided therefore to employ the 8th Virginia Cavalry dismounted until he could replace it with an infantry regiment.[86] The authorities in Richmond could not meet
Heth's request for additional troops, but they did authorize him
to levy on the local militia; this brought on the most difficult
problem of all.

The people of the mountain counties under Heth's jurisdiction
held mixed sentiments about the war: some were strong

Unionists; others, probably the majority, wanted to avoid involvement; still others, motivated as much by the prospects of loot as patriotism, preferred to serve on an informal basis as guerrillas. Only a small minority was willing to enlist in the ranks of the regular Confederate forces. This being the case, Heth's attempt to call the militia to the colors did little to solve his existing problems; worse, it created new ones by increasing the hostility of some of the local citizens.

The militia units which did answer the call gave a good account of themselves in their first engagement under Heth. On 9 May 1862, he divided his force into two brigades, giving Colonel Walter Jenifer command of one and John McCausland (VMI '57) the other. The same night, the entire force marched north from Floyd's Mountain, near Dublin Depot, toward Pearisburg, also known as Giles Courthouse; at that point Heth's leading units made contact with the pickets of an invading force under the command of Jacob Cox. Heth, deploying his troops rapidly and smartly, drove the Federals beyond the Narrows of New River, killing twenty and wounding eighty.[87] Henry Heth's Confederates had performed with professional élan, and their commander was justifiably proud. As he stated in his report,

> The force under my command was composed chiefly of the recent levies; they, as all others, acted like veterans. I have never witnessed better or more determined fighting.[88]

Heth's joy was short-lived. The term "signal disaster," which he used to describe the next engagement, was painfully accurate. Flushed with their victory at Giles Courthouse, Heth and his men immediately marched on Lewisburg, then occupied by the 36th Ohio Infantry under the command of George Crook. The Federal force at Lewisburg numbered approximately 1,500 infantry and 150 cavalry, supported by two mountain howitzers. Heth had at hand 2,000 infantry, 100 cavalry and three batteries. This preponderance would have been sufficient for the Rebels, provided they had taken Crook by surprise. Initially, all went well. Heth began his attack at 5 A.M. The Confederates quickly drove in the Union pickets east of the town and seized a ridge from which they could launch their final assault against the main body of the enemy, located on a hill to the west of Lewisburg. Had the Rebels moved quickly, before the enemy had time to react, they could have seized this hill, which would have guaranteed their success. However, Heth had overestimated the capabilities of his own command and had failed to consider the mettle of his opposite number—George Crook.

Crook, on hearing the warning shots, rapidly deployed his forces. Then, instead of waiting to receive Heth's assault, he launched an attack himself. With consummate skill the Federals moved forward, taking a knoll from which their riflemen could enfilade the Confederate left. Under fires from this position the rebel line began to give away. As it did, Crook pressed home the attack and drove the Confederates off the ridge. Heth's men broke and ran.[89]

The actual Confederate losses were not heavy: thirty-eight killed, sixty-six captured, and four field pieces plus three hundred small arms lost; but from the standpoint of morale, Lewisburg was a disaster. This time Heth was not laudatory in his report:

One of those causeless panics for which there is no accounting seized my command. Victory was in my grasp, instead of which I have to admit a most disgraceful defeat. The only excuse that can be offered for the disgraceful behavior of the regiments is that they are filled with conscripts and newly officered under the electoral system.[90]

The defeat at Lewisburg was not the last of Heth's troubles with the militia. On 9 July, his patience tried to the breaking point by the continued refusal of some of the local troops to join the Confederate ranks, he issued a proclamation ordering all males between the ages of eighteen and thirty-five to report for duty immediately. Those who failed to comply were to be "shot as deserters wherever found." The proclamation also nullified all previous exemptions granted by local magistrates and medical examining boards.[91] Legally, Heth was within his rights, for Richmond had declared the ten counties in his jurisdiction to be under martial law. Even so, the proclamation was a rash act, one that could only damage the Confederate cause in this highly sensitive area. The local population lost no time in making its sentiments known in the capital. So intense was the pressure that the Secretary of War rescinded the offending order, and Heth was soon on his way to another front.[92]

Understandably, Heth devotes little space in his memoirs to Lewisburg. It was a black and frustrating period in his career, marked by two defeats, one military, the other political. Both raised questions about the soundness of his judgment.

"Brigadier General Heth has been ordered to report to you for duty at Chattanooga and I hope is en route. I regard him very highly and am sure he will meet your requirements."[93] Thus did Jefferson Davis notify Edmund Kirby Smith of Heth's assignment to his command and at the same time reaffirm his faith in the Virginia brigadier, despite that officer's recent failures. Perhaps, the Confederate president was also hoping that the change would stop those irate complaints from western Virginia.[94]

Upon his arrival in Chattanooga on 1 July, Heth was given command of a mixed division of two brigades of infantry and two of cavalry, one of the latter under the command of an obscure colonel named Nathan Bedford Forrest.[95] Heth, however, had little time to ponder the oddities of the legion-type organizational structure he had inherited or the capabilities of his subordinates. He arrived to find Kirby Smith sick and out of action with a Federal force threatening Chattanooga. As the ranking officer present for duty, the Virginian also found himself in temporary command of the city's defenses. Actually, nothing came of the confusing and potentially dangerous situation. The Federals withdrew and, on the 14th, General McGown arrived to take over the command from Heth.[96]

Soon afterward, Smith recovered and led an invasion of Kentucky in conjunction with Braxton Bragg. The initial phase of this operation consisted of turning the Federal defenses at Cumberland Gap and seizing London, Kentucky in order to cut the lines of communication. To accomplish this Smith organized his force in two columns, one to pass into Kentucky via Rogers Gap, the other by way of Big Creek Gap. Heth's division, together with the artillery and supply trains, was to take the Big Creek Gap route. Smith gave the order to march on 14 August.[97]

When G. W. Morgan, the Federal commander, learned that his flanks were threatened, he abandoned his position at Barboursville, Kentucky, and soon thereafter evacuated Cumberland Gap as well. Kirby Smith's advance reached Barboursville on the 18th, but Heth had great difficulty moving the trains over the poor roads and did not close on the town until four days later.[98]

Smith next moved on Richmond, Kentucky where he made contact with Federal troops under the command of William "Bull" Nelson on 29 August and routed his opponent on the next day. Heth, slowed again by the pace of the trains, arrived too late to participate in this victory which he considered to be the most significant of the war.

In the memoirs, Heth relates in considerable detail the subsequent phases of the invasion and the reasons for its ultimate

failure. Like so many other Confederate operations, this campaign had all the requisites for success except one—cooperative
generals.

On 22 October 1862, the worn-out Confederates passed
through Cumberland Gap and reentered Tennessee. The following month Kirby Smith moved into middle Tennessee, leaving
Heth in charge of the eastern portion of the state. But an inactive command at this particular time was not what the Virginian
desired. In October, the Confederate senate had refused to confirm Davis' nomination of Heth for promotion to major
general.[99] Obviously, the only hope of retrieving the reputation
he had lost at Lewisburg lay in an active theatre. Heth made
it clear in his request for a transfer that there was no animosity
between Smith and himself; he also left no doubt as to under
whom he wished to serve. "General Lee has always been my
personal friend, and I should much like to join him for many
reasons."[100]

On learning of this desire Lee, who took an unusual personal
interest in Heth's career, wrote the adjutant general in
Richmond,

> General Heth, for particular reasons is desirous of active
> field service, and has expressed to me the wish to join the
> Army of Northern Virginia. I should be very glad of his
> services at this time, and if ordered to report to me, I can
> give him a command.[101]

Kirby Smith, for his part, appeared to have been satisfied
with Heth's performance of duty while serving under him. In
a farewell note the Floridian stated:

> I wish you success, and in bidding you farewell, thank you
> for the able manner in which you have always supported

me. Whether in front of the enemy . . . or commanding
a department, you have always performed all your duties
with zeal and ability.[102]

This plaudit from his former commander may have alleviated
to some degree the bitterness Heth felt at having been passed
over by the senate. But in spite of Kirby Smith's praise and
the continued faith of Lee and Davis, the Virginian's joy at
the prospects of returning home and serving with personal
friends must have been tinged with apprehension. The chal-
lenges which he had previously met with mixed success were
nothing compared to what he was about to face. How would
Henry Heth measure up to the standards of that most exacting
of taskmasters, the Army of Northern Virginia?

Heth reported for duty on 5 March 1863 and was given command of the first brigade of A. P. Hill's "Light Division,"
Jackson's Corps. The other brigadiers of Hill's command, Dorsey Pender and William Archer, were both junior to Heth; consequently, his assignment lessened their chances for eventual
promotion. But if either man resented this fact, he did not show
it.[103]

In all probability the Virginia brigadier heard of the difficulties between Stonewall Jackson and A. P. Hill soon after
his arrival, if not earlier. Undoubtedly, Heth who set great store
by personal loyalty, took the part of his fellow aristocrat, classmate, and close friend against the taciturn, up-country Presbyterian. This bias in favor of Hill may explain why the
memoirs, which otherwise are full of anecdotes about and
sketches of Confederate leaders, make so few references to
Jackson. Indeed, partisan sentiment is the only logical explanation for Heth's slighting of this "Great Captain" who was his
corps commander until Chancellorsville.

Perhaps Heth witnessed some of the snowball fights with
which the Army of Northern Virginia amused itself in the early

spring of 1863; if so, it was not for long. Across the Rappahannock, his old roommate, Burnside, had just been relieved of
command for his bloody failure at Fredericksburg, and a new
Union commander was about to test his skill.[104]

Heth's brigade, along with the other units of the Light Division broke camp before dawn on Friday, 1 May 1863, and took
up the order of march, behind Robert Rodes' division, toward
Chancellorsville. About three miles from the tavern there Hill
ordered Heth to take his own, Lane's, and McGowan's brigades
and proceed north to the Old Turnpike, at which point he was
to deploy and feel his way along the road in the direction of
Chancellorsville. In compliance with this order Heth sent the
14th South Carolina and Orr's Rifles ahead as an advance
guard, and then moved out with the main body. On reaching
the turnpike, however, Heth's men struck heavy Federal resistance and halted. By this time it was almost dark, and Jackson,
when he came up, ordered Heth to remain in place for the
night.[105]

Later the same night Lee and Jackson planned their famous
flanking move around Hooker's exposed right flank. Early the
next morning Jackson's corps marched west to execute it.[106]
Heth accurately relates Archer's countermarch to rescue the
Confederate supply train and Rodes' sweep down the Federal
right flank, but his statement that Hill's division "did not fire
a shot in this attack" is wrong. Actually, soon after Hill took
over the advance from Rodes late in the afternoon, his leading
brigade became hotly engaged and remained so until dark. In
fact, some of Hill's North Carolinians probably shot Jackson
and later, Hill himself.[107]

When Hill was wounded, Heth took command of the Light
Division and performed well the next day, 3 May. As he mentions in the memoirs, the division, after two unsuccessful
attempts, succeeded in driving the Federals from their works.
Heth does not mention, however, that he was wounded during

the action but refused to quit the field. J. E. B. Stuart, then in temporary command of Jackson's corps, did think Heth's devotion worthy of special note, stating in his report, "In Sunday's battle . . . Heth and Ramseur, though painfully wounded, persisted in retaining command to the close of the fight."[108]

Hill also took official note of Heth's contribution to the Confederate victory at Chancellorsville: "Generals Heth, Pender and Ramseur contributed greatly to the success of our arms."[109] When it came to recommending an officer to succeed to the command of the Light Division in the reorganization following Chancellorsville, however, Hill preferred Pender over Heth. Lee, cognizant of Hill's desire, and aware of the senate's earlier refusal to confirm Heth's promotion, hesitated to recommend him again, particularly when there was some question that this might be unjust to Pender, a particularly gallant and competent officer. In the end, the same reorganization which gave Hill a corps produced a solution to the Pender-Heth dilemma. Lee proposed, and Davis approved, the creation of a new division, thus creating vacancies for two major-generals. Both of Hill's brigadiers were named to fill these vacancies. On 23 May 1863, Henry Heth received his appointment as a major-general, and this time the Confederate senate confirmed it. A few days later he assumed command of the new division, consisting of Pettigrew's, Archer's, Cooke's, and Davis's brigades, together with his old brigade, now led by Brockenbrough.[110]

Heth's first battle as a major-general was Gettysburg, a name that would haunt him the rest of his life. Some idea of the burden he bore ever after can be gleaned from the memoirs, but it can be seen even more clearly in his unending efforts to seek reassurances from other old Confederates and from his unseemly attacks on the long-dead J. E. B. Stuart. In one respect Heth's feeling is difficult to understand; his share of the blame was minor compared to that of the corps commanders and Lee.

Furthermore, except for a garbled account of the battle which appeared in the Charleston *Mercury*, there was never an attempt to make Heth the scapegoat for the Confederate defeat; neither his former commanders nor the men he had led seem to have held him responsible for the loss. Yet, from another standpoint, one can appreciate Heth's feelings. After all, he personally had set into motion the chain of events which culminated in disaster.[111]

In the memoirs Heth accurately describes Pettigrew's expedition to Gettysburg in search of shoes, and the report the brigadier rendered on his return. Heth also makes it clear that Hill, knowing the substance of Pettigrew's report, approved Heth's plan to march on the town with his entire division the next day. What Heth fails to explain is why he committed his division to action without attempting to ascertain what lay ahead. This was inexplicable conduct on the part of an old Indian fighter, particularly when one of his trusted and seasoned brigadiers had reported enemy activity. Despite the advance warning, however, and despite his having had an entire night to investigate before moving forward, Heth, as far as can be determined, never thought to send out a reconnaissance or combat patrol. This was indeed a peculiar oversight on the part of one who later was to take such pains to point out the evil results of Lee's failure to obtain information. As it turned out, Henry Heth's oversight was costly as well as peculiar—2700 Confederate casualties in 25 minutes.[112]

Once Heth had engaged the enemy in force the responsibility for what followed passed to other shoulders. Had Hill or Lee seen fit, they could have withdrawn Heth's command or at least have refrained from becoming more heavily committed. Nor was Heth in any way responsible for the course of events after 1 July when he was absent from the field with a head wound. Still, those factors do not completely exonerate Heth; he had failed to evaluate the terrain and the strength of the enemy just as he had done at Lewisburg. His commanders' errors in judgment cannot obscure his own.

Henry Heth recovered in time to command the rear guard on the dreary march back into Virginia. This retreat continued without incident until the morning of 14 July, when a squadron of Federal cavalry attacked his division at Falling Waters.[113] There are several conflicting versions of this action. Two Confederate eyewitnesses maintained that in obedience to Heth's orders, the men had stacked arms and were resting when the Federals struck. Another Confederate who was also there refuted this. His version was that Archer's and Pettigrew's brigades were both on line, ready for action.[114] All agree, however, that Heth mistakenly assumed that Confederate cavalry was protecting his rear and had not taken the proper precautionary measures.

Heth mentions this first phase of the action in the memoirs, but he does not mention the flanking attack executed by dismounted Federal troopers soon afterwards. This attack was carried out by Judson Kilpatrick who, according to his account, netted one of Heth's brigades.[115] Heth denied this loss in his report, maintaining that Brockenbrough's brigade drove the Federals off and that not even a squad of his was captured. He went on to accuse Kilpatrick of lying in order to further his own ends. The Federal commander, according to Heth, counted in his total, stragglers, who had been collected for several days.[116] Colonel B. M. Mayo, a regimental commander in Brockenbrough's brigade, gave a third version, more accurate than either of the others. He reported that the Federal cavalry did successfully outflank his brigade and captured 230 prisoners, but not the entire unit.[117] This appears to be what actually happened.

Heth's coverage of his next action at Bristoe Station requires little amplification. This was a defeat for which A. P. Hill accepted complete and sole responsibility. In his report the corps commander candidly admitted: "I am convinced that I made the attack too hastily, and at the same time a delay of half an hour, and there would have been no enemy to attack."[118] Perhaps Henry Heth drew comfort from the other generals' mistakes, but Hill's confession was of little consolation to the soldiers. The price of his mistake was 1361 killed, wounded, or captured.[119] Many III Corps veterans maintained that it had been a slaughter.[120]

After Bristoe Station Hill's corps returned to winter quarters at Orange Court House and, except for the inconclusive Mine Run expedition in late November, remained inactive until the spring of 1864. It was while III Corps was in winter quarters that Hill, apparently feeling it necessary to bolster his lieutenant's morale, wrote:

Having been informed that it was probable some misapprehension existed in regard to your management of your division at Gettysburg, Falling Waters, and Bristow [sic], it is but simple justice to you that I say, your conduct on all these occasions met with approbation. At Gettysburg the first day's fight, mainly fought by your Division was a brilliant victory. . . . At Falling Waters the enemy were kept at bay until the army had crossed the Potomac and the prisoners taken by the enemy were stragglers, and not due to any fault of yours. At Bristow the attack was ordered by me and most gallantly made by your division.[121]

Heth relates his part in the opening stage of the Wilderness Campaign in minute detail, pointing out how, after having repulsed seven Federal assaults, he decided to take the offensive in conjunction with Cadmus Wilcox. He admits, moreover, that this was a blunder, then goes on to describe the confusion which

existed at the close of the day's fighting. This is readily understandable as in the Wilderness it was almost impossible for units
to maintain any kind of alignment; moreover, there had been
attacks, repulses, and skirmishes all day long. Undoubtedly, the
men in the ranks were worn out after the hard day's fighting
over difficult terrain. But these factors do not absolve the commanders concerned for the failure which followed.

It is almost inconceivable that Hill, even though he expected
Longstreet to relieve him momentarily,[122] should have permitted two of his divisions to remain disorganized in the face
of the enemy throughout the night, knowing that the men were
exhausted and would likely be far less vigilant than normal.
Then, if ever, forceful leadership was essential; but instead of
attempting to rectify the situation, the corps commander relaxed
on a camp stool in the rear, refusing to allow the men to be
disturbed because they were tired.[123]

At least Hill could claim illness as an excuse. His subordinates did not have even this flimsy alibi. Instead of acting
on their own initiative, they spent the night pacing nervously
up and down from pillar to post, seeking authority they should
have been ashamed to ask for. A moderately diligent corporal
could be expected to organize his position and maintain contact
with neighboring units. What manner of generals were these
who did not do such things automatically? Granted, aligning
divisions in the dark in difficult terrain is not an easy task and
can be risky, but veteran commanders such as Heth and Wilcox
could have accomplished it. As for Hill's order, it should have
been disobeyed. It would have been far better to suffer a
reprimand or court-martial than to risk disaster.

Heth's account of the rest of this campaign is difficult to follow because he shifts the chronology of events and digresses
to relate anecdotes. On the morning of 10 May, Jubal Early,
then in temporary command of the corps, dispatched Heth to
deal with Federal forces which had crossed the Po beyond the

Confederate left flank. Heth struck Hancock's troops in the vicinity of White's Shop, and the Federals fell back with little resistance. In the afternoon, however, the enemy stiffened and twice repulsed Heth before retiring across the Po.[124] Furthermore, contrary to Heth's contention in the memoirs, the Union forces withdrew on orders from higher headquarters in order to undertake another mission.[125]

After this action Heth returned to his position on the Confederate right. Here, on 11 May, he beat off Burnside's attacks. It was on the same day that Ewell moved the guns supporting his troops in the "Mule Shoe" salient to the rear.[126] The next morning, 12 May, the Federals attacked the northern nose of this salient on the Confederate left, capturing Generals Johnson and Steuart. Heth did not participate in this action.[127]

The same afternoon Burnside launched an attack against Heth's sector of the salient, but Mahone with two brigades executed a spoiling attack, striking Burnside's column in its left flank and beating the Federals back. Heth supported Mahone's attack with artillery and musket fire although he does not mention it in the memoirs.[128]

Hill resumed command of the corps on 1 June[129] and the same day sent Mahone and Wilcox to Cold Harbor, leaving Heth to hold the Confederate left.[130] It was also on this day that Heth repulsed two Union attacks. On the next day, 2 June, Heth, along with two of Jubal Early's divisions, attacked and drove the Federals to Bethesda Church, after which the Confederates remained on the ground. Thus, as of 2 June, Hill's lines extended six miles from Wilcox on the right at Cold Harbor, to Heth on the left at Bethesda Church. Here, on 3 June, Heth again repelled a Federal attack against the Confederate left flank.[131]

No significant actions occurred after the bloody Battle of Cold Harbor until Lee, surmising that Grant had crossed the James and was moving toward Petersburg, followed suit. Hill's troops crossed on the pontoons at Drewry's Bluff during the night of 18 June, then headed down the turnpike toward Petersburg. The following day they went into the lines south of that town.[132]

As with the Wilderness Campaign, Heth's account of the actions around Petersburg suffers from an excessive number of anecdotes and a lack of continuity. In addition, he telescopes the description, omitting several important battles. Finally, his versions of the actions do not always coincide with the official records.

On 23 July 1864, Grant sent Hancock's II Corps with two cavalry divisions to demonstrate against Richmond. His purpose was to draw Confederate troops away from Petersburg, thereby weakening the lines preliminary to detonating Burnside's mine. Lee, in response, dispatched Heth's and Anderson's divisions to deal with this threat: Thus, Heth and his division were away from Petersburg when the Battle of the Crater took place; in fact, the explosion occurred in the sector he had previously occupied.[133] Consequently, it is strange that Heth, who frequently violated his self-imposed rule against discussing events he did not witness, omitted this dramatic action in which he was almost involved. The only logical explanation is that at the Crater "Little Billy" Mahone rose to new heights as a leader, and Heth, as his memoirs illustrate, had another self-imposed rule: he never mentioned this fellow division commander in Hill's corps by name.

On the other hand, Heth was not reticent when it came to attacking Mahone by inference. In the account of Globe Tavern, Heth's next combat action, which took place on 21 August, he maintains that the officer commanding the flanking force, obviously Mahone, disobeyed orders and failed to press the attack. Heth could not have witnessed this operation since at the same time he was commanding the force making the frontal assault. His allegation, as indicated in the memoirs, is based on a conversation with some unidentified Federal officer after the war. This charge does not coincide with the reports of Hill and Grant, or that of Orlando Willcox, another Federal participant.[134] None of the three indicates that Mahone was derelict. More important, Heth's version does not conform to the aggressive nature of Mahone as portrayed by Freeman, and by Hassler, A. P. Hill's biographer. Orlando Willcox's version, which should be authentic, is that Mahone's men successfully executed the flanking maneuver and drove the Federals back; however, then they encountered strong enemy reinforcements and were forced to give way themselves.

Heth's action in this operation reflected great courage and tenacity. When Mahone gave way, Heth stood his ground, his division being the last Confederate unit to fall back. In addition, he executed another attack the same afternoon, one delivered with gallantry even though it failed to dislodge the Federals.[135]

Grant's next assault on the Weldon Railroad came at Reams Station. Here, on 25 August, Heth displayed conspicuous bravery as he participated in the Confederate attack against the right flank of the Federal "U". It was on this occasion that Heth personally planted the colors of the 26th North Carolina on the Union breastworks. This battle, as the memoirs indicate, inflicted heavy casualties on Hancock's II Corps.[136]

On 31 September, Hill's Corps parried another of Grant's thrusts, this one aimed at the Southside Railroad to the west of Petersburg. The Confederates made contact with the enemy at Jones's Farm and drove him from the field. Early the next morning the rebels again attacked and forced the Yankees to retreat in disorder. On 1 October, the Federals launched a counterattack, but Heth beat them off. This action, variously known as the Battle of Jones's or Peebles's Farm, was another costly affair for the Federals; they lost about 3,000 in comparison to negligible losses on the Confederate side.[137]

In spite of these tactical victories, there was by this time no

real hope of success. Grant, heedless of the cost, was determined to bring the war to a conclusion, and the Union superior-
ity in manpower and material made Confederate defeat inevitable. Even the men in the ranks were beginning to sense this,
some likening Yankees to mosquitos: "Kill one and two more
take his place."[138] But there was still plenty of fight left in
the hard core, as Heth's next operation, Burgess's Mill,
showed.

For the first three weeks in October 1864, Heth's division
was busy constructing breastworks along Hatcher's Run on the
Confederate right.[139] Just after they had completed this task,
Grant, on 27 October, sent six divisions of infantry and one
of cavalry across Hatcher's Run in an effort to pass around
Heth's right flank and cut the Southside Railroad.[140] In addition to his own division, Heth commanded, temporarily, two of
Wilcox's brigades and Dearing's Cavalry Brigade along with
600 more dismounted troopers who held the Confederate
right.[141]

As the Federals approached, Heth quickly reinforced the dismounted cavalry with an infantry brigade, and a little later
shifted the rest of his force to the right also. The troops on
the Confederate right checked the advancing Federals temporarily, but they continued to come on, and Heth's position became
precarious. Hill, learning of the Federal movement, dispatched
Mahone with two brigades to reinforce Heth. "Little Billy"
arrived about 3 P.M. Heth and Wade Hampton, who was commanding a cavalry division nearby, decided to attack
immediately afterwards. In the ensuing engagement the Confederates almost encircled the advancing Federals with Mahone
and Hampton attacking the advancing column on opposite flanks
while Heth's troops struck it in front. At the same time Davis,
one of Heth's brigadiers, held off another Federal column which
was coming up in support of the first. The Confederates, however, were too weak to close the gap completely, and when

Heth called a halt to the operation at dark, the Federals fell back.[142] During the night of 27 October, Heth and Hampton planned another attack for daylight the next morning, but when dawn came, they discovered that the Federal force had retreated across Hatcher's Run.

In his report Heth gave due credit to Mahone for the part he played in the operation but then proceeded to take "Little Billy" to task. Mahone, apparently, had filed a report of his own which indicated that he had acted independently during the operation and had not been under Heth's command; furthermore, he had cast aspersions on some of Heth's men and had hinted that the victory was primarily the result of his own intervention.[143] This was too much for Heth. In his report he stated:

> During the day's operation he was under my command. He was not ordered, as he states, to my support by Lt. Gen. Hill, but ordered to report to me. . . . He so reported to me and acted under my orders during the day.[144]

Unfortunately, neither Mahone's nor Hill's reports can be found, so the justice of Heth's allegations cannot be weighed. Logic dictates that in this instance Heth would have been in command as he was the senior of the two. Equally important, Heth was on the scene when the action started; consequently, he was in a better position to direct operations. All this Hill knew, and he must also have been aware of the feelings between the two; therefore, he would have been more likely to have placed Mahone under Heth's command than rely on a cooperative effort. Regardless of who was in command, this was the last major victory for III Corps.[145]

Hill's men again were called out of the lines to counter a Federal threat at the end of the first week in December 1864. Warren's V Federal Corps, with a division from II Corps and Gregg's Cavalry, had begun to advance along the Petersburg-

Weldon Railroad. Initially, Wade Hampton moved to cut them off, and on 7 December, Hill's Corps climbed out of the trenches to follow in support of the cavalry. As it turned out, the Confederate exertions went for naught. Before they could make contact, the Federals had come under the fire of guns defending the ford over the Meherrin at Hicksford and had turned back. On the night of 11 December, Heth's exhausted veterans countermarched and headed back to Petersburg.[146]

There were still occasional forays to beat back Union advances, but for the most part Heth's men spent the rest of that dreary winter in the trenches. For the high-ranking officers who had their families with them in Petersburg, life may have been tolerable, but for the soldiers in the trenches it was unrelieved misery. Rations were short, and warm clothing was almost nonexistent. But far worse was the news from home. A man could stand privations himself, but the thought of a hungry wife and children was another matter. Desertions now climbed at an alarming rate.[147] The end was in sight.

On 20 March, Hill took sick leave, and Heth assumed command of the corps, but only for a short while. Hill returned to duty 1 April;[148] his remaining time in command was not long. On the morning of 2 April, Wright's Federal division drove around Heth's right flank, then proceeded to roll up his line, capturing Davis's Mississippi Brigade and many of McComb's Tennesseans and Cooke's North Carolinians as well. It was while Hill was en route from Petersburg to Heth's position that a Federal soldier shot him through the heart.[149]

Heth, his position having become untenable, ordered the remnants of his command to withdraw westward to Sutherland's Station where he hoped to make a stand. On reaching Sutherland's, the division formed line of battle. At this point Heth learned Hill had been shot; leaving Cooke in charge of the division, he headed toward Petersburg to report to Lee. Cooke, while Heth was absent, managed to repulse two Union attacks;

in the end, however, the Federals succeeded in outflanking the Confederate ragamuffins, and they had to give way. Many were captured, but a few managed to escape and assemble at Amelia Court House on 5 April. There Heth joined them, and on the next day they marched toward Appomattox.[150]

An Appraisal

In assessing Henry Heth's performance as a general, certain factors must be kept in mind. First, he was a professional soldier, schooled at the highest institution of formal military training then extant in the United States. Furthermore, prior to the war Heth had spent most of his fourteen years of active service on the frontier, and during this period had held several independent commands. Thus, he was no novice when the Civil War began. On the other hand, he had never commanded a unit larger than a company, and although he had seen combat against Indians, he had not participated in the Mexican War. Consequently, he had to make the sudden transition from captain to general with no experience in larger command and without having fought in a full-scale war.

Other men, of course, had made even more radical transitions and emerged with better records of performance. Bedford Forrest, Turner Ashby, Wade Hampton, and John Mosby, for instance, had been civilians without military education or experience in 1861. Then, there was a large group of younger professional officers, such as J. E. B. Stuart, John Pegram, Stephen Ramseur, and Fitzhugh Lee.[151] These men held commands comparable to or larger than Heth's and on balance did better. Nor can it be ignored that Kirby Smith graduated from West Point only two years before Heth, Stonewall Jackson one year earlier, and A. P. Hill on the same day.[152] Not only did these close contemporaries outstrip Heth in rank, they outshone him as commanders. Obviously, then, Heth's performance fell short of what it might have been. In this respect he was far from unique.

If achieved rank can be considered a rough indicator of ability, however, Heth stands high. Of the sixty-five Confederate officers who graduated from the Military Academy between 1844 and 1850, inclusive, one became a general; three reached lieutenant general; and nine, including Heth, became major generals.[153] Thus, in this contemporary group of Confederates who were West Pointers, Heth stood in the top 20 percent according to rank. Focusing even closer, of his immediate contemporaries in the classes of 1846-1848, twenty-four entered the Confederate service; two then became lieutenant generals and six became major-generals. Again using rank as the criterion, Heth stands in the upper third of a group whose backgrounds closely approximated his own.

Admittedly, such comparisons are valid only within broad limits. They do not give weight to political influence, a critical factor in some cases; nor do they take into account the fact that some of the group were killed before they had a chance to demonstrate their capabilities fully. Moreover, these comparisons overlook the varying conditions of service in the different theatres of operation, and they fail to allow for differences in the competence of the men who commanded the officers in Heth's peer group, another critical factor. All this notwithstanding, it is still possible to say that Heth definitely ranked below the top level of Confederate leadership, but still in the upper third of that broad spectrum of generals whose performance of duty was neither consistently good nor poor.

A clearer, though more subjective view of the memoirist emerges when he is compared with his fellow division commanders in III Corps. During Heth's tenure under Hill, comparable commands in the same organization were held by Richard H. Anderson, W. Dorsey Pender, Cadmus Wilcox, and "Little Billy" Mahone. Anderson's performance at Gaines's

Mill and Chancellorsville alone[154] would undoubtedly place him higher on the scale of command ability than Heth. Pender must be eliminated from the comparison since he died of wounds after Gettysburg, but all the evidence indicates that had he lived, he too would have stood higher.[155] Although Mahone got off to a slow start, he progressed rapidly once he obtained high command, and by the last year of the war had become the best division commander in III Corps, and possibly the best in the entire Army of Northern Virginia.[156] Wilcox seems to stand closest to Heth in ability, but of the two even he appears to have been more able and diligent than Heth.[157] In summary, Heth stands last in professional ability when compared to his four closest contemporaries.

Douglas Freeman characterized Heth as capable but unlucky.[158] At best this is an oversimplification. Heth may have been capable in comparison with the average West Pointer in the Confederate service, but at the same time he was less effective than his immediate contemporaries in III Corps. As for luck, Heth was unfortunate in losing several battles through no fault of his own, but he was exceedingly lucky in having both the commanding general and the Confederate president as friends, for on more than one occasion they saved him from the consequences of his own rash acts.

The question arises as to why Henry Heth, with a better military background and more experience than many of his brother officers, did not perform more ably than he did. A close analysis of his personality reveals the answer. First he had a persistent tendency to act on impulse before evaluating his own and the enemy's capabilities. A second consistent defect, closely allied with the first, was Heth's inability to foresee with any degree of accuracy what the enemy would do to counteract his moves; in fact, more often than not he seemed to disregard the opposing force altogether. Some of Heth's occasional defects were lack of initiative and want of vigilance. For example, in the Wilderness he failed to correct a situation he knew to be potentially dangerous; at Falling Waters he did not remain on the alert even though commanding a rear guard in the face of the enemy; and at Petersburg, Lee had to reprimand him for neglect of duty.

To be sure, there were admirable traits as well. Heth was unquestionably a brave officer; never did he put self-preservation above duty. Also, Henry Heth was a hard, tenacious fighter. Frequently he and his men were called upon to do battle under severe handicaps against a much more powerful enemy; yet with few exceptions the units under his command acquitted themselves nobly, exhibiting a fighting spirit that could only have been engendered by inspired leadership. Another of Heth's admirable traits was a fierce loyalty to his subordinates. This is apparent, not only from the memoirs, but from his official reports and correspondence as well. Heth also deserves high marks for moral courage. Throughout a long lifetime he personified the flinty integrity which was once associated with the profession of arms. Finally, Heth possessed in full measure that most endearing of human traits, a sense of humor. Not only could he endure disappointment and defeat with stoic calm, he could even joke about his plight. Surely, this was the mark of an indomitable spirit.

But this was Henry Heth the soldier, and that man died at Appomattox. It was not the dashing young general who went home to Norwood in April 1865, but a tired, beaten man of forty.

The Closing Years

Chronologically, the Civil War marked the halfway point in Henry Heth's life, but it was actually a much more significant milestone. He never managed to settle down and come to grips with the problem of earning a living after the war. At times success seemed almost within his grasp, but inevitably the bright prospects would dim, and Heth would move on to something else. Some of these failures were his own fault, but just as often they resulted from factors beyond his control. In any case, Heth's postwar life was unsuccessful insofar as material wealth was concerned.

In the memoirs Heth discusses his coal mining venture at Norwood, his father-in-law's estate on the James River. Burnside sponsored the project, advancing $50,000 initially; Heth, who supervised operations, began construction work at the mine in January 1866. Expectations were high in the beginning. The first ore samples consisted of excellent coal, and there seemed to be ready markets for it locally and in New England.[159] Soon troubles began to appear: subsequent samples contained excessive sulphur; some adjacent property which had been leased for development failed to produce; and drainage of the mines proved a serious problem. These factors, coupled with a tightening money market, doomed the Norwood mines.[160] Heth also may have been at fault for the failure as he did not keep his northern partner fully informed of the situation; moreover, had he more carefully explored the sites before plunging in, he might have discovered their limitations sooner than he did.

The mines closed in the early spring of 1869, but Heth apparently had anticipated failure even earlier, for he was already seeking employment elsewhere several weeks before the mining operation shut down. Again, the West Pointer turned to Unionist friends for help, this time to George B. McClellan and Winfield S. Hancock. They tried to render assistance but were unable to do so.[161] In desperation, Heth considered migrating to California and wrote a friend in San Francisco for help in finding work, again without success.[162]

In the memoirs Heth badly scrambles the chronological sequence of events subsequent to the mining fiasco. For example, he relates his adventures as a treasury agent in Brownsville,

Texas, immediately following his discussion of the ill-fated joint
venture with Burnside. Although it is impossible to determine
precisely where he was from the summer of 1869 to January
1872, the available evidence indicates he did not go to Texas
then, but almost ten years later.[163] The most plausible explanation of his whereabouts for the two years following the closing
of the mines in 1869 is that he left Virginia and went to Raleigh,
North Carolina, where he remained for about a year, and then
returned to Richmond.

It can definitely be established that by January 1872 Henry
Heth and his family were living in Richmond and that he
remained there, working as an agent for a life insurance company, until 1878.[164] This venture also went sour, and the com-
ments of Heth's immediate superior, the general agent, leave
no doubt as to why. According to his supervisor, Heth ignored
inquiries from the headquarters of the company, let policies
lapse, and failed to process his clients' claims. Another stark
indicator that Heth did poorly during this period was that his
wife had to take in boarders in an effort to make ends meet.[165]

Although he may have neglected business, Heth took an
active interest in the social life of the Virginia capital. In March
1877, he was elected president of the new Westmoreland Club,
which was organized at that time by a group of men who had
formerly been members of the Richmond Club.[166] Then, in July
of the same year the State Agricultural Society appointed him
to a committee that called on President Hayes at the White
House and invited him to Richmond. Hayes accepted and visited
the Confederate capital the following fall; Heth was a member
of the escort of honor on that occasion.[167]

Heth also contributed an article on the Battle of Gettysburg
to the *Weekly Times* of Philadelphia while he was living in
Richmond. In this account he freely violated his self-imposed
stricture against commenting on events he had not witnessed,

and as a result found himself embroiled in a heated skirmish with two of Stuart's old troopers, John Mosby and Henry B. McClellan. Both wrote articles flatly denying Heth's allegation that their dead leader had exceeded the bounds of Lee's discretionary orders during those fateful July days of 1863, and pointing out that more than half of Stuart's cavalry had, in fact, accompanied the Army of Northern Virginia in the invasion. The cavalrymen scored at least a minor victory, for Heth eventually wrote an apology to McClellan, maintaining that Stuart's partisans had misunderstood the intent of his article and that he had not desired to "reflect on the cavalry or cast the slightest blame on our friend, General Stuart."[168]

In the spring of 1878 Heth tried his hand at another business venture. He became a director of the Great Southern Railway, a corporation being organized to construct and operate lines in Florida and Georgia. The company lost out in competition with another new line for a government franchise, however, and was unable to progress past the embryonic stage.[169]

At this juncture, having suffered defeat in his several jousts with the private enterprise system, the West Pointer turned again to old army friends for help. Burnside, then a senator, Sherman, and General Devens all sought employment for him. One of them, probably Burnside, secured a post for Heth in the summer of 1878 as treasury agent in Brownsville, Texas; he held this position until 1880 when he received an appointment as a government civil engineer.[170] Heth's headquarters while serving in the latter capacity was Georgetown, South Carolina. He was employed as an assistant engineer, supervising surveying and dredging operations on the Waccamaw, Greater Pee Dee, and Watersee Rivers and the harbor of Winyah Bay. This job lasted until 1885.[171]

A former Confederate helped Heth obtain his next appointment. In March 1885, Custis Lee recommended him to another ex-Rebel, Secretary of Interior L. Q. C. Lamar, for a position in the Bureau of Indian Affairs. Heth was commissioned as a special agent in that bureau on 26 June 1885.[172] For the most part he spent his time inspecting Indian schools, but on occasion he also investigated general agency administration as well. As a special agent Heth visited most of the western states and territories from Kansas to California. This was probably the happiest period in his postwar life. The job enabled him to return to the scenes of earlier, more enjoyable days and to renew old acquaintances, red and white alike. Certainly, Heth fulfilled his duties with dedication and vigor. He wrote numerous reports evaluating complaints against whites, recommending the removal of incompetents, suggesting improvements in administration, and describing the ways in which the schools could be improved.[173] In their totality these documents reveal that whatever else Henry Heth may have been, he was not a mindless bureaucrat, but a conscientious public servant sincerely concerned for the welfare of the people under his charge. This being the case, he must have felt some sadness when he resigned in June 1889.[174] He was bidding farewell to a land he loved, and he had to leave, knowing what the future held in store for the once-mighty warriors whom he had admired. Who better than an ex-Confederate could so fully appreciate the futility of naked valor against industrialized might?

Heth's next task must have evoked even more poignant memories. In February 1891 he was named a Confederate representative to the War Department board for marking the battlefield at Sharpsburg, a position he held until his final illness.[175] Nor was this his only reminder of the past. In May 1892 the people of Virginia erected a monument to A. P. Hill in Richmond, and Heth acted as Chief Marshal at the ceremoney, looking "every inch a soldier as he sat erect on his prancing charger."[176] A year later Jefferson Davis was brought back to his old capital and buried in Hollywood Cemetery. On that occasion Heth commanded a section of the escort and also

served as an honorary pallbearer.[177] We can only guess what
ghosts the city of Richmond, Jefferson Davis, and A. P. Hill
must have conjured up in the mind of the aging veteran.

During his service with the Sharpsburg Commission, Heth
also assisted in collecting Confederate documents for the *Official Records*. . . . In fact, he was probably so engaged while
writing the memoirs in 1897.[178] This would explain several of
the direct quotations from that source which the memoirs contain.

In February 1899, Bright's Disease struck Heth down.
Paralyzed and penniless, he fought to the bitter end, as always.
But this time he faced an enemy even more ruthless than Grant,
and on 27 September 1899 Henry Heth died in Washington,
D.C. Two days later, old comrades, blue and grey, escorted
him back to Richmond where he lay in state in the capitol building on the morning of the 29th, with large crowds coming to
pay him tribute. In the afternoon of the same day, the Confederate veterans, their sons, the Richmond "Blues" and the
"Howitzers" joined the governor of Virginia in accompanying
him to Hollywood Cemetery.[179] There Henry Heth bivouacs
beneath a granite cross inscribed, "In action Faithful and In
Honor Clear," a fitting epitaph.

Notes to Introduction

1. Ida J. Lee, "The Heth Family," *The Virginia Magazine of History and Biography*, XLII, No. 2 (July 1934), 280.

2. Act of Incorporation, Heth Manufacturing Company, 24 February, 1836, F 233 3H5, Virginia State Library.

3. Robert A. Brock, "Orderly Book of Major William Heth of the Third Virginia Regiment, May 15-July 1, 1777," *Collections of the Virginia Historical Society* (new ser.) XI (1892), 320-21.

4. John W. Boitnott, "Secondary Education in Virginia" unpublished Ph.D. dissertation, University of Virginia, 1935, 258-259.

5. Alfred J. Morrison, *The Beginnings of Public Education in Virginia, 1776-1860* (Richmond: State Board of Education, 1917), 101.

6. Boitnott, "Secondary Education," 316.

7. Edward I. Devitt, "Georgetown College In The Early Days," *Records of the Columbia Historical Society* (Washington: Published by the Society, 1909), XII, 21-37.

8. Anne Ayres, *The Life and Work of William Augustus Muhlenberg,* (New York: Anson D. Randolph & Co., 1883), 125-128.

9. Hamilton Basso, *Beauregard the Great Creole* (New York: Charles Scribner's Sons, 1933), 16-17.

10. Letter, William Gibbs McNeill to Honorable Henry A. Wise, 6 February 1843, Adjutant General's Office Military Academy File 152-42, National Archives.

11. Letter, Gouverneur Kemble to the President, 18 January 1843, Adjutant General's Office Military Academy File 152-42, National Archives.

12. Letter, William G. McNeill to Honorable Henry A. Wise, 6 February 1843, Adjutant General's Office Military Academy File 152-42, National Archives.

13. Ibid.

14. Letter, Henry Heth to Secretary of War, 15 March 1843, Adjutant General's Office Military Academy File 152-42, National Archives.

15. "Circumstances of Parents of Cadets, 1842-1879;" "Descriptive List of New Cadets," U.S. Military Academy Archives.

16. Ibid. James L. Morrison, Jr., "The United States Military Academy, 1833-1866: Years of Progress and Turmoil" (unpublished Ph.D. dissertation, Department of History, Columbia University, 1970), 57-58.

17. John C. Tidball Papers, Chapter i, 15-16, U.S. Military Academy Archives. Morrison, "Military Academy," 58-59.

18. Ibid., 59. Lewis, Lloyd, *Captain Sam Grant* (Boston: Little, Brown & Co., 1950), 68.

19. "Descriptive List of New Cadets."

20. "Staff Records," III, 146, U.S. Military Academy Archives. Order No. 62, 27 July 1843, Post Orders No. 2, U.S. Military Academy Archives.

21. Special Order No. 28, 16 February 1844, Post Orders No. 2, U.S. Military Academy Archives. Regulations, U.S. Military Academy 1839, 9.

22. George C. Strong, *Cadet Life at West Point* (Boston: T.O.H.P. Burnham, 1862), 112-21.

23. *Register of Graduates and Former Cadets of the United States Military Academy* (West Point, New York: West Point Alumni Foundation, 1963), 234-35.

24. Regulations, U.S. Military Academy, 1839, 18-20; Morrison, "Military Academy," 103.

25. "Staff Records," IV, 11-13, 104, 133-78, 203, 230. "Staff Records," III, 228-29, 263.

26. "Register of Delinquencies, 1843-1847," U.S. Military Academy Archives, 33, 40, 105, 108. "Staff records," IV, 230.

27. Special Orders No. 1, 2 January 1844, U.S. Military Academy Post Orders, No. 3, 138-39, U. S. Military Academy Archives.

28. Letter, Superintendent to Chief of Engineers, 23 September 1846, Superintendent's Letter Book, 1 1/2, Part 2, U.S. Military Academy Archives. Letter, Superintendent to Mrs. Margaret Heth, 30 September 1846, ibid. "Register of Delinquencies," U.S. Military Academy Archives.

29. Dabney H. Maury, *Recollections of a Virginian In the Mexican, Indian and Civil Wars* (New York: Charles Scribner's Sons, 1894), 23.

30. Morrison, "Military Academy," Appendix VII.

31. Letter, R. S. Ewell to Rebecca Ewell, 29 August 1836, MS 1084, U.S. Military Academy MSS.

32. Strong, *Cadet Life,* 297.

33. Maury, *Recollections,* 22. Ulysses S. Grant, *Personal Memoirs* (2 Vols., New York: Charles L. Webster, 1885), I, 38-9. Lewis, *Captain Sam Grant,* 71. Letter, W. T. Sherman to Philomen Ewing, 1 December 1839, Sherman Papers, U.S. Military Academy MSS.

34. Ben-Perley Poore, *The Life and Public Services of Ambrose E. Burnside* (Providence, R.I.: J. A. and R. A. Reid, 1882), 36-39. John C. Tidball Papers, Chapt. i, 124-27, U.S. Military Academy MSS.

35. Letter, Henry Heth to the Adjutant General, 18 June 1847, Engineer Department Letters, "Application of Graduates for Promotion," U.S. Military Academy Archives. "Cadet Applications for Branches," 18 June 1847, Adjutant's Letters Received, U.S. Military Academy Archives. "Staff Records," IV, 230.

36. Order No. 42, 19 June 1847, U.S. Military Academy, Post Orders, III, 93, U.S. Military Academy Archives.

37. Horatio Gibson, "History of the Class of 1847," 2-5, 40, U.S. Military Academy Archives. Display of class rings, U.S. Military Academy Library.

38. *Official Army Register, Corrected to August 31, 1847,* (Washington: Adjutant General's Office, 1847), 51. Ibid., *1848,* 63.

Ibid., *1849*, 39. Thomas H. S. Hamersly, *Army Register of the United States* (Washington: T. H. S. Hamersly, 1880), 213. Francis B. Heitman, *Historical Register and Dictionary Of The United States Army, 1789-1903*, (2 Vols., Washington: Government Printing Office, 1903), II, 282, 626.

39. *Official Register, 1848*, 27, 66, Ibid., *1853*, 53, 39. Ibid., *1855*, 31, 46.

40. Morrison, "The United States Military Academy," 24, 25.

41. Letter, Secretary of Interior to Adjutant General, 15 June 1899, "Mexican Dependents," Record Group 15-A, Mexican War Claims, 2452, National Archives. Letter, Henry Heth to Capt. H. L. Scott, Assistant Adjutant General, 24 January 1848. Adjutant General's Correspondence File, Record Group 94, National Archives.

42. Letter, Henry Heth to Elizabeth Heth, 6 January 1850, VIH M552H 472 a 40, Virginia Historical Society.

43. Report, Henry Heth to Adjutant General, 24 May 1850, Adjutant General's Office Letters Received, No. 26, National Archives. Report, Heth to Adjutant General, 1 October 1850, ibid.

44. Letter, Henry Heth to Adjutant General, 1 October 1850, ibid. George B. Grinell, *The Fighting Cheyennes* (New York: Charles Scribner's Sons, 1915), 116 fn. Robert M. Utley, *Frontiersmen in Blue: The United States Army and the Indian, 1848-1865* (New York: Macmillan & Co., 1967), map facing 60, 67; Hamersly, *Army Register*, 123.

45. U.S. War Department, *Annual Report of the Secretary of War, 1851*, 161, 194-95, 298.

46. Grinell, *Fighting Cheyennes*, 109. Leroy R. Hafen and W. J. Ghent, *Broken Hand: The Life Story of Thomas Fitzpatrick* (Denver: The Old West Publishing Co., 1931), 223-25. David Lavender, *Bent's Fort* (Garden City, New York: Doubleday, 1954), 320.

47. Lavender, *Bent's Fort*, 320. U.S. War Department, *Annual Report of the Secretary of War, 1852*, 56. Letter, Henry Heth to Adjutant General, 8 October 1852, Adjutant General's Letters Received, No. 28, National Archives. Report, Henry Heth to Adjutant General, 1 March 1853, ibid., No. 29. Report, Henry Heth to Ass't Adjutant General, 6th Military Department, 20 March 1853, ibid. Report, Henry Heth to Adjutant General, Adjutant General Letters Received, No. 28, National Archives. Report, Henry Heth to Adjutant General, 4 September 1851, Secretary of War, Register of Letters Received, LXXIII, No. 123, National Archives. Report, Henry Heth to Adjutant

General, 31 July 1851, Adjutant General Letters Received, No. 27, National Archives.

48. Letter, Henry Heth to Elizabeth Heth, 30 November 1852, VIH MSS IH 471a43, Virginia Historical Society.

49. Letter, Henry Heth to Elizabeth Heth (undated), VIH Mss 2 HN 71a46, Virginia Historical Society. Grinell, *Fighting Cheyennes,* 116. Utley, *Frontiersmen in Blue,* 67. U.S. War Department, *Annual Report of the Secretary of War, 1853,* 116, Chart D, and *Annual Report of the Secretary of War, 1851,* 161.

50. Henry Heth, Commission as First Lieutenant, 6th Infantry, signed 9 February 1854, Adjutant General's Office Records, XIV, p. 654, National Archives. Heth's date of rank as a first lieutenant was backdated to 9 June 1853, a common practice.

51. Letter, Commanding Officer, 6th Infantry, to Adjutant General, 14 March 1854, Adjutant General's Office Letters Received, 106H 1854, National Archives.

52. Letter, Henry Heth to Adjutant General, 20 June 1854. Army Commands, Letters Sent, Fort Kearny, 1848-1855, Record Group 95, National Archives.

53. *American History Atlas* (Maplewood, N.J.: C. S. Hammond, 1953), A-15. Utley, *Frontiersmen in Blue,* map facing 60, 65-66.

54. Letter, Heth to Adjutant General, 22 September 1854, Adjutant General Letters Received, 1854, No. 30, National Archives. Report, Heth to Ass't Adjutant General, Department of the West, 15 November 1854. AGO Letters Received, Record Group 94, National Archives. U.S. War Department, *Annual Report of the Secretary of War, 1854,* 1-6, 56-57.

55. *Official Army Register,* 1855, 24. Item No. 224, 1 December 1854, Secretary of War, Letters Received, LXXX, National Archives. Telegram, Adjutant General to General N. S. Clarke, 23 February 1855. Adjutant General, Letters Sent Book, 1854-55. XXIX, National Archives. Henry Heth, Commission, Captain 10th Inf., 30 April 1855.

56. Franklin H. Mackey and Charles C. Ivey (authors of Heth's obituary), *Confederate Veteran,* VII, No. 12 (Dec. 1899), 569-70. Horatio Gibson, "History of the Class of 1847," 40, U.S. Military Academy MSS.

57. Doane Robinson, *A History of the Dakota or Sioux Indians* (Minneapolis: Ross and Haines, 1956), 224. L. U. Reavis, *The Life and Military Service of General William Selby Harney* (St. Louis:

Bryan, Bird & Co., 1878), 247-48, 255. Letter, Commanding Officer, Fort Kearny to Adjutant General, 28 August, 1855, Army Commands, Letters Sent—Fort Kearny, National Archives. Otis E. Young, *The West of Philip St. George Cooke* (Glendale, Calif. Arthur H. Clark Co., 1955), 266-71. U.S. War Department, *Annual Report of the Secretary of War, 1855,* 4, 49-51. Utley, *Frontiersmen in Blue,* 115-116.

58. Eugene Bandel, FRONTIER LIFE IN THE ARMY 1854-1861 (Glendale, Calif.: The Arthur H. Clark Co., 1932), 29-31. U.S. War Department, ANNUAL REPORT OF THE SECRETARY OF WAR, 1855, 4. Utley, *Frontiersmen in Blue,* 115.

59. *Annual Report of Secretary of War, 1855,* 49-51. Utley, *Frontiersmen in Blue,* 116. Young, *The West of P. St. G. Cooke,* 266. Bandel, *Frontier Life in the Army,* 84.

60. *Thirty-First Annual Reunion of the Association of Graduates of the United States Military Academy* (Saginaw, Mich.: Seemen and Peters, 1900), 87.

61. *Annual report of the Secretary of War, 1855,* 50. Young, *The West of Philip St. George Cooke,* 268.

62. Young, *The West of Philip St. George Cooke,* 270-71. *Army Register, 1855,* 13.

63. Letter, Henry Heth to Elizabeth Heth, 5 May 1853, VIH Mss H41a44, Virginia Historical Society.

64. Letter, Henry Heth to "Teny" Selden, 26 January 1857, Heth Papers, 5071, University of Virginia MSS. Pension Claim, Harriett Heth, 22 May 1901, Mexican Dependents Branch, National Archives.

65. Ibid.

66. Letter, Henry Heth to Elizabeth Heth, 5 May 1893, VIH Mss IH47a44, Virginia Historical Society.

67. Letter, Henry Heth to the Adjutant General, 15 October 1857. A.G.O. Letters Received, 1857, No. 33 National Archives Letter, Henry Heth to the Adjutant General, 8 February 1858, (37H), Record Group 97, National Archives.

68. Letter, Henry Heth to Adjutant General, 10 June 1856, with endorsements, A.G.O Letters Received, 1856, No. 32, National Archives.

69. Letter, Henry Heth to Adjutant General, 8 February 1858, Adjutant General's Office Records, Record Group 94 (37H), National Archives.

70. Ibid.

71. U.S. Senate, Report of the Secretary of War, 35th Cong., 2d Sess., 1858, 118-121.

72. Drafts with these titles are in the Heth Papers, 5071, University of Virginia MSS.

73. *Annual Report of the Secretary of War, 1859,* I, Part I, 139-159.

74. Letter, Henry Heth to the Adjutant General, 26 November 1860, Adjutant General's Office Records (289H), Record Group 94, National Archives.

75. Letter, Henry Heth to Adjutant General, 17 April 1861, Adjutant General's Office Records (289H), Record Group 94, National Archives.

76. Letter, Henry Heth to Jefferson Davis, 17 April 1861, Confederate Records, Record Group 109, National Archives.

77. *The War of the Rebellion, A Compilation of the Official Records of the Union and Confederate Armies* (4 Ser., 70 Vols., Washington: Government Printing Office, 1880-1901), Ser. 1, LI, Part II, 36; cited hereafter as *O.R. Official Army Register,* 1861, 73. Confederate Archives, Chapt. i, File No. 88, National Archives.

78. Register of Appointments, Confederate States Army, II, 781, Confederate Archives, National Archives. Clement A. Evans, (ed.), *Confederate Military History* (12 Vols., Atlanta: Confederate Publishing Co., 1899, reprinted by T. Yoseleff, 1962), III, 124. Douglas S. Freeman, *Robert E. Lee* (4 Vols., New York: Charles Scribner's Sons, 1934), I, 77. *O.R.,* Ser. 1, LI, Part II, 121.

79. Roster, 45th Regiment of Virginia Volunteers, 31 July 1861, Confederate Records, No. 19076, Virginia State Library. *O.R.,* Ser. 1, LI, Part II, 121. Ibid., 5, 153. Ibid., 2, 236-37. Ibid., 5, 772.

80. R. U. Johnson and C. C. Buel (ed.), *Battles and Leaders of the Civil War* (4 Vols., New York: The Century Co., 1914), I, 143-46. *O.R.,* Ser. 1, LI, Part II, 290, 325, 368.

81. *O.R.,* Ser. 1, LIII, 191.

82. Ibid., 761-62.

83. Ibid., VIII, 88.

84. Ibid., V, 1038. Register of Appointments, Confederate States Army, File No. 86, Chapts. I, VI, Confederate Archives, National Archives.

85. Ibid.

86. *O.R.,* Ser. 1, V, 1073, 1077-78. Ibid., LI, Part II, 480, 494.

Letter, Heth to Adjutant & Inspector General, CSA, 6 February 1862, Confederate Archives, National Archives.

87. *O.R.,* Ser. 1, XII, Part I, 513. Ibid., Part III, 204. Ibid., LI, Part II, 511. *Battles and Leaders,* II, 278-81.

88. O.R. Ser. 1, XII, Part I, 492.

89. Robert White, "West Virginia," *Confederate Military History* (12 Vols., New York: Thomas Yoseloff, 1962), II, 56-60. Jacob D. Cox, *Military Reminiscences of the Civil War* (2 Vols., New York: Charles Scribner's Sons, 1900), I, 220. *O.R.*, Ser. I, XII, Part I, 812-13.

90. *O.R.,* Ser. 1, XII, Part I, 213.

91. Ibid., LI, 584.

92. Edward Younger (ed.), *Inside the Confederate Government: The Diary of Robert Garlick Hill Kean* (New York: Oxford University Press, 1957), 42-43.

93. *O.R.,* Ser. 1, XVI, Part II, 707. Repeated in Dunbar Rowland (ed.) *Jefferson Davis, Constitutionalist: His Letters, Papers, and Speeches,* (10 Vols. Jackson, Miss.: Mississippi Department of Archives and History, 1923), V, 286.

94. *O.R.,* Ser. 1, LII, Part II, 326-28.

95. *O.R.* Ser. 1, XVI, Part II, 719. Joseph H. Parks, *General Edmund Kirby Smith, C.S.A.* (Baton Rouge: Louisiana State University Press, 1954), 195.

96. *O.R.,* Ser. 1, XVI, Part II, 721, 722.

97. Ibid., 752. *Battles and Leaders,* III, 4-7.

98. *O.R.,* Ser. 1, XVI, Part II, 777.

99. The senate probably refused to confirm Heth's promotion because of his failure at Lewisburg and the criticism he had incurred as a result of his militia proclamation. The senate, in executive session, voted against the promotion without discussion on receipt of the negative recommendation of the Committee on Military Affairs. *Journal of the Congress of the Confederate States of America, 1861-1865,* (7 Vols., Washington: Government Printing Office, 1904-05), II, 471. Martin Schenck, *Up Came Hill* (Harrisburg, Pa.: Stackpole Co., 1958), 266.

100. Letter, Henry Heth to Adjutant & Inspector General Confederate States Army, 21 November 1862, Confederate Archives, H2240, Record Group 109, National Archives.

101. Douglas S. Freeman, *Lee's Lieutenants: A Study in Command*

(3 Vols., New York: Charles Scribner's Sons, 1949), II, 506-7.

102. Letter, E. Kirby Smith to Henry Heth, 27 January 1863, Heth Papers, 5071, University of Virginia MSS.

103. Freeman, *Lee's Lieutenants,* III, 506-7. William W. Hassler, *A. P. Hill, Lee's Forgotton General* (Richmond: Garrett and Massie, 1957), 127. *O.R.,* Ser. 1, XXV, Part II, 654. Schenck, *Up Came Hill,* 239.

104. Hassler, *A. P. Hill,* 125.

105. Ibid., 132-33. Freeman, *Lee's Lieutenants,* II, 533, 536-37. *O.R.,* Ser. 1, XXV, Part I, 889-92. Rodes was a VMI graduate, Class of 1848.

106. Hassler, *A. P. Hill,* 134.

107. Ibid., 138-39. *O.R.,* Ser. 1, XXV, Part I, 916, 920.

108. *O.R.,* Ser. 1, XXV, Part I, 886-89.

109. Ibid., 885-86.

110. *O.R.,* Ser. 1, XXV, Part II, 840. Clifford Dowdey (ed.), *The Wartime Papers of R. E. Lee* (Boston: Little, Brown & Co., 1961), 448-49. Douglas S. Freeman ed., *Lee's Confidential Dispatches to Davis, Unpublished Letters of General Robert E. Lee, C.S.A. to Jefferson Davis and the War Department of the Confederate States of America, 1862-65)* New York: G. P. Putnam's Sons, 1915, 91-93. *O.R.,* Ser. 1, LI, Part II, 716-17. Register of Appointments, Confederate State Army, Chapt. i, File No. 86, 4. Freeman, *Lee's Lieutenants,* II, 698-712. Ibid., Part II, 685. *O.R.,* Ser. 1, XXIX, Part I, 400.

111. Letter, James Longstreet to Henry Heth, 14 January 1897, Heth Papers, MC3 H480, Confederate Museum MSS. Henry Heth, "Why Lee Lost at Gettysburg," Philadelphia *Weekly Times,* 22 September 1877, Henry B. McClellan Papers, MSS. Henry Heth, "The Gettysburg Campaign Official Reports," *Southern Historical Society Papers,* VI, 258. *Lee's Confidential Dispatches to Davis,* 108-11.

112. Hassler, *A. P. Hill,* 156. Fitzhugh Lee, *General Lee* (Vol. IV, Great Commanders' Ser., New York: D. Appleton Co., 1894), 269-73. E. P. Alexander, *Military Memoirs of a Confederate* (New York: Charles Scribner's Sons, 1912), 380-84, 444. *O.R.,* Ser. 1, XXVII, Part II, 637-39.

113. Wayland F. Dunaway, *Reminiscences Of A Rebel* (New York: Neale Publishing Co., 1913), 96-97; and Spencer G. Walsh, *A Confederate Surgeon's Letters To His Wife* (Marietta, Ga.: Continental Book Co., 1909), 154.

114. Walter Clark (ed.), *Histories of The Several Regiments and Battalions From North Carolina In The Great War, 1861-65,* (Goldsboro, N.C.: Nash Bros., 1901), 559.

115. *O.R.,* Ser. 1, XXVII, Part II, 639-42.

116. Ibid. Freeman, *Lee's Lieutenants,* III, 167. *O.R.,* Ser. 1, XXIX, Part II, 326, 428. "Report of Maj-Gen. Heth of the Affair at Falling Waters," *Southern Historical Society Papers,* VII, 196-99.

117. Report of Heth's (old) Brigade in the Battles of Maryland and Penn., Hq. Walker's Brigade, 14 August 1863, Heth Papers, MC 3 H 479, Confederate Museum, Richmond.

118. *O.R.,* Ser. 1, XXIX, Part II, 427. Hassler, *A. P. Hill,* 179.

119. *O.R.,* Ser. 1, XXIX, Part I, 430-33.

120. Hassler, *A. P. Hill,* 179.

121. Letter, A. P. Hill to Henry Heth, 13 January 1864, MC 3, H 479, Confederate Museum, Richmond.

122. Hassler, *A. P. Hill,* 152.

123. Ibid.

124. Freeman, *Lee's Lieutenants,* III, 392.

125. Ibid., 393.

126. Ibid., 398.

127. Ibid., 402.

128. Hassler, *A. P. Hill,* 201-2.

129. Ibid., 205.

130. Ibid., 206-7; and *O.R.,* Ser. 1, XXXVI, Part III, 863, 1047.

131. *O.R.,* Ser. 1, XXXVI, Part I, 1031, 1032. Hassler, *A. P. Hill,* 209, 210. Dowdey, Clifford, *Wartime Papers of R. E. Lee* (Boston: Little, Brown & Co., 1961), 760.

132. Hassler, *A. P. Hill,* 214-15.

133. *O.R.,* Ser. 1, XL, Part III, 506, 520, 552, 563, 619. Ibid., Vol LI, Part II, 1082.

134. *O.R.,* Ser. 1, XLII, Part II, 302, 940. *Battles and Leaders,* IV, 568.

135. *Battles and Leaders,* IV, 568. Hassler, *A. P. Hill,* 226-27.

136. *History of North Carolina Regiments,* II, 388-89. *O.R.,* Ser. 1, XLII, Part II, 525.

137. Hassler, *A. P. Hill,* 231.

138. Ibid., 213.

139. Freeman, *Lee's Lieutenants,* III, 623.

140. Report, Henry Heth to Adjutant General, III Corps, 27 October 1864, MC 3 H 480, Confederate Museum, Richmond.

141. Ibid.

142. Ibid. *O.R.*, Ser. 1, XLII, Part I, 853. Freeman, *Lee's Lieutenants*, III, 615.

143. Report, Henry Heth to Adjutant General, III Corps, 27 October 1864.

144. Ibid.

145. Freeman, *Lee's Lieutenants*, III, 617.

146. Ibid., 616 and Report, Henry Heth to Adjutant General, III Corps, 1 February 1865, MC 3 H 480, Confederate Museum, Richmond.

147. Ella Lonn, *Desertion During the Civil War* (Gloucester, Mass.: Peter Smith, 1966) 27, 230. Dowdey, *Wartime Papers of Lee,* 910.

148. Hassler, *A. P. Hill,* 236. Ibid., 239. *O.R.,* Ser. 1, XLVI, Part II, 19.

149. Ibid., 242.

150. Report, Henry Heth to Adjutant General, Army of Northern Virginia, 11 April 1865. Robert E. Lee Papers, 1855-1878, MS 3L 515a, Virginia Historical Society. *O.R.,* Ser. 1, XLVI, Part I, 1272.

151. Warner, Ezra B., *Generals in Grey* (Baton Rouge: Louisiana State University Press, 1955), 13, 92, 143, 178, 231, 296, 348, 502.

152. *Register of Graduates and Former Cadets of the United States Military Academy* (West Point: West Point Alumni Foundation, 1963), 232-35.

153. *Register of Graduates,* 231-38. Eliot, Ellsworth, Jr., *West Point in the Confederacy* (New York: C. D. Baker Co., 1941), 31.

154. Freeman, *Lee's Lieutenants,* III, xxxiii. Eliot, *West Point in the Confederacy,* 51.

155. Ibid.

156. Freeman, *Lee's Lieutenants,* III, xxxviii.

157. Ibid., II, xiv; III, xxvi.

158. Ibid., xxiv. Letter, Douglas S. Freeman to Mrs. Emlyn H. Marstellar, 9 June 1942, Heth Papers, University of Virginia.

159. Letters, D. H. Larned to Henry Heth, 22 May 1866 and 17 March 1868, Heth Papers 5071, University of Virginia.

160. Letters, D. H. Larned to Henry Heth, 30 March 1866 and 14 March 1868, Heth Papers, 5071, University of Virginia.

161. Diary, Miles Selden, entry of 1 April 1869, Heth Papers 5071,

University of Virginia. Letters, George B. McClellan to Charles P.
Stone, 9 March 1869, and Winfield S. Hancock to Henry Heth, 30
May 1869, Heth Papers 5071, University of Virginia.

162. Letter, John C. Maynard to Henry Heth, 8 May 1869, Heth
Papers, 5071, University of Virginia.

163. *Dictionary of American Biography,* XVII, 84. General
Records, Treasury Department, Special Agents and Inspectors Appli-
cations, 20 June 1878, Record Group 56, National Archives.
Obituary, *Confederate Veteran,* VII, No. 12, 569-70. Diary, Miles
Selden, entries 1 January 1872-23 April 1873, Heth Papers, 5071,
University of Virginia.

164. Diary, Miles Selden, 1 January 1872-23 April 1873.
Richmond City Directory, 1874-1878, Virginia State Library.

165. Letter, C. Pickett to Henry Heth, 26 January 1878, Heth
Papers, 5071, University of Virginia. Letter, N. R. Selden to Mrs.
General H. Heth, 10 May 1877, ibid.

166. *The Constitution, By-Laws, and House Rules of the Westmoreland Club of Richmond, Virginia* (Richmond: Bell Book and Stationery Co., 1909), 1-6.

167. *The State* (newspaper), Richmond, 21 July 1877, 1; and *The
Richmond Dispatch,* 19 October 1877, 1.

168. *The Weekly Times,* Philadelphia, 22 September, 6 October and
15 December 1877. Letter, Henry Heth to Henry B. McClellan, 27
March 1878, Henry B. McClellan Papers, M1 1324a 18, Virginia Historical Society.

169. Letter, J. C. Maynard to Henry Heth, 5 March 1878; Bill,
S. 899, 45th Cong., 2d Sess., 11 March 1878, Heth MSS Paper,
5071, University of Virginia.

170. Special Agents and Inspectors Applications 1878-79, General
Record, Treasury Department, Record Group 56, National Archives.
Cullum, *Register,* III, 343. *Official Register of the United States, con-
taining list of Officers and Employees in the Civil, Military, and Naval
Service on the First of July 1883* (Washington: Government Printing
Office, 1883), I, 318.

171. U.S. War Department, *Annual Report of the Secretary of War,
1881,* II, Part I, 1030-37. Ibid., 1882, II, Part II, 1108-12. Ibid.,
1883, II, Part I, 869. Ibid., 1884, II, Part II, 1048-49.

172. Indian Office Executive Appointments Register, I, 199 and

certificate, No. 14261, Record Group 75, National Archives. Letter, G. W. C. Lee to L. Q. C. Lamar, 12 March 1885, Heth MSS, MC 3 H 480, Confederate Museum.

173. Office of Indian Affairs, Index of Letters Received, 1881-1886, Vols. E-K, Record Group 75, National Archives, and various specific entries referenced therein, in particular, report, Henry Heth to Office of Indian Affairs, 30 August 1888, 22215, ibid.

174. Resignation, Henry Heth to Office of Indian Affairs, June 1889, Register of Letters, R-161, National Resources Record Division, Bureau of Indian Affairs, National Archives.

175. Letter, General J. C. Kelton, Adjutant General, U.S. Army, to Quartermaster General, 13 February 1891, Document File 8586, Record Group 92, National Archives. Letter, Henry Heth to Quartermaster General, 29 October 1894, Document File 10048, Ibid.

176. Richmond *Dispatch,* 31 May 1892, 1.

177. *The New York Times,* 1 July 1893, 5.

178. Letter (draft), Henry Heth to A. C. McClung, October 1897, Heth MSS, 5071, University of Virginia.

179. Richmond *Times,* 27 September 1899; Washington, *The Evening Star,* 27 September 1899; *The Washington Post,* 30 September 1899.

The Memoirs of Henry Heth

Contents

officer nearly produces war. Colonel Sumner settles the trouble. Brevet Captain Buckner in command. My brother John joins me. Major R. H. Chilton. Grey hounds. Fight with Pawnees. How Indians scalp the dead. Incantations. Find an Indian baby in the grass. Mason purchases Mexican woman and child.

regimental quartermaster. General Harney to command Sioux expedition, appoints me his aide-de-camp. At Leavenworth. Appointed a captain in the Tenth Infantry. Ordered to Washington. See Adjutant General and Secretary of War. Ordered on Sioux expedition. Company mounted. Leave Fort Leavenworth. Famous buffalo hunt.

CHAPTER XV *127*

Reach North Platte. General Harney attacks Indian village. The fight. Charges against A. P. Howe. Obituaries. Winter at Laramie. Antelope not good. A duel. Ordered to Platte Bridge. My company improved in accuracy of fire. March to Fort Snelling. Visit my friend Captain Bee. Horses sold. Major E. R. Canby. Apply for leave. Visit to Secretary of War. Target practice. Determine to secure a wife. Am married. On a Board at West Point. Burnside's unanimously pronounced the best. Board visits New England. Burnside in high spirits, but fails to receive the award. Joins McClellan. Target practice. Approved by Secretary. Ordered to Utah. In command of recruits. Camp Floyd, Utah. About Mormons. Pratt shot. In revenge, Mountain Meadow Massacre.

CHAPTER XVI *145*

Judge Cradlebaugh. Company ordered to Provo. U.S. Courts a travesty. Brigham Young, judge, and jury. Position becomes hazardous. Major Paul sent to Provo. Mormon Church, how organized. General Johnston leaves Utah. Col. C. F. Smith in command. Captain Burton, English Army, makes me a visit. On leave. War fever increasing. Virginia secedes. Resign. Expedition to Norfolk.

General Lee seizes flag. Longstreet arrives and drives enemy. Spottysylvania Court House. What happened there. North Anna. Bethesda Church. General Grant moves to Petersburg.

CHAPTER XXI *190*

Battle of the 18th, 19th, and 20th of August, 1864 on Weldon Railroad. A brave but silly girl. General Grant extends his left. Objective point South Side Railroad. My headquarters. A wagon load of good things. Red Eye colt. General Lee objects to my wife riding Red Eye. General Lee frequently visits my Headquarters. A reprimand. My daughter secures valuable mementoes. Col. William J. Pegram. General Lee would gladly command brigade or regiment. General Wise at General Lee's Headquarters. General Grant's successful flank movements. Surrender Appomattox, April 9, 1865. Note to Seth Williams. Visit from Seth and Rufus Ingalls.

CHAPTER XXII *198*

Interview with General Grant April 9, 1865 at Appomattox. Reach home. Visit St. Louis. Sent for by General Pope. Visit General Hancock. Am his guest. What occurred. Visit to Burnside. What occurred. Special Agent, Treasury Department. Life at Brownsville, Texas. General Sykes. A hunt. Work on Rivers and Harbors. Special U. S. Indian Agent. Take census of Indians in Washington and Oregon. With Hancock at Governors Island. Reams Station fight. Meade's letter to Hancock. Hancock refuses to make a promise.

The Memoirs of Henry Heth

Written at the request of my wife and children.

I

I was born at Blackheath,[1] Chesterfield County, Va., December 16, 1825. My father served as a midshipman in the United States Navy during the War of 1812 with Great Britain and was in the U. S. ship "The President" commanded by Commodore Decatur when captured by the English fleet outside of Boston. My father and several young officers were taken to Bermuda and held as prisoners of war, until they made their escape by boarding and seizing a small vessel in the harbor, and thus escaping to the United States.

As soon as peace was declared, my father resigned from the Navy[2] and took charge of the very valuable coal mines in Chesterfield County owned by his father.[3] These mines deserve to be mentioned in this brochure. The coal mines of Chesterfield

9

"Blackheath"

and contiguous counties were the only bituminous coal fields
near the Atlantic coast of the United States; their nearest com-
petitors were the bituminous mines in the British provinces
north of Maine; consequently, we find the owners of Virginia
coal fields petitioning Congress to place a duty on foreign
bituminous coal. Having a monopoly of bituminous coal, the
producers fixed their own price. The city of Richmond was
supplied from these mines with fuel, and for their gas works
when gas came to be used. Likewise Baltimore, Philadelphia,
New York and Boston were compelled to purchase from these
mines. All the large foundries procured their coal from the Virginia coal fields. The West Point foundry for years used no
other. I have often heard my father say that he would rather
own a coal mine than a gold mine.

My earliest recollections were among coal mines, and my
greatest desire was to descend into one of the perpendicular
shafts. I was forbidden descending into any mine. The desire
to do what was forbidden, combined with the curiosity, was
too strong, so I saved what money was given me for several
weeks; with this and some cake that I got from my mother's
storeroom I bribed a foreman of the mine, an old "darkey,"
to take me down into the mine seven hundred feet deep.
Remaining in the pit some two hours, I asked the old "darkey"
to take me out. The illusion of a coal pit was dispelled from
that day.

Until I was ten years old I went to school in Virginia, the
first being at Mr. Medijah Meade's in Amelia County, from
there to Mr. Hugh Nelson's in Charles City County, and then
to Mr. Page's in Cumberland County.

My father was passionately devoted to blooded horses, his
large means enabling him to indulge in the expensive sport of
racing. At that time racing was conducted very differently from
that of the present day. The Jockey Clubs were managed by
gentlemen. Richmond boasted of three race courses, a week's

racing at each, spring and fall. The wealth and fashion of the State collected in Richmond to witness the races, and participate in the gayeties of the same; dinners, balls, and parties of various kinds followed each other thick and fast. No questionable characters were admitted in the race course or race stand; these were sacredly kept for the aristocracy of the Old Dominion and surrounding states. Gentlemen were the owners of the horses. Many of the gentlemen who could afford to do so owned race horses, or were interested in blooded horses.

Racing has changed since then; now it is followed as a profession extensively by gamblers. After the racing was over in Richmond, Va., (which lasted three weeks) the gentlemen took their horses to Washington, Baltimore and New York, to participate in the races near those cities. Returning home they were put in training for the fall season.

One condition I made on going to school was that I would be sent for and permitted to attend the races. As a boy I always had a horse in training, but do not recollect that my horse ever won a race.

I was sent when about twelve years old to Georgetown College, D. C.; I remained there one year and was then sent to Dr. Wm. A. Muhlenberg's school at College Point, Long Island, a fine school and largely patronized by South Carolinians and Virginians.

During the winter of 1841 I attended Mr. Peugnet's school in New York City. Mr. Puegnet was a Frenchman who had served in Napoleon's army, and coming to this country after Napoleon's overthrow, opened a school in New York City.[4] General Beauregard and General Delos B. Sackett,[5] "Beau" Whistler,[6] now on the retired list, Charles Choteau,[7] and many other St. Louis boys, among whom were the Pratts and Nidletts,[8] Frederick Prime[9] of New York, who led the class of 1850, and General W. H. F. Lee,[10] son of General Robert E. Lee, were eleves of this accomplished gentleman and good old man. I remained at Mr. Peugnet's nearly two years, and acquired a fair knowledge of French and the rudiments of mathematics.

I have often doubted whether this knowledge was beneficial to me or not at West Point. For the first six months I scarcely ever opened a book; I thought I knew it all, but often found, to my sorrow, that I was sadly mistaken when the X-rays of the professor were turned on my perfunctory knowledge of the subject.

In 1842 the most severe calamity I had ever felt came to me. Mr. Peugnet received a letter from Virginia saying that my father was dead,[11] and requesting that I should be sent to my mother in Virginia. My father had just returned from England and died of consumption, after a short illness, at Norwood,[12] Powhatan County, Va. He was buried in the family vault at that place. I believe there was no man in Chesterfield and surrounding counties more esteemed and beloved than my father. Generous to a fault, no deserving person in need ever applied to him for assistance who was refused. He was the captain of the Chesterfield Cavalry Troop as long as his health and business permitted him to perform the duties. When he was buried the Chesterfield Troop came to Powhatan County and escorted his remains to the grave.

I remained a month with my mother and returned to Mr. Peugnet's. Immediately after my father's death, President Tyler wrote to my mother offering me an appointment as a midshipman in the Navy. My mother declined the offer; two nieces had married naval officers who happened to be dissipated, and I believe she imagined this was a characteristic failing in the Navy. In the latter part of 1842[13] the President (Tyler) sent me an appointment to West Point, to enter the class of 1843.

II

It was a sad day for me when I bade adieu to my schoolmates, and the dear Peugnets, and was placed on a boat and
consigned to West Point.[1] There I found my cousin George E.
Pickett,[2] afterwards General Pickett of Confederate fame, the
first man to scale the walls of Chapultepec and raise the American flag over that stronghold. Pickett extended to me, a plebe,
his cousinly protection and thus I escaped many of the rough
tricks played upon new cadets.

My four year career at West Point as a student was abominable.[3] My thoughts ran in the channel of fun. How to get to
Benny Havens[4] occupied more of my time than Legendre on
Calculus.[5] The time given to study was measured by the amount
of time necessary to be given to prevent failure at the annual
examinations.[6]

During the early part of my third class encampment I, was
engaged with a number of my classmates in the enjoyable occupation of deviling a plebe on his post; the plebe became enraged
and threw his musket, bayonet foremost, into the crowd. The
bayonet struck me in the thigh, missing the femoral artery by
about an eighth of an inch, and passed through my leg. I fell
as though I had been shot by a cannon ball. I was taken to
the hospital, fainting several times before reaching there. I
remained there flat on my back for weeks. The strangest part
of this escapade on my part was that the only punishment I
received was the confinement in the hospital. The cadet who
threw his musket into the crowd of teasers was severely
punished, as he was informed by the commandant of cadets,
not because he had hurt me, for he would have been justified
in killing me, but for a soldier to part with his gun was criminal.

The summer encampments of the cadets at West Point were

View of West Point in 1841 by Kollmer

Courtesy of the U.S. Military Academy Archives and Special Collections, West Point

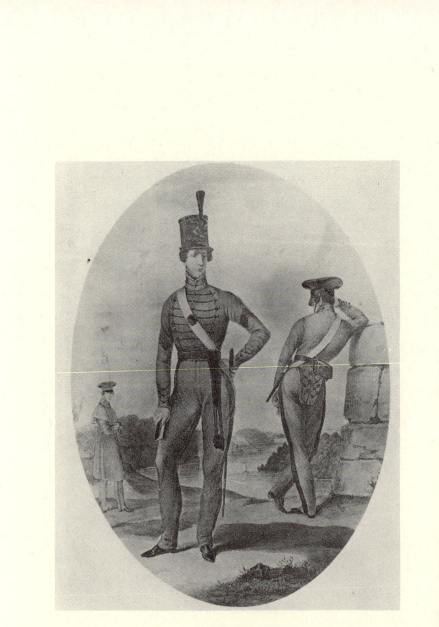

*Courtesy of the U. S. Military Academy
Archives, West Point*

Cadet Uniform of the Early 1840s

Kosciuszko's Monument in the 1840s by Kollmer

Courtesy of the U. S. Military
Academy Archives and Special
Collections, West Point

looked upon as the most enjoyable part of their four years' course. The summer of 1845, being now second classmen,[7] we were permitted to go to our homes for two months. I think those two months were among the most enjoyable of my life. The Duke of Wellington, after defeating his great adversary at Waterloo, could not have felt more exalted, or more pleased with himself, than the West Point cadet dressed in his furlough coat, with brass buttons, when strutting along the streets, or on entering the parlor of some young miss who had given a party in honor of his return to his native city or village.

When I entered West Point in 1843 there were many cadets in the corps who subsequently made brilliant names for themselves. Grant graduated the year I entered; I do not remember having seen him as a cadet, but subsequently became well acquainted, as will be told in its proper place. Generals S. B. Buckner, Winfield S. Hancock,[8] W. H. C. Whiting, W. F. Smith, Fitz John Porter, E. K. Smith, Delos B. Sackett, Bernard F. Bee,[9] George B. McClellan, Jesse L. Reno, Darius N. Couch, S. D. Sturgis, George Stoneman, George F. Evans, Dabney H. Maury, D. R. Jones, Cadmus M. Wilcox, George E. Pickett,[10] made honorable names for themselves during the Civil War 1861-5. Those of my own classmates who became general officers during the war were Daniel T. Van Buren, Orlando B. Willcox, John S. Mason, James B. Fry, Ambrose P. Hill, Ambrose E. Burnside, John Gibbon, Romeyn B. Ayres, Charles Griffin, Thomas H. Neill, W. W. Burns, Egbert L. Viele, Lewis C. Hunt.[11] There was but one thing I excelled in at West Point. I was acknowledged to be the best rider in my class.

After passing my second class examination and becoming a first classman, we went into camp.[12] I was looking forward to my first class encampment with great pleasure. My submaxillary glands were somewhat swollen. I determined to consult the post surgeon; he told me I must come to the hospital and be treated.

That meant being confined to a ward in the hospital during the summer. I thought I saw an opportunity, by which I could have a better time by being on the sick list, and in the hospital, than in camp, so I interviewed the doctor and told him my general health was very good, that for the past year I had attended to all military duties, as well as to my studies, and I was unwilling to be subjected to strict hospital rules, which I thought would be injurious rather than beneficial; but I was willing and anxious to be treated, and would take his prescriptions, etc.; that I would like to attend artillery drills, riding, and the pyrotechnic class. To this the doctor consented. By this arrangement, if the doctor came to my ward and found me absent, I was supposed to be attending some of these duties and nothing was said. I was thus enabled to visit New York and Newburg, and go pretty much where fancy and inclination prompted; of course I was running a great risk, but I was so in the habit of taking risks, that I presume I became callous. Fortunately for me I was never caught, or even suspected of being guilty of these unpardonable violations of Academic Regulations.

During the summer of 1846 the hospital steward at West Point, Stoddard by name, was a Scotchman by birth and a graduate of a medical college in Edinburgh. Stoddard was a man of intelligence, and well educated. On his arrival in this country it was necessary for him to find some occupation which would enable him to lay up money preparatory to becoming a practitioner of medicine; he heard of the vacancy of hospital steward at West Point, applied for it and was appointed to the position. Stoddard and I became great friends. Stoddard was inclined to frolic, and he would prescribe for me toddies, never failing to take some of his own medicine.

One night he proposed that we should pay a visit to Benny Havens. I was always ready for a trip to Benny's. We soon found ourselves safely ensconced in old Benny's bar room. We remained there for several hours when I perceived that my

friend was becoming very shaky. I took him up the hill from
Benny's; on reaching Buttermilk Falls, a small village, he said,
"You go on, I propose visiting a friend in the village." I saw
him to the house of his friend, and continued my walk up the
road. On nearing a lane I discovered two horses. I said to myself, "It is useless to walk when kind Providence has supplied
me with a horse;" so I caught one of them and, improvising a
bridle from my neck and pocket handkerchiefs, I mounted my
"Rosanante" and galloped up the road, fully intending to turn
my steed loose on reaching the gate which entered the reservation. It occurred to me that there was more fun on hand; and
I determined to charge the encampment which was guarded by
six sentinels. The midnight charge had never occurred before;
the sentinels challenged. I made my way through the encampment, concealing my horse and self among the ruins of Old
Fort Clinton,[13] and awaited developments. Patrols were sent out
in various directions, but none came near my hiding place. After
a while quiet was restored and I again charged the encampment;
this was repeated a third time. After the last charge the officer
of the day, the army officers in charge of the cadets, came out,
had their several companies paraded and the rolls called; sentinels were doubled and Patrols sent out. The mysterious horseman was not found.

After quiet was restored in camp I quietly made my way to
the hospital. On reaching there the thought occurred to me that
I had better ride to Buttermilk Falls and bring my friend Stoddard home on horseback. I found Stoddard very much intox-
icated. He insisted on getting a stick before mounting behind
me, and at once commenced using the stick vigorously on the
horse. The road made a sharp turn at the bridge over Buttermilk
Creek. As we were crossing the bridge, dogs appeared, barking
and snapping at the horse, who shied; off fell Stoddard, pulling
me with him. Stoddard was knocked senseless. I was not hurt.
I carried Stoddard to the house of the former steward of

West Point, who was practising medicine in Buttermilk Falls. Stoddard was put to bed and was soon asleep. As I could be of no further assistance I made my way to the hospital and went to bed.

Sick call beat every morning shortly after Reveille, when the doctor, accompanied by his steward, was due in one of the rooms in the old North Barracks to prescribe for ailing cadets. On this particular morning the Doctor (Southgate) had no steward to assist him. During the morning the missing steward appeared. He was much cut about the head and face. Doctor Southgate was furious; he came to my room and said, "I had no steward at sick call this morning. I find that he was off last night frolicking with cadets." I said, "Can that be so, who would have thought it!" "I shall have him tried by a court martial and severely punished."

Under the bank of the river near the hospital was a cove, known as the "Pirate's Cove," so named from the fact that a man known by the cadets as "The Pirate" was in the habit of coming there with his boat and trading whiskey, tobacco and other contraband articles with the cadets for shoes, old clothes and what not, in the absence of money. Stoddard saw the Pirate and arranged to have his boat at the cove on a given night to carry him down or across the river. I assisted Stoddard to get his books and belongings to the boat and bid him God speed. I have heard that he went to Illinois and became a successful practitioner of medicine, and subsequently a minister in the Episcopal Church. The part I played in this night's frolics was never discovered by the authorities, and *I never told them.*

My first roommate at West Point was A. H. Seward,[14] a son of Mr. Seward, Secretary of State under President Lincoln. We both had demerits by the score. Governor Seward wrote to the superintendent to know why it was his son received so many demerits. About the same time Mr. Gouverneur Kemble,[15] who had been, during his life, a particular friend of my father, and feeling an interest in me, wrote and made the same inquiry about me. The answers of the Superintendent were identical. The letter to Governor Seward was that his son was rooming with a very wild and bad boy from Virginia, and that he intended to separate them. In answer to Mr. Kemble he said that I was rooming with a very wild and bad boy from New York and that he intended to separate us. Governor Seward sent the Superintendent's letter to his son, and Mr. Kemble sent his letter to me. The idea of calling Seward a bad and wild boy amused his classmates and no one more than myself. Of all the quiet, reticent human beings I ever met, Gus Seward was the most so. I was, as all our classmates were, devoted to Gus Seward.

The cadet assigned to my room, who by his example was to redeem me and cure me of my wicked ways, was Ambrose Everett Burnside. Burnside and I had been, since we first knew each other, warm friends. The assignment was agreeable to both of us. Burnside had but few demerits when he came to live with me; in a few months he had over a hundred. I presume I must have been the Jonah of that room, but I must say I found Burnside a very ready pupil. We continued to be roommates and tentmates during our four years at West Point. This friendship continued until his death. A truer friend, a bigger-hearted man, never lived than Ambrose E. Burnside. From the day we met at West Point, until his death in 1881, our friendship and intimacy was only interrupted by the four years of the Civil War; as soon as the war was over it was resumed as though nothing had happened to separate us.

When in the hospital, a very hot day in the summer of 1846, clad in my shirt sleeves, and white cadet pants, I was on the front porch. I saw a cadet coming down the walk; he stopped under an apple tree loaded with green apples, and took a seat on the grass. I went into the passage leading to my ward, and threw myself into a rocking chair and was soon enjoying a delightful siesta. I was awakened by footsteps in the hall. The intruder was the same short plebe I had seen take his seat under the apple tree, and he had both hands pressed on his abdomen. I at once saw a chance for fun. He had mistaken me for the doctor. I started from my chair, assuming the most ferocious look I could put on, and said, "What is your name?" "Brown,"[16] he answered. "Plebe Brown," I said, "have you studied the Academic regulations?" He answered, "Not much." "So I supposed," I replied; "if you had done your duty you would have informed yourself that it is a dismissable offense to awaken the chief surgeon of this post when taking his evening nap. What is the matter with you, sir?" "Oh, doctor, my belly! my belly!" "Let me see your tongue; let me feel your pulse."

Starting back, I said, "Plebe Brown, you have been eating green apples." This he denied. I said, "Don't tell a falsehood; every beat of your pulse to the skilful surgeon says, 'Green apples! Green apples! Now, sir, tell the truth, the whole truth, and nothing but the truth; how many green apples did you eat?" After some hesitation he said, "I suppose about my cap full." I started back, exclaiming, "About a cap full! Plebe Brown, the only way I can save your life is to cut your abdomen open and take out those green apples. Come with me to the dispensary. Sit on that chair."

I found a case of surgical instruments, took them out of the case and examined them. Brown was turning very pale. I said to him, "Plebe Brown, I regret very much I can't cut you open now, as both my assistant surgeon and steward are absent, and I find I will need their assistance to hold you and keep you from wriggling. Brown," I said, "Do you think I could trust you not to wriggle?" Brown said he was afraid he would wriggle. "Yes," I said, feeling his pulse, "I find you are a wriggler, and though I am disappointed not to cut you open, I will defer the operation for the present, and see the effect of medicine. If medicine does not relieve you, come here after sick call tomorrow morning and I will have my assistant surgeon and steward here and proceed to cut.''

I mixed in a pretty large glass some of every medicine on the shelves which I knew not to be poisonous—castor oil, sweet oil, epsom salts, common table salt, and red pepper I remember were some of the ingredients. I told Mr. Brown that I would excuse him from drill and evening parade, on one condition, that he was not to bother me any more that day, nor was he to come to sick call next morning. I was afraid of his seeing the real doctor and being exposed.

I made Mr. Brown drink every drop in the glass. I watched him as he went up the walk leading to the encampment. He had not gone a hundred yards when he stopped, laid hold of the fence on the side of the walk, and I thought before he got through, he would throw up everything inside of him. When the steward, my friend Stoddard, returned I told him what I had done and he excused Mr. Brown according to my promise. Brown never put in an appearance again.

General Scott and his two eldest daughters[17] visited West Point almost every summer during the encampment. The general delighted in getting a dozen or more cadets around him in the hotel parlor and fighting over to them his battles in 1812. Niagara, Chippewa and Lundy's Lane we knew well. When telling us about the battle of Niagara, at a certain point in his narrative, he would throw his hand up to his shoulder and, assuming a look of pain, exclaim, ''Oh, Niagara! Niagara!'' This was to inform us that he was wounded at Niagara. General Scott was a very vain man and was called by his political enemies, ''Old Fuss and Feathers,'' but no one can discount his great military ability. For daring, and ability in execution, his march from Vera Cruz to the City of Mexico has rarely been equalled, never excelled.

On one occasion he was surrounded by a number of cadets

in the riding hall and asked whether there was any other cadet
besides Hancock who was named for him. I said, "Yes,
General, there is a new cadet just arrived who is named for
you." "Bring him," ordered the General. The plebe was produced. The General said, shaking the hand of the plebe, "I
am glad to learn, my young friend, that you were named for
me, Winfield Scott." "That is not my name," answered the
plebe, "My name is Walter Scott."[18] "Named for a great man,
sir, a great man," said the General.

Mrs. Scott came to West Point during the encampment, and
was there the summer of 1844. She was well acquainted with
my family and relatives in Richmond, Va.[19] I received from
her many tokens of kindness during my third class encampment
when I was in the hospital from the bayonet wound described
elsewhere. Cologne and many delicacies, such as jellies, etc.,
were sent me daily.

Mrs. Scott was an exceedingly bright and well-read woman.
She was a Miss Mayo, of Richmond, of one of our best and
oldest families, and was a great belle. General Scott, it is said,
addressed her several times before he was accepted, and then
only after he had acquired great military reputation in the war
of 1812, when for gallant service in 1814 he was brevetted a
major general. Mrs. Scott and the General were said not always
to harmonize. Her definition of ennui was, "A tallow candle,
a game of whist, and General Scott."

It was the custom when I was at West Point for the Army
officers stationed there to give a grand dinner on the 22d of
February. To this dinner, in order to recognize the near
approach of the first class as commissioned officers, the cadet
first captain and cadet adjutant had been for many years invited.
My class was not thus recognized. Several small indignation
meetings were held by us, and we voted that the class had been
grievously insulted. I asked, "Well, what do you propose to
do about it?" The answer was, "We can do nothing."

There was some eight or ten of my special friends in this conclave. I said, "Boys, I will get even with these fellows." They wanted to know how. I answered, "I have no information to give now, but all of you be in McAllister's room tonight soon after taps and you will find out."

McAllister[20] (dear old Julian) was the adjutant; he and Hill, A. P., had a room over the commandant's office, and it was never inspected. I disclosed my plan of operations to W.W. Burns,[21] my classmate. Burns, though not large, was one of the most powerful boys in our class and he was very fleet of foot; these were requisites indispensable in my proposed campaign against our common enemy. I had already made a thorough reconnaissance of the ground of my operations. The officers' mess hall was at that time in the west end of the building used as the cadets' messhall; in the rear of the officers' mess hall was a small yard in which their kitchen was located. A window communicating with the storeroom of their mess opened upon this yard. It was protected by wooden bars and a window, usually fastened but on this night it happened to be left open. The wooden bars were sufficiently far apart to enable one to get his hand between them and to reach the shelves inside, on which were stored wines, cigars, sweetmeats, etc. I told Burns to provide himself with a clothes bag; each cadet had a bag of this kind in which to put his soiled linen. I got mine, and we made a most successful raid on the enemy's stores, wine, brandy, cigars, sweetmeats, nuts, oranges, apples, etc. These we soon stored away in one of the barrack rooms. I told Burns that we must make another trip in order to successfully complete our foraging expedition.

The kitchen door of the officer's mess opened into the yard described. I saw in the stove one of the most beautiful turkeys I ever looked upon. Ah! the recollection of the sight of that beautiful bird makes my mouth water today, as it assuredly did then. How to get it and not be discovered was the problem.

We returned to our foraging ground. I peeped through the fence and saw our bird being dished to be eaten by our natural enemies. I said to Burns, "Now is our time, stand in the shadow of that wall; I will stand here, and when that fellow comes out give him a good clip," and a clip it was. He struck against the fence near me as though he had been shot from a catapult. I seized the coveted prize; my recollection is that it never touched the ground. It was soon in my bag and Burns and I were safe at the barracks before that menial fully recovered his senses.

Never were ten boys happier; never did ten boys enjoy a supper more, never did a turkey have, before or since, the flavor of this turkey. Burns and I were the heroes of the occasion, for could we not exclaim, as the great Roman general did, "Veni, vidi, vinci"? Had we not wiped out the outrageous and uncalled for indignity heaped upon the class of 1847? The wine, though drunk from a tin dipper, had a bouquet far superior to the old Madeira in my father's vaults which had been buried during two wars; and were ever oranges so juicy, or apples of such flavor? Many of our enemies, the officers stationed then at West Point, became in after years my warmest friends. We talked over this night's escapade and it was as much enjoyed by them as by myself. It was not robbery or petty larceny we committed, simply *foraging* on our enemies, which in all wars is commendable.

When we became third classmen and the candidates for admission appeared, I noticed a tall, dark plebe, weighing, I should say, one hundred and seventy-five pounds. I pointed him out to some of my pals as a fit subject upon whom to play a practical joke. Jesse Valentine[22] was the boy's name. Some one started the story that Jesse had left behind him in North Carolina a wife and several children. How shocking! Jesse deserved to be punished. After taps I went to Jesse's room and asked him to lend me his citizen clothes to wear to Benny's.

He readily consented. As I was receiving the clothes, a squad, my pals, in charge of a presumed noncommissioned officer, knocked at the door and came in. I dodged behind the door but was discovered and asked what I was doing there. I replied that I came to borrow Cadet Valentine's clothes to wear to Benny Havens. "Did he lend them to you?" I replied "He did." Now Cadet Valentine was placed under arrest, and so was I, and ordered to my quarters. About two minutes after I appeared with a file of the same cadets and ordered Jesse to dress and follow me. I informed him that the superintendent, on learning of his grave violation of the regulations, was very angry and had ordered a drumhead court martial for his trial.

A room in the cockloft of the old North Barracks was prepared for Jesse's trial. The windows of the room had blankets tacked up to prevent any passing officer of the Army from seeing the lights. A long table covered with green baize[23] was improvised. Burnside, personating the president of the court, sat at the head of the table, and on his right and left were arranged twelve cadets, dressed in blue coats, such as the cadets wore on furlough, cadet officers' hats with black plumes, swords and red sashes,—a formidable looking body. I was ordered to produce the prisoner. We had hardly taken our positions when the president of the court (Burnside) arose and reprimanded me severely for neglecting to make the prisoner assume the regulation position of a soldier—heels together, toes turned out, little finger behind the seams of his pants, palms of hands to the front, and eyes striking the ground at a distance of fourteen paces. The judge advocate read the charges; First, was desertion. In this, that new cadet Jesse Valentine did, on a certain day, desert his wife and three small children, who were now starving in Buncombe County, N. C. Second, Lending his clothes to an old cadet to enable said cadet to deceive his officers by appearing in the dress of a citizen. Then followed a long list of absurd charges which I do not remember.

Some one was appointed to defend the prisoner. The prisoner was asked how he plead to the first charge. He replied, "Gentlemen, before God I am not married; I suppose the mistake occurred in my being engaged to be married, and I would have been married but my mule died and I could not make a crop." "What was the name of the girl you were engaged to marry?" was asked by one of the court. "Nancy Hicks," replied Jesse. Several of the court cried out, "Bigamy! Bigamy!" "Bigamy of the worst kind," exclaimed the president. "Mr. Judge Advocate, add the charge of bigamy to the charges." Jesse's counsel here objected; his objection was unanimously overruled. Jesse plead guilty to lending his clothes to an old cadet. His counsel told him to plead "Not guilty." Jesse replied, "I have never told a lie." The president said, "I commend you, plebe, for never having told a lie; by doing so you are following in the footsteps of him who is without Paladin, the great and good George Washington." The room was very hot; the perspiration was trickling down Jesse's cheeks; he raised his hand to wipe his face. Several of the members of the court cried out, "Mr. President, won't you make that sergeant do his duty? the prisoner raised his hand." I was reprimanded and told if the prisoner dared to raise his hand again to his face to run him through with my bayonet.

Speeches were made by the judge advocate, who asked that this hardened sinner, convicted of having deserted wife and children, this would-be bigamist, this violater of the constitution, lending his clothes to an old cadet, should receive the extreme penalty of the law. Jesse's counsel asked for mercy, dwelling upon the youth, beauty and inexperience of the prisoner. (Jesse was the ugliest, most misshapen plebe I ever saw.) The court was finally cleared. Jesse, escorted by his guard, was taken into the passage. In about five minutes I was ordered to bring the prisoner in to receive sentence. The president arose from his seat and said, "Plebe Valentine, the court, after mature deliberation, have pronounced in your case the following sentence: that you be taken tomorrow morning to the statue of the great and glorious Washington, and at sunrise precisely to be shot to death with musketry, and may God have mercy on your soul.'' Jesse turned as pale as a sheet. I was ordered to take the prisoner outside and await further orders. When in the passage Jesse fell on his knees, and raising his eyes to heaven said, ''Oh! my God, shall I never again see my mother or sisters? Oh! if my mule had not died.''

We were again summoned into the court room. The president said, ''Plebe Valentine, you are a great sinner and deserve to die, but as Christian soldiers we cannot send you, with all your sins to eternity. You must be given time for repentence, and instead of being shot tomorrow we grant you a respite; you will stand with your head in a mortar until reveille tomorrow morning.'' I put Jesse's head in a mortar and left him, where he was found the next morning by an army officer who asked him what he was doing there. He explained, and was informed that some third classmen had played this trick upon him. Jesse straightened himself up and said, ''I can whip any boy on this hill!'' We had no doubt of that fact, and no one accepted the challenge.

I have given an account of what a good time I had in the hospital during my first class encampment. I must now relate how it suddenly terminated by my being placed in arrest and ordered to camp. At a class meeting held before going into camp a half dozen cadets were selected from the first and third classes to represent their classes at the dances which took place in the academic building three times a week. This entitled the cadets so chosen to visit the hotel[24] at pleasure to look out for new arrivals and extend to them invitations to the dances, and, if the ladies had no escort, to accompany them or to provide escorts. A ball was given at the end of the encampment with a supper.

During the summer of 1846 two young ladies with their mother spent the summer at the West Point hotel. The Misses M. were wild girls, though not bad. A. P. Hill, Burnside and myself were always among the number to represent the class as party managers. Hill was very devoted to the elder Miss M., I equally so to the younger (Miss Josephine).

About a week before the encampment broke up I was at the hotel and suggested to Miss Jo. that after she finished her supper we should take a stroll around Flirtation Walk. She consented. After supper Miss Jo. came into the hotel parlor with a package in her hand. I asked her what it was. She said, "Gingerbread." She knew my weakness for gingerbread, saying we would have "petite supe" on Flirtation Walk. We walked and talked, and finally found one of the numerous benches, provided for lovemaking and flirtation, which adorn that beautiful walk. We took seats and Jo. produced the cake.

It was a square cake, about ten inches wide, and say about an inch thick. Jo. asked me if I knew the latest and most delightful way to eat cake baked as that was. I professed my ignorance. She said, "I will show you." She borrowed my knife and cut off a strip of the cake the whole width of it, and about an inch thick. She put one end of this strip of cake in her mouth; the other I put in mine, and the result of this manner of eating cake, it will be readily seen, brought our lips close together. The entire gingerbread was after a while consumed. I found it the most delightful way to eat cake I ever tried, and I must say after the cake disappeared, our lips came together a good many time minus the gingerbread.

Time passed very rapidly. Miss Jo. suggested it was the hour to return to her mama. We approached the hotel by passing in rear of the encampment and by Kosciusko's monument. When nearing the hotel I noticed many lights on the Plain, and there appeared to be considerable consternation in and about camp. Miss Josephine had just given one of her ringing laughs when I heard some one with a light cry out, "Here they are; here they are." We took the hint and made rapidly for the hotel. I deposited Miss Jo. at the foot of the stairs leading to her room and she disappeared. Soon the hotel was filled with my pursuers, and, worst of all, Madam M. and her elder daughter, weeping and wringing their hands, for Josephine was drowned in the Hudson River. I told her her daughter had retired and was safe in her room. For some time Madam M. was inconsolable, insisting that Josephine was a corpse floating in the North River. I insisted she was in bed asleep. "Where have you been and what doing?" I answered, "Taking a walk and eating cake." "Have you any idea what time it is?" asked the old lady. I said, "I suppose about ten o'clock." "Look at the clock," she said. I looked and to my horror found the clock indicated two o'clock and fifteen minutes. I insisted that the clock was hours too fast. I was ordered to the hospital. I did not sleep much that night; I was thinking what that horrid old Mama was saying to my dear Josephine. When I saw her next she said she had caught fits from her mother and sister. The following morning I was ordered to report for duty in camp, and very soon after was placed under arrest and confined to my tent.[25]

The grand ball I was looking forward to was to come off in a few days. My card was filled up for every waltz and polka, every quadrille. Mrs. Scott and Mrs. Captain F. A. Smith,[26] Engineer Corps, came to see me in my troubles. I asked them to see the superintendent[27] and beg him to let me to attend the ball. They did so. The superintendent was obdurate—I was the worst boy in the corps, deserved no leniency, and none would be shown me. All this trouble I attributed to ginger cake. Should this ever read by an aspirant for military glory at West Point, let him beware of a pretty miss, ginger cake, and Flirtation Walk.

III

How a bad boy was put ahead ten years in his profession!
Before closing with West Point episodes I must relate a rather
singular incident which happened in the winter of 1848-9. During this winter Mr. Archer Campbell, Chief Clerk of the War
Department, was detailed to take to West Point and deposit
there the flags captured by our army in Mexico. It appears that
Campbell and Captain Cullum,[1] Engineer Corps, on duty at the
Academy, one cold night called on the assistant surgeon
stationed at the Point; the ground was covered with snow a foot
or two deep; the snow had been shovelled from the sidewalks
and banked in the road near the walk.

When leaving the house of the assistant surgeon, as Cullum
and Campbell descended the steps, a cadet with the cape of
his overcoat thrown over his head, appeared in their front with
a jug of whiskey slung over his shoulder; the cadet was returning from Benny Havens. Cullum seized the cadet and asked
his name; no answer was given: Cullum, still holding his cap-
tive, determined to take him to the barracks, where there was
a stationary lamp, and ascertain who he was. The cadet, a First
Classman, knew that discovery meant dismissal; he was an
athletic and powerful young man; he turned, seized Cullum,
who was a small man, lifted him from his feet and threw him
into a pile of snow near the walk, jumped on him and covered
him with snow.

While this was going on, Archer Campbell, who took in the
situation, was holding on to the fence bordering the walk and
laughing to kill himself. The cadet seized his jug of whiskey
and ran like a deer. When Cullum had sufficiently recovered,
he cried, "Catch him, Archer!" But Archer was too much con-

vulsed with laughter to do anything of the kind, *and I think* his sympathies were with the cadet. Cullum caused an inspection of barracks. The cadets were all in their rooms deeply engaged in their studies; no whiskey could be found. This incident was too good to be kept a secret; after the cadet graduated, he told the story as it occurred and the laugh was on Cullum.

In 1855 Congress created four new regiments,[2] two of cavalry, two of infantry. It appears Archer Campbell, still Chief Clerk of the War Department, and the Secretary, Mr. Jefferson Davis, were examining the Army register to find a suitable second lieutenant to promote as first lieutenant in the first Regiment of Cavalry. When James McIntosh's[3] name a second lieutenant, low on the list, came under discussion, Archer Campbell told Mr. Davis the incident connected with Cullum, and suggested the name of McIntosh for promotion. Mr. Davis, I heard, never fancied Cullum, McIntosh was made the senior first lieutenant of the First Regiment of Cavalry and he became a captain in two years or less; he was thus advanced ten or twelve years in his profession.

McIntosh was descended from fighting stock; his father[4] was a conspicuously brave and gallant officer, who was desperately wounded in one of General Taylor's first battles with the Mexicans, and subsequently killed in the storming of Molino del Rey, Mexico; his son, James McIntosh, our cadet here, was killed March 7th, 1862, at the battle of Pea Ridge, Arkansas, on the Confederate side.

During the encampment of 1846, my sister,[5] a beautiful girl, and as graceful as she was beautiful, accompanied by Mrs. John Butler and her daughter, also a beauty, came to West Point. They were, of course, great belles. Julian McAllister, of my class, and adjutant of the corps, became much enamored with Miss Lizzie Butler. This was reciprocated by the young lady, and Julian was to come and see her when he passed through Philadelphia after graduating. Half a dozen of my class reached

Philadelphia together. We stopped at Jones's, then the famous hotel in that city. As soon as I arrived in Philadelphia, I went to Mrs. George Cadwalader's[6] the home of my sister during her school days in that city, and ever afterwards when visiting Philadelphia. Mrs. Cadwalader was the aunt of Miss Butler. I found Miss Butler at her aunt's, also my sister. Miss Butler could talk of nothing but Julian McAllister. It was apparent she cared for my tall, fine looking friend. I hurried back to the hotel, and found McAllister, Hill, A. P., and Burnside entering a carriage to go to the theatre. I pulled McAllister out of the carriage and told him to come with me, that I was going to Mrs. Butler's, he would find Miss Lizzie there, and to court her. I added, "If you don't I will!" This determined his course, I think; he did as I suggested and they became engaged that evening, and were married after his return from Mexico.

Mrs. Smith,[7] wife of Captain F. A. Smith, Engineer Corps, a very bright lady, had many friends in my class. She adopted our class as her own and wrote a song, dedicating it to the class of 1847, which I have always thought the best of the kind ever written. I give it here.

A SONG.[8]

Dedicated to the Graduating Class of the United States Military Academy of the Year 1847.

By Mrs. Capt. Frederick A. Smith, Corps of Engineers.

Hurrah! for the merry, bright month of June!
    That opens a life so new;
When we doff the cadet and don the brevet,
    and change the grey for the blue.

To the struggles of youth, to the mimic of war,
        To our sports, to our follies, adieu!
We are now for the strife in the battle of life—
        We must change the grey for the blue.

We may find this world a rough hard world,
        As we travel its mazes through,
But with right stout hearts we'll play our parts
        When we change the grey for the blue.

And some will be bound to far Oregon's shore,
        And some to the famed Vera Cruz;
We'll see Matamoras, and the fair senoras,
        Though not as the greys, but the blues.

When the bugle is calling on Mexico's plain,
        May we all to our colors prove true;
Be cool and be steady, with "Old Rough and Ready,"
        Nor Tarn'sh the grey nor the blue.

For the "hero of Lundy" again takes the field,
        The scenes of his youth to renew;
When we stand by his side let it be our first pride
        To show that his greys are true blue.

Though broken the tie that here bound us a while,
        Fate n'er shall discover the few
Of a true hearted band who, linked hand-in-hand,
        Changed together the grey for the blue.

The grey of the morning is warmed by the sun,
        To the azure of noon's bright due,
As the morn of our time ripens fast to its prime,
        When we change the grey for the blue.

This verse, complimentary to General Scott, was not in the original version, but was added after the omission had been temporarily supplied by the following verse written by Cadet Beltzhoover.[9]

With Niagara's hero, the brave General Scott,
    The stout-hearted soldier and true,
We will triumph in victory, or fall in its arms,
    Lamented by grey and by blue.

There were three young ladies who, during my cadetship, were visitors at the Point during and after the encampment,—the two Misses Coleman, visiting their sister, the wife of Colonel Alden,[10] the Commandant of Cadets, and Miss Nora Bankhead, daughter of Colonel Bankhead,[11] Second Artillery. Miss Sarah and Miss Isabelle Coleman[12] were high bred, aristocratic, kindhearted ladies. The above applies equally to Miss Bankhead. The Misses Coleman belonged to a very wealthy family in Pennsylvania, their wealth being in iron mines. Miss Isabelle died early, Miss Sarah lived to an old age and never married. Her life and large means were spent in relieving the wants of the destitute, the deserving poor and needy. Her life if written would constitute a grand epic of real events. Her princely mansion still remains, facing the most beautiful square in this city, but that spirit which was its greatest ornament has been called by its Maker to a still more beautiful mansion.

My last day at West Point was spent in taking a final look at the beautiful views to be had from that picturesque place. I have crossed and hunted in the Rocky Mountains, the mountains of Virginia, Tennessee and North Carolina but to me no view equals the view from the back porch of Roe's Hotel on a moonlight night. General Maury, in his exquisite and charming book, *Recollections of a Virginian in the Mexican, Indian and Civil Wars,* says the four years he spent at West Point were the most unhappy of a happy life.[13] My experience was just the reverse. Some one had said, "Be virtuous, and you will be happy," but, added the girl, "you will not have a good time." Dabney was a good boy at West Point, he was not happy;[14] I was not good, I was happy, and had a good time. My classmate and dear friend, Burnside, accompanied me to Virginia; we went by way of Old Point and the James River visiting many of the old family residences, owned by my relatives and friends. Burnside remained a couple of weeks with me in Richmond. We had a jolly good time. After remaining a month in Richmond with my mother and sisters, I determined to hie me to the haunt of my boyhood, the White Sulphur Springs, one of the most beautiful summer resorts in America.

My father and his family visited the White Sulphur Springs every year. He owned a cottage there; Jack Miller, the grandson of Mr. Caldwell, the owner of the White Sulphur, was as a boy and man my boon companion. Mr. Caldwell had half a dozen grown sons. Jack, like most grandchildren, was indulged and spoilt by his grandparents and uncles, went to school when and where he liked, and came home when it suited him. He had his own cottage, horses, dogs, guns and servant. I always shared Jack's cottage.

A pack of some thirty or forty hounds were kenneled at the Springs. Lewis or James Caldwell took the pack out once or twice a week on a day's drive which all the gentlemen at the Springs desiring to participate were invited to attend. Jack and I, until we were about fourteen, preferred accompanying James and Lewis in the drive, in other words handling the dogs, in starting the deer from its lair. The hunters took stands at the base of the mountains and abided their time for the chance of a shot.

When about fourteen years old I proposed to Jack that we take a stand. A stand was assigned us. We took a pack of cards with us and were engaged in a game of seven up, our guns resting against a tree; we heard a splash in the creek about twenty paces from us; the next moment an immense buck, heavily antlered, passed within twenty feet of us. We ran for our guns, the deer quickened his pace; we both fired; the buck was two hundred yards from us when we shot. I said, "Jack, I am certain we hit him." "So am I," said Jack, "Did you not notice how he kicked up his heels when we fired?" About five minutes after we heard a shot on the creek above us; a little while after, two of the gentlemen hunters passed, and we inquired who had fired the shot we had heard, and the result. They informed us that some one had killed a fine buck. "Our deer!" we exclaimed. We were soon where the dead deer lay. I found my uncle there and asked him why he shot our deer. He said to put the poor beast out of its misery. He said, "Boys, as this is the first deer you have killed, you know what must be done; you must be blood-marked." My uncle marked our faces well, but we did not think we were sufficiently marked, so Jack put more blood on my face; I performed the same office for him. The buck was tied fast on a led animal, and Jack and I, by turns, led back to the Springs; large crowds of the visitors assembled to see the deer which we never knew until several years later we had not even hit when we fired.

When I was at school in New York my especial chums were Edgar and Alfred Grymes, sons of the celebrated lawyer, John Randolph Grymes of New Orleans. Mrs. Grymes lived in New York with her two daughters. I frequently Sunday evenings visited Mrs. Grymes. Her oldest daughter Medora was esteemed the most beautiful woman I ever saw. Some years after she married the celebrated Sam Ward,[15] a widower whose first wife was a daughter of John Jacob Astor. When Ward married Miss Grymes he was a member of the firm of Prime, Ward & King, rich bankers of Wall Street, New York. Several years after the firm failed, and I do not think Sam made another fortune.

I found at the Springs this summer Mrs. Grymes, Mrs. Ward, and Athenais, the younger daughter who had just been taken from the convent in Baltimore. How could I help falling in love with the graceful Athenais, the "Maid of Athens?" Did I not memorize Byron's "Maid of Athens, ere we part," etc? Athenais danced better than any girl at the Springs, and did we not have a standing engagement for all waltzes, etc? We planned a visit to the Old Sweet Springs, twenty or twenty-five miles from the White Sulphur.[16] The stage left early. Half way between the White and the Sweet Springs was a noted hostelry kept by a famous character, Jim Crow. Crow's breakfasts were famous. I told Crow who the ladies were; he had known Colonel Grymes, and knew my father and uncle well. Crow disappeared and presently returned with a large goblet of delicious julep; Jack Miller was with us. The ladies sipped a small quantity of julep; Jack and I finished it. The *piece de resistance* at breakfast was fried chicken. I never saw a party enjoy a meal more; the chicken was pronounced absolutely perfect.

The day after reaching the Springs, Mrs. Ward proposed a walk to the Old Sweet Springs, a mile or so from the new Sweet Springs where we were stopping. I was Athenais's escort; Jack Miller, Mrs. Ward's. The road was dusty. Mrs. Ward was walking in front. I said to Athenais, "Go and tell Mrs. Ward that she is holding her dress too high." Athenais stopped and said, "Are you a fool? don't you suppose Medora knows exactly how high her dress is? She practices that before her glass." This taught me a lesson not to interfere with ladies' dresses; it matters not how high they hold them. Athenais parenthetically remarked, "Medora is said to have the most beautiful ankle of any one in New York." "Oh, that is the reason she raises her dresses so high," I said. I came to the conclusion then and there, that I had yet much to learn that my professors at West Point had not taught me.

IV

From the Virginia Springs I returned to Richmond, where I received orders to report for duty at Fort Hamilton, New York Harbor. I found there Burnside, McAllister and Van Buren, my classmates. Recruits were coming in very fast. Our duty was to drill these recruits; as soon as a sufficient number were assembled we were to sail with them to Vera Cruz. (When at West Point, Burnside, my roommate, religiously went on a spree two nights in the week; when in this condition he had an insane desire to roam around the barracks visiting friends; if caught by an inspector when in this condition, dismissal was certain. I was the only one of his class who could manage him. I would put him to bed and frequently stood at my door with my musket clubbed, threatening to knock him down if he attempted to leave the room.)

When at Fort Hamilton, Burnside made a visit to New York, and met a naval officer, Lieutenant Hunter,[1] who had been serving with Commodore Perry's fleet in the Gulf of Mexico, and had acquired the sobriquet of Alvarado Hunter from having captured the Mexican town of that name with the vessel he commanded. This got Alvarado into trouble; he was relieved from his command and came to New York. Alvarado was a great toast in New York; he was wined, dined and feasted. Alvarado and Burnside found each other to be *par nobile fratrum,* and they got on a protracted spree.

Being uneasy about my friend, I went to New York, found him, and brought him down to Fort Hamilton. After recovering from his debauch he said, "Heth, old fellow, I have gotten myself in an awful scrape with Miss Nora Bankhead. When Hunter and I were returning to New York from Albany I, like a fool, stopped at West Point to see Miss Nora and when talking to her fell out of my chair on the parlor floor; when I woke up I found myself in bed at the hotel. I was ashamed to see Miss Nora before I left. Here is a note from her breaking off our engagement. Now I want you to see Miss Nora and straighten out this trouble."

I went to West Point, and saw Miss Nora. We took the usual stroll around Flirtation Walk and a seat on the same bench where I had eaten cake with the fair but faithless Josephine the year previous. I need not say no cake was eaten on this occasion; Miss Nora was not one of the cake-eating girls. I dilated on the noble qualities of my friend. I ended by saying in my peroration that I did not believe there was a man living calculated to make so good a husband and make a woman so happy as Burnside. As I believed all that I said to Miss Nora, I thought I had straightened out matters, but alas! I was doomed to disappointment. Miss Nora had during my eloquent appeal been looking down, playing vacantly with her fan; she raised then her beautiful brown eyes, looked me squarely in the eyes, and said, "I want you to answer me candidly one question." I thought I had certainly won the day. Her question was assuredly a plumper, and what I believe the lawyers call an *argumentum ad hominum.* "Mr. Heth," she said, "If you had a sister who was engaged to Mr. Burnside would you advise her to marry him?" I hesitated for a few seconds and said, "Oh, not just now, not just now; but, I assure you, Miss Nora, Burnside and I, not an hour before leaving Fort Hamilton, took a solemn vow that when we joined our regiments we would turn over a new leaf, and our every energy would be devoted to duty, to acquiring the esteem and confidence of our superiors and rising in our profession," and as a last shot I added, "I am certain Burnside will in time become a general." She replied, "Please say to Mr. Burnside that I shall always be a warm friend of his and pray for his success in life but I can never marry him." We returned to the hotel; it was a sad walk, and I do not know which was the sadder of the two, Miss Nora or I.

I took the first passing boat for New York. Burnside was much chagrined at the result of my visit to Miss Bankhead. Burnside, however, was much of a philosopher. A few days after he said, "Heth, do you know the sutler's daughter?" I replied "No." "Well, come with me to see her; she is a daisy." We saw the sutler's daughter; she was at least five feet nine inches high, very fat, weighing, I would say, one hundred and seventy pounds, with a remarkably beautiful face and a beautiful neck.

On our way back to the Fort Burnside said, "Heth, I am rather in love with that girl." I said, "If you fall in love with her, for heaven's sake don't go to see her when you are drunk and fall out of your chair and have to be put to bed." Knowing to what I alluded he said, "Oh, Heth, I can never love any one as I loved Miss Nora. No, I can never love again." Burnside did not know how much love he had stored away after being, as General Maury said, "immured"[2] for four years at West Point. I can't say what might have happened between him and the sutler's daughter had he not been suddenly ordered to Mexico.

At that time in New York balls were not *en regle*. The entertainments that were given by what was then, I suppose, the four hundred, were called matinees. They commenced at about two o'clock and broke up not later than ten o'clock. Mr. Stevens, a wealthy New York gentleman, was to give the grand matinee of the season. His palatial residence was in rear of Columbia College. The ground was given Mr. Stevens by the college on the condition that the ground and building should revert to the college at his death. Mr. Stevens' service was of gold. All New York, that is, the four hundred of that day, were talking about this matinee.

An invitation to the affair had been sent me. A few days

before this grand function I called to see a young lady in the city. She was a very queer, eccentric girl. She was going to the matinee and invited me on that day to breakfast with her at twelve o'clock and accompany her in her carriage. I accepted. The day named I was on time and was shown into the young lady's boudoir, a beautiful little room; the furniture was covered with blue satin, the curtains to the windows were of the same, and the carpet was blue. A small table large enough for two was set; the china was blue.

Presently, in walked Miss————, robed in a beautiful blue morning wrapper, looking charming. We took our seats. The first course was oysters, then a plump, delicious pheasant. Miss —— must have known my partiality for pheasant. I certainly enjoyed this breakfast, but all pleasures must come to an end. Breakfast over, she said, "Now you go down into the parlor and amuse yourself looking at the paintings, books, etc. I will go up and put on my new Paris dress just received, and will join you very soon." She went out but immediately returned and said, "I forgot to tell you that it is considered quite proper for a young lady to ride in a carriage with a young gentleman in the day, but this matinee will not be over until ten o'clock, when it will be dark; then it is not proper for a young lady to be alone in a carriage with a young man so you must not accompany me home." I said, "All right, I will observe the established proprieties."

In the parlor I found many beautiful paintings and much to admire. Very soon I heard some one rushing down the steps, and in walked my "blue girl." She said "Heth, we are late." (I had known her at West Point, hence, I suppose, she did not say Mr. Heth.) "We are very late; hook my dress, and be quick about it." "Hook your dress!" said I. "Yes, hook my dress," said she, "quick! quick!" Now, I had never hooked a girl's dress—that part of my military education had been shamefully neglected by my professors at West Point.

If you have ever been in battle, or if you unfortunately should ever go into one you will find your thoughts run very fast. My first thought was to bolt and run; the door was open and I could have escaped, then I thought, "Heth, you are a Virginian. State pride, old fellow! Were you not educated a soldier? Are you not en route to Mexico, to fight the battles of your country?" Had I not vowed to win many, many brevets, by slaying hecatombs of "Greasers"? Had I not on my full dress uniform, worn now for the first time (by request) to adorn the great matinee of the season? If I fled from hooks and eyes, would I not only disgrace myself but the great class of 1847? Like Cortes who burned his ships I determined to cut off all chance of a bolt. I turned, closed and locked the door.

My great fear was pins, needles, and other things which Providence, or the Devil, has provided woman with in order to annoy man. I fully expected then and there to die from laceration by needles and pins. I closed my eyes for a second or two, said a short prayer I had composed to be said on going into battle, and then charged. My first attack, like that of a brave soldier, was on the works in front. I was about to demolish all obstructions I saw defending the works. I had already captured half a dozen yards of lace, when my "blue girl" said, "Stop! Stop! What are you doing?" I said, "Hooks and eyes." She said, "my dress fastens from behind, hook it quick." I picked up the lace and said, "Shall I restore this lace from where I pulled it?" "No," she said, "give it to me, I will arrange that, you hook my dress, and be quick about it."

I went to the rear; she was arranging the lace. I leaned over her shoulder and asked, "Shall I commence hooking at the top, middle, or bottom?" She said, "Bottom, of course, Stupid." There seemed to me to be a hundred hooks and eyes on that dress. I commenced to hook up; I got along pretty well until I got half way up when I came to one hook and eye which were very obdurate. I could not get the hook and eye to meet.

I came to the conclusion that the trouble was due to some obstruction in front, so I like a prudent and good soldier, determined to make a reconnaissance. She was still arranging that lace, I saw where the obstruction was, but though "immured at West Point for four years," I knew those obstructions were on forbidden ground. I returned to my duty. Finally, patience and perseverance were rewarded; the dress was hooked up.

Before announcing the completion of my task I determined to see how far she had progressed in hers. I leaned forward and looked over her shoulder; I must have leaned too far; the bullion of my epaulettes touched her beautiful neck and tickled her, she turned her head and said, "What are you looking at? I wish you would look at my back and those hooks and eyes, then you would get on faster." I said, "I have finished, but I do not think you can wear this dress to the matinee; the dressmaker has made one side of it six inches too long." She went to a mirror, inspected my work, and I inspected hers. She wheeled on me and said, "You stupid fellow, you have hooked up my dress all wrong." I offered to unhook it and said I was good at unhooking dresses and felt confident a second attempt would prove a success. She said, "No, I will go upstairs and make Marie (Marie was her French maid) hook it." She was with her during the summer at West Point.

I became well acquainted with Marie. Marie every evening when her mistress went to supper (cadets were not admitted to the dining room) would take a seat on the porch. I would sit by Marie, who had a beautiful foot and a lovely mouth, filled with pearls. My object in sitting by Marie was to improve my French. I spoke French then tolerably well; before the summer was over I had learned more French than old "Claudy," "Angel" and D'Oremieulx[3] taught me during the years I recited to them. We conjugated French verbs; amour and baiser were the favorites, and thus improved our grammar.

After she left, I reflected and came to the conclusion that

time would have been saved by making Marie dress her before coming down. Soon she made her appearance again. Marie must have been an expert in hooking dresses, for she came down in one tenth of the time it took me to hook it up "all wrong."

My "blue miss" had rouge on her cheeks, and chalk or powder on her shoulders. We got into the carriage and soon reached the palatial residence of Mr. Stevens. The dancing had commenced. The ball room was the finest I had ever seen, extending the entire length of the building. Mrs. Sam Ward and her sister Athenais were present. Of course I devoted myself, as I was duty bound, to my "hook and eye girl." We waltzed and polkaed ever so many times. I had learned that girls like a change of partners sometimes; several of my friends were present whom I knew to be beautiful dancers. I saw them and asked them to take a turn with "hooks and eyes," though I did not call her "hooks and eyes" to them; they all acquiesced.

This gave me an opportunity to request a waltz with the most beautiful woman in New York. To my request, Mrs. Ward said, "No I will not waltz with you, Jack." (Jack I was called by her brothers and my schoolmates.) "And pray, Madam," I said, "how have I offended you?" "Oh you have not offended me in the slightest, but Jack, I have some regard for my dress which I think beautiful." I replied, "We have often waltzed and I am not aware that I have ever injured a dress of yours." She said, "I have been waiting for an opportunity to advise you to go to the gentlemen's dressing room wash your face and brush your coat. How did you get rouge on your nose and powder on your coat sleeve?" I looked at my coat sleeve and the under part was as white as if I had put my arm in a flour barrel. I could not deny the powder but I did deny the paint business. She wrapped the end of her handkerchief around her finger, rubbed my nose, and held it before me. Horrors on horrors! it was as red as vermilion.

"How did you get powder on your coat sleeve and the rouge

on your nose?'' I said, ''When we were coming here, our carriage was run into by a heavy dray. Miss ——— fell forward
and had I not caught her she could have had a dreadful fall.
I suppose in catching her my arm came in contact with her
cheek.'' She replied, ''But the rest of your story Jack, is an
unmitigated . . .'' I replied. ''A soldier at West Point never
lies! The great George is our model.''

I went to the dressing room and repaired damages. I then
had a delightful waltz with the ''most beautiful woman in New
York,'' and two with Miss Athenais. She was my best girl,
whom I had loved without interruption for years, and was ever
constant except when I ate cake with the fair but faithless
Josephine, and, possibly, I had been derelict on one or two
occasions. I have heard it said that a sailor has a sweetheart
in every port—why should not a soldier? Does a sailor belong
to a preferred class?

General Scott told some of us at West Point that when he
attained the rank of Major General, he was in Philadelphia, and
when his Major General's uniform was sent to his hotel, he
engaged a large parlor, with large mirrors at both ends, dressed
himself in full uniform and strutted up and down the room half
the day admiring himself. I could see the girls smile and nudge
each other as we passed them—they were calling attention evidently to my soldierly appearance and new uniform. I was
happy, as happy as General Scott was in his parlor. After Mrs.
Ward pointed out to me the condition of my coat sleeve and
nose, I concluded those girls were not admiring me and my
uniform but were laughing at my color and were making fun
of me, having no soldier as an escort.

About seven o'clock we went down to supper. A most beautiful feast it was; the tables were effulgent with gold plate,
dishes, waiters, spoons, forks—all gold. During the supper Miss
———, who of course, I had accompanied, said, ''Madame
De Trobriand will ride in the carriage with me, so you can

accompany me home if you wish." I accepted the invitation.

When the matinee was over I saw my young lady to the carriage and helped her in. I kept the carriage door open. After standing at the door some minutes, Miss ——— said, "Why don't you get in—what are you waiting for?" I said, "I am waiting for Madame De Trobriand." My "blue girl" caught hold of the door, slammed it to with a crash, at the same time ordering the driver to drive home. I had in some way offended her; that was evident. I went to my friend Mrs. Sam Ward and related to her all that had happened, the hooking business, etc. I asked her to find out how I had offended Miss ———. Mrs. Ward said, "Well, Heth, you are certainly the biggest fool I ever met; I wonder that you ever graduated at West Point." I replied, "That has mystified many, and no one more than myself." (I never saw my "hook and eye girl" from that day to this; she married and got a divorce, or rather her husband did.) "But," I said, "I should like to know what act of omission or commission I have been guilty of; please find out." Mrs. Ward replied, "You have hit it, Jack, omission! omission!" I said, "I certainly paid her every possible attention this evening. I was her partner in every waltz and polka, or I saw she had a partner." "Well," replied Mrs. Ward, "if you have not sense enough to solve the riddle, I don't propose to assist you. Omission, Jack, omission."

V

We embarked from New York on a sailing vessel with some four or five hundred recruits bound for Vera Cruz. The officers were Captains Luther and Roland, Second Artillery,[1] Lieutenants McAllister, Van Buren and myself. Nothing of interest occurred on the voyage. We were becalmed two or three days off the "hole in the wall." We were well supplied with fruit brought to us by the natives of the islands we passed. The voyage was made in about twenty-five days. The captain, a gruff "old dog," informed us one day that if we had luck the next morning, we would be in sight of Orizaba, one of the highest mountains in Mexico. The next morning we saw Orizaba, clad in snow, apparently not more than ten or fifteen miles distant. The captain informed us that it was one hundred and fifty miles off.

The captain about noon that day changed the course. We found he was running directly away from Vera Cruz. Captain Roland remonstrated but was informed very plainly by the captain that he Roland did not command the ship, but that he (the captain) did, and he would tolerate no interference. I thought the captain was right. Soon we knew why he had changed his course,—a norther struck us. I thought nothing could save us; the ship tossed, the timbers creaked, and the waves broke over us. I was awfully seasick. I went to my bunk, fell asleep, and slept all night. In the morning when I awoke, it was comparatively calm, and that evening we reached Vera Cruz.[2] I obtained a room at the principal hotel on the plaza. One of the first questions we asked was, "How about yellow fever?" "No yellow fever here now," was the answer. The next morning on leaving my room I heard the shuffling of feet in the room next to mine; the door was thrown open, and out walked six men bearing a coffin. I asked what the man died of; the answer was, yellow fever.

The First Regiment of Infantry, Colonel Henry Wilson,[3] commanding, was then stationed at Vera Cruz. General Scott had left it there to garrison the town and the castle of San Juan

De Ulloa. I was assigned by the War Department as a brevet second lieutenant to the First Infantry. I reported for duty on my arrival and was assigned to Captain Granger's[4] company. Guard duty came quite often and I was much exposed to the hot sun of that hot place. I suffered as I never suffered before with the most violent headaches. One morning after marching off guard, I felt so unwell that I went to bed. I soon had a high fever; the doctor was sent for, and I had a regular attack of yellow fever, but in order not to alarm me he said it was a slight attack of acclimating fever. A nurse was provided. I soon became delirious and remained so for several days. Very stringent orders were given by the doctor to the nurse about giving me my medicine at stated intervals. When I was delirious the nurse went on a spree and for twelve hours no medicine was given me.

Lieutenant Denman[5] of the First Infantry, a kind, humane man, came in to see how I was getting on; he at once took in the situation and sent for the doctor. The doctor said that if I had gone without remedies much longer, I certainly would have died. Dear, kind Denman, now assumed the place of nurse, watched over me as though I had been his brother, and saved my life. In about two weeks I commenced to convalesce, and rapidly recovered. I noticed that after recovering from this attack I could expose myself to the sun with impunity, and never again had a headache. I was acclimated.

When well, I was ordered to the Castle of San Juan De Ulloa to report to Captain (Brevet Major) Backus.[6] Major Backus married the daughter of General Brady. He was a crossgrained old fellow, never had a good word to say of any one. I came to the conclusion that the only beings in the world he cared for were General Brady,[7] his wife, "little daughter," and Fop, his dog. If the accusations brought by him against many of the officers were true, they were a disgrace to the Army. I asked my friend Denman about these stories; he said, "Every one understands old Backus; he is the most complete cynic in existence; pay no attention to his cynicism."

In January or February orders were received directing the First Infantry to proceed to the City of Mexico. This was most acceptable to all. The march for the first two days was over a sandy road; the heat was excessive. We soon, however, got out of the *tierra caliente* and commenced to ascend to Jalapa. My feet were a mass of blisters; the quartermaster of the regiment had some led horses,[8] and let me have one. Old Backus, who, I believe, delighted to see any one suffer, snarled and growled, but I was fortified by the surgeon's certificate that I could not march. On reaching Puebla, the most important city in Mexico next to the City of Mexico, we rested two or three days in order to give the men an opportunity to have washing done, and to recuperate somewhat.

My company was quartered in a convent abandoned by the monks, or possibly they were made to leave their dirty dens to be occupied by their conquerors. A room was assigned me. I unbuckled my sabre and rested it against the wall a few feet from the door. The room had a tilted floor, and was as filthy as a pig pen. There were fleas galore; my trousers were soon covered. I went out of the room—my sabre was gone. I had seen several monks prowling around, and felt certain that one of them had appropriated my sabre to his own use. I recollected that John Randolph of Virginia had once said in a speech in the House of Representatives, "Mexico, Sir, is a nation of blanketed thieves." John Randolph, I concluded, was right. The blankets they wear give them an opportunity to conceal their plunder. I never met but one other people who could steal as quickly and conceal their thefts as readily, as Mexicans. They were the Pawnee tribe of Indians. I have thought that the Pawnees must be directly descended from the Aztecs.

When at Puebla a party was made up to visit the ruins of

the City of Cholula.[9] Cholula at one time, three or four hundred years before the Mexican War, is said to have contained a population of two hundred thousand souls. We only found a few houses, or rather adobis huts, standing (an adobis is a sun-dried brick.) The huts appeared not to have been inhabited for some time. I presume the inhabitants had fled on the approach of the army. The attraction here was what was, a thousand years before, one of the chief Aztec temples, a pyramid some hundred of feet in height on the altar of which was kept a fire perpetually lighted.

The Spaniards had erected where this altar stood, a chapel, now not in good repair. Cortez on a visit to Cholula on some trumped-up charge massacred five or six thousand of the inhabitants, possibly to keep his hand in, and to satisfy the penchant of the inhuman race to which he belonged, for blood, cruelty and atrocity.

We found around the base of the pyramid many pieces of broken pottery but nothing worth bringing away. We resumed our line of march for the City of Mexico, crossing Rio Frio, the highest point between Vera Cruz and the City of Mexico, where I passed the most uncomfortable night in my life, suffering from severe cold.

I should have stated before that when my class (the class of 1847) reached Mexico the war was over. The City of Mexico had been captured and all the country and cities General Scott chose to occupy were in our possession. Negotiations were being carried on leading to peace. Not one of our class ever heard a hostile shot fired in Mexico. It was something we could not comprehend, that General Scott could have captured the City of Mexico without the assistance of the class of 1847. How were any of us to gain the brevets for gallant conduct which we had assured our sweethearts we would do? The class voted that the hero of Niagara and Lundy's Lane had made a mistake in not awaiting the arrival of the class of 1847.

Being much of a Virginian, I thought the only reason General Scott made this mistake was, being a Virginian himself, he felt certain of success, having in his army such as R. E. Lee, Joseph E. Johnston, "Old Joe" Selden,[10] Edward Johnson, Lewis A. Armstead, T. J. Jackson (afterwards "Stonewall"), Dabney H. Maury, R. S. Ewell, George E. Pickett, and others. With those alone he knew he could have driven before him Santa Anna and as many "greasers" as would have filled the national highway between Cerro Gordo and the capital of Mexico.

We had hoped that we might be attacked by guerrillas when en route. One day we saw in the distance what we thought were guerillas. Now came the chance to gain one, maybe two, brevets. I drew my sword, felt its edge, examined my pistol to see that it was all right. I was ordered, being mounted, to reconnoitre the enemy. I dashed off; I was determined to kill a dozen or more "greasers" and to bring in a score or more of prisoners. I was at a loss to know which of my sweethearts should be honored by my calling her name when I slew my first "greaser." I had approached near enough to my enemy to use effectually my field glasses. The glasses almost fell from my hands, disclosing as they did, instead of guerillas, burros, jackasses, loaded with firewood for the good people of Puebla. The burros were in charge of two filthy, half-clad "greasers." Should I slay these guerillas and scalp them then and there? The Mexicans were each riding a burro, one in front, the other in the rear. I approached the vile wretch in front; as I did so the burro he was on gave a most unearthly yell that started the whole pack. My horse had never seen a burro or heard his screech. He became frightened and uncontrollable; he wheeled suddenly and made for the column a mile away. I reported to my colonel, told how the "greaser" had made his burro yell, which was followed by the whole pack doing the same; that I was sure that it was intended as an insult to our flag, his command, and myself. I asked that I might be permitted to return and annihilate those two "greasers." His only reply was, "Take your place in the column, sir, you have done all I wished you to do." "Too tender-hearted," I thought, "and too old to have a sweetheart at home."

VI

I found much to see of interest in the Mexican capital. The palace, the halls of the Montezumas, now occupied by our troops, the grand plaza in front of the beautiful cathedral occupying one side of the plaza, the queer shops, the beautiful articles of silver work, which these people excel in manufacturing. The markets were well worth seeing, containing many curious and, to me, strange edibles. I was never tired of gazing at the volcano of Popocatapetl, which I believe has been quiescent for many years, but always emitting more or less vapor which hangs above the crater. My chief pleasure, however, was in meeting again many of my classmates and old friends.

On reaching the City of Mexico I found I had shed my rank as brevet second lieutenant in the First Regiment of Infantry and been promoted to a full second lieutenant and assigned to the Sixth Regiment of Infantry[1] commanded by Bvt. Brig. Gen. N. S. Clarke.[2] I was sorry to part with my friend who had saved my life at Vera Cruz, Lieutenant Denman, but otherwise I liked the change. I was assigned to Captain W. H. T. Walker's[3] company. Walker was a graduate of West Point and a Georgian. He had been desperately wounded in the battle of Molino del Rey. He was spoken of as one one of the bravest of the brave. No one, not even the surgeons, believed he could survive his wounds, but Walker's indefatigable will saved him. He said, "I am not going to die; I am going to New York to see my wife and children." Walker was placed on a litter and carried safely to Vera Cruz and thence by steamer to New York; he lived until killed in a sortie from Atlanta, Ga., July 22, 1864.

First Lieutenant Lewis A. Armistead,[4] a Virginian, had been assigned to the command of Captain Walker's company and I reported for duty to dear old Lewis, a kinsman of mine. I found several officers I knew well in the Sixth Infantry. Lieutenant Edward Johnson,[5] whose mother owned a place adjoining my father's in Virginia, also Lieutenants Simon B. Buckner[6] and Winfield Scott Hancock, both of whom I had known as cadets at West Point. Armistead, Hancock and I were messmates, and never was a mess happier than ours.

If you ever visit the field of Gettysburg, you will find, near what is known as the "high water mark," *inside* the Federal lines, a piece of marble some eighteen inches square with the inscription on it, "Here fell Brig. Gen. Lewis A. Armistead, C. S. A., July 3rd, 1863." If ever there was a man absolutely without fear, it was Armistead. Napier's celebrated eulogy on Ridge, who fell in the Siege of Badajos, may with all truth be said of General L. A. Armistead: "No man died on that field with more glory than he, yet many died and there was much glory."[7] Armistead lived a short time after being shot; his last words were, "Please say to General Hancock I would like to see him." Hancock, however, had been severely wounded and taken to the rear, so those two regimental associates, messmates and devoted friends, never met on earth, but I am sure have met again. I think Armistead was killed by Hancock's troops, and Hancock was wounded by one of Armistead's command. What a commentary on Civil War!

After spending two or three days in the City of Mexico sight seeing, I thought it behooved me to look up my dearest friend

and classmate, Lieutenant Burnside,[8] and see if he had gotten
into any more scrapes. I found he was with his company,
stationed at Tacubaya some three miles from the capital. He
was delighted to see me, as I was to see him. I said, "Old
Man, have you gotten into any scrapes since you have been
here?" He replied, "Heth, old fellow, I want to caution you
about having anything to do with these Mexican girls; they are
she-devils, the most jealous beings on earth; when angry they
would not hesitate to knife you, or to cut your throat." "Have
any of them attempted to knife you or cut your throat?" "Yes,"
he said, "Annita is her name; she is the prettiest thing in this
valley; well I made love to Annita, went to see her several times
and she came to see me. Oh, Heth, she is a daisy!" ("So was
the sutler's daughter at Fort Hamilton a daisy," I said.)

"Yesterday I was coming to my quarters; I passed Annita's
house, looked in; she was not there; at least I did not see her.
I crossed the street and called to see Bonita, with whom I had
commenced a quiet flirtation. As I was about to leave, I kissed
Bonita. Annita saw me go into Bonita's room; she followed
me, and it was my luck, she was looking in through the window
when I kissed Bonita. She rushed into the room, and, Heth,
she made the fur fly; she pulled out enough hair from that girl's
head to have stuffed a pillow, and then drew out a stiletto—they
all carry stilettos, I believe,—turned and made for me. I took
to my heels, she after me; I outran her, but she was close behind
me. I ran into this room; she got in before I could lock the
door, so I bolted through the window and ran across the garden,
she still after me. How I managed to get over that fence I can't
tell, but I did get over it and did not stop until I got to the
convent where my company is quartered."

Burnside then proceeded to lock the door. "I always keep
the door locked now. What would you do if you were in my
place?" "Go to the convent; stay there; shave your head, and
become a monk; that is the best thing you can do." "No, Heth,

be serious and advise me, for my life is in danger." "Well,"
I said, "let us go to the convent, order your first sergeant to
place a sentinel at the gate of your corral with instructions to
let no woman pass, and see you keep away from Bonita."

This was done, at least a sentinel was placed at the gate;
whether Burnside kept away from Bonita I can't say. I advised
him to send some dulces (candies and sweetmeats) to Annita
for several days and see how that would work. In about a week
or less Annita, as I supposed she would, relented, and Burnside
and she were great friends again, but he said, "Heth, she
watches me like a hawk." I said, "She is right, and you will
bear watching, Burn. I say let her watch; one Mexican daisy
is enough at a time." I loved Burnside more than I ever loved
a man, and I know my love for him was reciprocated. I told
his wife, after he was married that she was the only person
of whom I had ever been jealous.

After being in the City of Mexico for some two months,
General Clarke was ordered with about two thousand troops to
occupy the town of Cuernavaca[9] (the English of which is cow's
horn), the object being to collect the taxes imposed. I was asked
by the General to be his aide-de-camp and accepted.

VII

Cuernavaca is situated south of the City of Mexico, by the
road we travelled about sixty or seventy miles, and on the edge
of the tierra caliente, very much such a climate as Jalapa, in
other words, delightful. Our mess consisted of General Clarke,

my old cynical commander Backus, Acting Adjutant General; Hancock, Regimental Quartermaster, and myself.

A short distance from Cuernavaca was a celebrated coffee plantation owned by the Duke of Monte Leon (a Sicilian nobleman descended from Cortez), but managed by a relative. The coffee raised here, as we were told, was esteemed the best in the world; it was never put on the market but was distributed among the crowned heads of Europe and the Duke's particular friends. General Clarke and his staff were invited to visit the Cortez plantation which was formerly owned by Cortez.

We were invited to partake of a Mexican breakfast, an elaborate affair. The table was beautifully decorated with flowers, much gold and plate in evidence. There must have been a dozen or fifteen courses; between each course sweetmeats were served. There were many kinds of light wines, and by all odds the best champagne I drank while in Mexico. The ladies did not appear at this breakfast. Hancock and I had seen one, a beautiful Spanish girl, the daughter of our host. Hancock was then a magnificent specimen of youthful beauty, as he afterwards was of manly looks. He was tall, graceful, a blonde, with light hair, the style of all others that at once captivated the Mexican girls. After breakfast Hancock and I walked into the garden surrounding the hacienda, and saw there our beautiful Spanish miss, sauntering among the shrubbery. I said, "Now is your chance, old fellow, pluck a rose and go for her. I will remain here, gather flowers and watch; If her duenna comes I will be seized with a coughing spell. You must do a heap of lovemaking in a short time for you may never have such a chance again." "I will," he said, and he did. I saw him make a bow to her that Chesterfield would have envied, present his rose and take her hand.

The following he told me on returning to Cuernavaca: "When I took her hand, I squeezed it just a little, and she returned it. I said, 'Usted as me amante;'[1] she said, 'Lieutenant, I speak

English, and my father is going to take me to England to finish my English education.' I told her pure English was only spoken in America, to come to America, complete her education there, and we would be married. She said she would try to persuade her father to change her plans, that she would greatly prefer being educated in the Estados Unidos. Heth, I looked and your back was turned towards us; I kissed her and told her that I had never loved before.'' I said, ''How could you have told such a story? I know you have said the same thing to half a dozen girls in the city of Mexico and God knows how many in the States.'' He replied, ''We are at war with Mexico, peace has not yet been made, and you know all is fair in love and war. She told me her father would be absent day after tomorrow, and at twelve o'clock she would be in the garden again; that she could manage her duenna.'' That Spanish beauty was in love with Hancock the moment she saw him. ''What is her name—did she tell you?'' ''Yes, she gave me her card; Isabella Garcia is her name; Isabella is a beautiful name, don't you think so?'' ''Well, yes, but any name by which that girl is called you would think beautiful.''

When in the City of Mexico Hancock and I were quite often invited to attend entertainments given by Mexican young ladies in the city. I owed my invitations to Hancock with whom these senoritas were in love. They were robed the same way, always in white, and the same colored ribbons decorating their dresses; if the hostess wore blue ribbons, all wore blue; if she wore yellow ribbons, all had yellow ribbons. We would find them in the parlor seated on the floor; they did not rise when we entered, only the hostess. After paying our respects to her we were at liberty to take our seats on the floor between any two of the young ladies we preferred. We only knew a few words of Spanish, they less of English. The first thing they would do was to roll a cigarette, light it and hand it to you, and when one was finished, another was offered; they always joined in the smoke. Thus I learned to smoke cigarettes and have kept up (some say) the vile practice for fifty years, so far as I know, without injury.

My duties as aide-de-camp were not onerous; the most disagreeable duty I had to perform was attending the punishment of Mexicans in the plaza and reporting the result to the General. John Randolph was right when he said they were a nation of "blanketed thieves." They would frequently be detected stealing horses, forage, etc., from the quartermaster's department. The culprits were tried by a commission appointed by the General; if found guilty a flogging was the result. I was to report if the punishment was properly administered and stop it if too severe. I often let "greasers" off with half the stripes they were to receive. I hate to see a human being flogged.

Among the officers at Cuernavaca who afterwards became distinguished were Mansfield Lovell,[2] Fitz John Porter,[3] and Orlando B. Willcox,[4] my classmate, all of the Fourth Regiment of Artillery. After a sojourn in Cuernavaca of some two months or more, we were ordered to return to the City of Mexico. The Sixth Regiment, my regiment, was ordered to Tacubaya[5] and quartered in one of the numerous convents. Burnside was still in Tacubaya with his company. He did not follow my suggestion, shave his head and retire to a cell in a convent, but was in his old quarters. He and Annita were fast friends; she, being a very pious Catholic, had taught him to say his beads, which she made him do three times a day. She was anxious to make me say my beads. I told her I had been taught to say them when at school at Georgetown, D. C.; besides this I had no idea of being involved in Miss Annita's meshes. I remembered how ready she was to use a stiletto. She was much improved in the way of dress; now she wore stockings and was very fond of displaying her stockings and ankles; she was fast becoming civilized and I hoped was making Burnside pious.

Before leaving West Point we (my class) agreed when we

captured the City of Mexico that we would have a West Point
Cadet hash in the halls of the Montezumas, and this was carried
out. We had a royal hash in the palace. In the absence of old
Benny's whiskey there was aguardiente galore. Burnside got
gloriously tight, as did others. I took him home; as soon as
Annita saw him, she cried out "Borracho! borracho!" I said,
"No, enfermo, real enfermo, dolor de cabeza, too much hash."
We put him to bed. I went to my quarters, leaving Annita to
watch my friend.

A number of our soldiers were assassinated in and around
the City of Mexico. Cowardly assassins were ever on the look-
out for a drunken soldier, and if time and place were propitious,
he would be killed and robbed.

Following the *"costumbre de país,"* I went one Sunday to
witness a bull fight. I was not enthused; my sympathy was with
the bull. The way the women behaved astonished me more than
anything else. The Sunday I went to the bull fight the place
was crowded; the women outnumbered the men, two or three
to one. When a bull frightened almost to death was turned into
the arena, and stood still refusing to fight, the women would
become furious, standing up and crying, "Cobarde! Cobarde!
(coward) matar el cobarde!" I only attended one of these
favorite Mexican exhibitions. They seemed to take the poor
bull's indisposition to fight as a personal insult to themselves.

A party was made up to visit the volcano of Popocatepetl,
ascend to the summit and plant the American flag on the highest
point of the mountain. I cannot recall the names of all who
were in this party of ambitious young men desirous of seeing
the stars and stripes float from one of the highest points in Mexico. Captain Andrew Porter[6] of the Rifles, U. S. Grant, 4th
Infantry, Lieutenant R. H. Anderson,[7] First Dragoons, Lieutenant S. B. Buckner of ours, Sixth Infantry, Lieutenant C. P.
Stone,[8] Ordnance Corps, Lieutenants R. H. Long,[9] Montgomery P. Harrison,[10] A. H. Seward and the writer were among

the party; there were several others, including a quartermaster and one or more assistant surgeons, and right glad we were, as it turned out, that those "saw-bones" were with us. My recollection is that we were told that Humboldt was the only man up to that time who had succeeded in ascending the summit of this extinct volcano.[11] Popocatepetl was supposed to be between sixteen and seventeen thousand feet high. I believe that more recent and accurate measurements have determined that there is another mountain in Mexico somewhat higher than Popocatepetl.[12]

The quartermaster's department furnished us with the necessary wagons, pack mules and riding horses. I think it was a two or three day journey from the City of Mexico to the base of the mountain. The morning after reaching the base, quite early, we commenced the ascent with burros packing our tents, bedding, edibles, etc., etc. The road, or rather, rugged path was the worst apology for a path I had ever encountered. About two hours before sunset we reached our camping ground, the limit of vegetation, and were informed we had ascended about ten thousand feet and were on the edge of the line of perpetual snow.

While waiting for our tents to be pitched and our supper to be cooked, we witnessed the grandest sight it was ever my fortune to behold. Below us, stretching out from the base of the mountain, was a beautiful valley, under the highest state of cultivation, fields of different grain, orange and lemon groves, and vast fields of every variety of fruit which the tropics furnish. The valley presented the appearance of a checker board. The sun was shining brightly, the green orange and lemon groves and the fields of yellow grain were brought out in the most beautiful hues. Very soon clouds appeared below us, casting their shadows over portions of the valley. We could see the lightning playing among the clouds and hear the crash of thunder following; some of the fields in the valley were being rained upon, while upon others the sun shone brightly. It certainly was a magnificent picture which spread itself out beneath us. If a genius, such as Church,[13] could only have beheld this grand panorama, he surely would have received an inspiration enabling him to produce a picture equal to his famous "Niagara."

Before we retired for the night the clouds began gathering over the summit of Popocatepetl. When we awoke in the morning, the sun was shining, but during the night a foot or eighteen inches of snow had fallen; this additional snow piled on that which has covered the mountain since its creation, made the ascent of six or seven thousand feet to reach the crater look, to me, very ominous. My idea was to wait until the snow which had fallen during the night had melted or disappeared, which the guides said would be in a few days, but it was decided to attempt the ascent at once. All started. The snow was up to the middle of my thighs. At that altitude the rarefaction of the air is very great and, of course, becomes more so as you ascend. I soon found that I could take only two or three steps before I had to rest and regain my breath. I determined that others might ascend the crater, but I could not, and suggested to those nearest me to return to our tents; this we did, but very soon others commenced to arrive. On counting noses we found that only three or four of our party were still on the mountain above us. Some hours after, the missing ones turned up—Lieutenants R. H. Anderson, S. B. Buckner, and C. P. Stone. Stone had become exhausted and so benumbed by the cold that he insisted upon lying down and going to sleep. This meant death, so his friends pulled, tugged and pushed him down the mountain and saved his life.

Very soon the above-named began to complain of pain in their eyes which rapidly grew worse; it finally became so excruciating that we had to guard them in their tents. They described the pain as one might suffer from having a red hot iron thrust into the eye balls. Fearing they might become delirious and attempt to injure themselves, their pistols, swords, etc., were removed from their tents. The length of time those gentlemen had remained on the mountain side subject to the glare of the sun on the snow, aggravated by the rarefaction of the air, produced this intense distress. The following morning we started down the mountain; our suffering comrades with their eyes bandaged were placed on led horses. On reaching the valley a hospital was improvised.

After resting a day or two, and seeing we could be of no further use, we left our friends in the hands of the doctors and nurses, and the party visited a celebrated cave two or three days' journey from Popocatepetl. It was not long before our afflicted friends recovered, and as the accumulated snow which had fallen on the mountain had disappeared, they determined to again make the attempt to reach the crater and this time were successful. The American flag was planted on the summit. There was nothing worth mentioning about this cave except its immense size. We were informed that its entirety had never been explored. All caves are pretty much alike; stalagmites and stalactites abound, differing only in the queer shapes, which they assume.[14]

We now by slow marches wound our way back to the capital, thence to our several commands. Hancock[15] piloted me over the battlefields of Contreras, San Antonia and Churubusco, and pointed out where our gallant soldiers carried the works, and especially where the gallant Sixth Infantry distinguished itself. My much beloved cousin and boyhood playmate, George E. Pickett,[16] visited with me the fields of Molino del Rey and Chapultepec. He pointed out where old Joe Seldon, when he reached the top of the wall when making the assault on Chapultepec, had an escopeta[17] put to his head and discharged, carrying away an eye and part of his skull. He showed me where he scaled the wall and where he shot a "greaser," thus saving his own life. He then conducted me to the roof of the citadel and pointed out the identical staff from which he lowered the Mexican flag and hoisted "Old Glory."[18] I think it was in an earthwork at Churubusco that our people captured some dozen or more American deserters[19] who fought like tigers. They were turned over to General Harney[20] for execution after being tried, convicted and sentenced. Harney had a scaffold erected in full sight of Chapultepec and told these wretches that as soon as the American flag was hoisted over that work, it would be the signal for their execution. In compliance with that order, when Pickett ran up our flag, on the flagstaff of Chapultepec, these miscreants who had been the cause of the death of many brave American soldiers, were launched into eternity.

Peace had been made.[21] My regiment was ordered to Jalapa to await transportation from Vera Cruz. I was appointed acting adjutant in the absence of the regimental adjutant, Lieutenant Kirkham.[22] Hancock was acting quartermaster, in the absence of Lieutenant Wetmore,[23] regimental quartermaster. We continued our old mess, Lewis Armistead, Hancock and myself. Armistead was a good-natured man, and I am afraid we teased him too much. Hancock had a joke on him which he often related to the officers. Armistead was the carver. Hancock said, "When we had a turkey, chicken or duck for dinner, Lewis would give us a very small piece and then say, " 'Boys, I will take the carcass.' "

VIII

Lieutenant-Colonel Loomis[1] was now in command of our regiment. Colonel Loomis was a good officer and kindhearted

man, although at times he had a queer way of showing his amia-
bility. He entered the army in the year 1811 as a second lieutenant and was awfully dissipated, a complete sot in his early
days. The story was told that he found himself asleep under
a billiard table, after playing billiards with the drummer boys
at the post. He was so ashamed of himself when he realized
what he had done that he determined never to use liquor again.
General Twiggs[2] once said to a number of officers, Colonel
Loomis being present, that he had never known, and did not
believe there ever was, a reformed drunkard. Loomis said,
"But, General, you have forgotten me." Twiggs replied,
"Loomis, you are not dead yet."

At the time of which I am writing Colonel Loomis was
absolutely abstemious and one of the most religious men in the
Army. An order came from Vera Cruz informing the Colonel
that a steamer was there, waiting to transport his regiment to
New Orleans. Our tents were struck. I saw Hancock and asked
him in what wagon my effects were to be placed. He replied,
"In the headquarters wagon, of course." I saw the colonel, who
informed me that my baggage could not go in the headquarters
wagon. I again saw Hancock, who reiterated what he had said
before. I was getting vexed. I said, "I am entitled to transportation; you and old Loomis must settle this business." Hancock
saw Loomis, and my baggage was put in the headquarters
wagon.

The Eighth Regiment of Infantry was also ordered to Vera
Cruz with the Sixth. As we were about commencing our march
Pickett, acting adjutant of the Eighth, said to me, "I am going
into Jalapa as we pass by to have a good time; can't you come
with me?" I said, "No, Old Loomis is as mad as a wet hen;
Hancock and he have just had a devil of a row." As we neared
Jalapa the Colonel said to me, "Young man, would you like
to ride into Jalapa?" I said, "Yes, Colonel." He then told me
to go to a certain house and I would find there a Mr. ———,

a colporteur, and tell him to have his baggage, etc., at a certain point on the road, and they would be put in the headquarters wagon. The reason for his not wishing my effects to be placed in the headquarters wagon was now explained.

I delivered my message to the colporteur and joined Pickett. We spent the day there and painted that town red before leaving.

There were several companies of the Second Regiment of Dragoons camped on the roadside a short distance out of Jalapa. The Sixth Infantry and Second Dragoons had, before the Mexican War, been stationed at the same posts, and a warm friendship existed among the officers. Knowing the Sixth Infantry would pass their encampment that morning, the officers of the Second Dragoons mixed several buckets of julep which were placed on tables near the roadside. The regiment halted conveniently near the aforesaid tables. The juleps speedily disappeared and were speedily replenished; in short, all got more or less under the influence of julep. This road was blocked with wagons in front of the regiment. Loomis came along, saw the condition of things, and was vexed. He found that Hancock's wagons were blocking the road and said in the presence of some of the officers of the regiment, "This is all Hancock's fault; if he had attended to his duty, this blockage would not have occurred; he has *shamefully* neglected his duty."

When I reached my regiment it had been in camp several hours. I reported to the Colonel who said, "Where have you been?" I replied, "You sent me to Jalapa to deliver a message." "Did I tell you to stay there all day? Do you not know that you should have been here to locate the encampment?" To the first question I answered "No;" to the second, "Yes." "Have you not done wrong, sir?" "Yes," I replied. "Sit down there and eat some ham and onions."

I went to my tent; soon Hancock came in and said, "Heth, I wish you would go with me to see Colonel Loomis." We found the Colonel in his tent, reading his Bible as usual. Hancock said, "Colonel Loomis, you said today in the presence of several officers that I had shamefully neglected my duty. Now, sir, by ——— I will not permit any one to say I neglected my duty." Colonel Loomis, replied, "Don't swear in my presence, young man." Hancock answered, "I will be G—— d—— if I don't swear." The Colonel said, "Go to your tent, sir, under arrest." On reaching his tent I found Hancock much more under the influence of julep than I had thought. I put him to bed, and soon he was asleep. The next morning I saw him and said, "Hancock, you drank too much of the Second Dragoons' julep yesterday, and you should not have used the language you did to Colonel Loomis; you owe him an apology and I am satisfied you will make it." He said, "Yes, I should not have sworn in the Colonel's presence." I saw the Colonel and asked him if he would receive an apology from Hancock; he said he would. We went to the Colonel's tent and Hancock made the *amende honorable*. The Colonel released him from arrest. His mess table was being set by his servant, and the Colonel said, "Wait a moment and have some *ham and onions*."

When I arrived in camp on the day of the julep celebration, almost every officer in the regiment was under its influence. Captain and Brevet Major Albemarle Cady[3] was detailed as officer of the day; he disputed the detail, and refused to march on as officer of the day. I reported this to Colonel Loomis who ordered me to arrest Cady. This was done. We all loved "Grandpa" Cady as he was called. In a few days this breach was healed; I forgot how. There was the greatest good feeling existing among the officers of the Sixth Infantry. The enthusiast of the regiment who created most amusement by his ardent imagination was Captain J. B. S. Todd.[4] He said on one occasion, "No sir, I would not marry that girl if every hair on her head was strung with diamonds;'' on another, ''She is a girl I would marry if I found her on a sandbar without a garment on her back.''

Ned Johnson and Hancock told the following story on Todd: When stationed in Arkansas, gamblers were numerous about the post. They found out that Todd was an enthusiast on horse racing. They put up a job on him and sold him, as they said, the fastest horse in the west. ''Billy Dixey'' had never been beaten before. They charged Todd a good round sum for ''Billy Dixey.'' In a few months the pals of those fellows appeared and bantered Todd for a race, one mile. ''Billy'' was, of course, beaten. They told Todd that no horse could possibly beat ''Billy'' at three miles; that at that distance he would get all his money back. Three miles were run, and ''Billy'' was again beaten. Todd exclaimed, ''Who knows! who knows! 'Billy' may be a four mile horse.'' By this time all of Todd's friends and every one else understood the game that these gamblers had worked on him. Todd was persuaded not to try ''Billy'' at four miles, besides Todd was broke and no one would lend him money to bet on ''Billy Dixey.''

On reaching Vera Cruz we found our steamer awaiting us, embarked, and arrived safely in New Orleans. From New Orleans we went by river steamers to Jefferson Barracks.[5] Soon we were joined by the Seventh and Eighth Regiments of Infantry. Each regiment gave a ball in turn, to which, of course, the young ladies in St. Louis were invited. Hancock's position as acting regimental quartermaster enabled him to go up to St. Louis any day.

A steamer plied between St. Louis and Jefferson Barracks, making one or more trips a day. Hancock frequently would say, ''Heth, get permission from 'Old' Loomis, and let us go to St. Louis and make some calls.'' Whenever I asked permission to go to St. Louis, I always received the same reply: ''No, sir, take your seat at your desk and attend to your work.'' ''But my work is all done, Colonel." "Then reflect on that text I read you this morning." "But I have reflected, Colonel." "Then reflect some more sir." Presently the second bell of the boat would ring, when the Colonel would say, "Young man, if you are going on that boat you had better hurry up or you will be left." I suppose the above conversation occurred a dozen or more times. Colonel Loomis was as good hearted a man as ever lived, but, as I have said before, a queer one. You will notice that I did not tell the Colonel that I had reflected upon the Bible text he read me that morning, but said, "I have reflected, Colonel."

I had a very susceptible heart at that time. At a ball the night before I had fallen desperately in love with the sweetest, and to me the most beautiful, girl in the world. I was reflecting what I should say to my charmer and how I could choke Hancock off from going to see her with me. I knew if Hancock accompanied me, my cake would be all dough; she would never look at me. In some way I managed to give Hancock the slip and I had a delightful time with my sweetheart, the beautiful Sallie W.

The time came for the distribution of the troops at Jefferson Barracks to their stations. The Sixth Infantry was ordered to the Upper Mississippi, headquarters at Prairie du Chien. That portion of the regiment that was to be stationed on the Upper Mississippi embarked one Saturday evening. We were to remain all night at St. Louis taking on stores.

I asked Colonel Loomis's permission to take the regimental band into the city to serenade our sweethearts. His reply was, as I expected, a refusal. Colonel Loomis was a Presbyterian of the strictest order. He gave me his reason for refusing. "I can't trust you; you will keep the band out after twelve o'clock." I assured him that not a tune should be played after twelve, that the Sabbath should be observed. "Can't trust you! Can't trust you!" About five minutes refusing to trust me with the band, as I expected, he came to me and said, "Young man, I suppose I must let you have the band and will do so if Hancock will go along." I told him Hancock was going with the party. "All right," he said. We serenaded our sweethearts, and of course, I gave my sweetheart more music than any other girl. As we were about to return to our boat, a friend of ours, a citizen of St. Louis, said that a young lady who had spent the summer in the east had just returned to St. Louis, that none of us had even seen her, adding, "She is the most beautiful girl in the West. Her residence was only a square off and would I not let the band give her one tune?" I assented. After the first tune was played, the window shutters of a room were slightly opened and something white was thrown out. I picked it up and handed it to Hancock who was nearest me. It was a kid glove. The glove was that of the lady who a year later became Hancock's wife.[6]

I was transferred to Captain Alexander's company, which was ordered to Fort Atkinson[7] in the Winnebago country, sixty miles due west from Prairie du Chien. Captain Alexander,[8] Doctor Charles Smith[9] and I were the only commissioned officers at the post and messed together. Captain Alexander was a noble gentleman, with fine taste and a natural born cook. About a week before the winter set in, a man with a wagon loaded with fine fat deer came to the post. Alexander purchased the load, cut it up and hung it in his cellar; in a few days it was frozen hard, and what was left remained until we abandoned the post in March.

I had contracted in Mexico the disease of the climate, dysentery, from which so many died after returning to the States. Doctor Smith would not permit me to partake of the delicious stews Alexander made; milk and rice was my diet and I was rapidly becoming worse. The company was ordered to Fort Crawford at Prairie du Chien. Finally I became so weak that the surgeons, McLaren[10] and Smith, determined to send me

home, as they afterwards informed me, to die. I was too weak
to travel alone. My good friend Hancock volunteered to take
me to my home in Richmond, Va. I had a very comfortable
trip down the Mississippi and up the Ohio to Cincinnati. The
change of water was beneficial. Hancock wished to stop over
in Cincinnati two or three days. There lived on the outskirts
of Covington a young lady whom Hancock had addressed, and
an understanding of some kind existed. Leaving Hancock to
adjust matters with Miss T., I determined to pay a visit to North
Bend, where my father's former private secretary lived. William
Taylor,[11] when I was a small boy, would take me to my school
in Amelia county, and come for me when the holidays began.
He went west and married a daughter of the first President Harrison and was now living at North Bend. I had a pleasant visit
with my friend and commenced to improve. I found on my
return that Hancock had adjusted matters to his satisfaction on
the outskirts of Covington; he and the lady were to be friends
for life, nothing more. From Cincinnati I went to Cleveland;
there I had a terrible setback and but from prompt attention
given me by Hancock I believe I should have died. When strong
enough to travel we left for New York and arrived there safely
and were soon ensconced in the New York Hotel. We met at
the hotel three Sixth Infantry associates, A. D. Nelson,[12] whose
sobriquet was "Sides" Nelson, C. T. Baker,[13] known as
"Betsy" Baker, and George W. Lay.[14]

McCready, the English actor, was to play at the Astor Opera
House that night. All determined to go and hear him. The year
previous Forrest, then the ideal of the "Bowery Boys," visited
England to star there. Forrest was not a success in England;
he was too much on the blood and thunder order to suit the
British public; the English papers were decidedly uncomplimen-
tary in their criticism. This, it appeared to the "Bowery Boys"
and toughs of New York was attributed to the jealousy of
McCready. We got a carriage and when within a square or two

of the theatre we found the street blocked with men and some women. Toughs were much in evidence; the theatre was in their possession; they determined to have their revenge and not permit McCready to act. In pushing my way to the door of the theatre I was separated from my friends. I was very weak, and I determined that was no place for me, feeble as I was. I worked my way to the opposite side of the street, intending to get a conveyance and return to the hotel as soon as I could get out of the crowd. There was terrible commotion going on inside of the theatre and still more in the street. Presently troops arrived, who attempted to clear the streets. The troops were attacked; the officers gave the command to fire. I jumped into an area of a basement window and was safe.

Several volleys were fired into the mob before they dispersed. Here I received my baptism of fire; here I heard the first bullet whistle. I did not enjoy the whistle of the bullet, and I must confess, though having heard many since, that I never could understand the pleasure the musical whistle the bullet conveys to some I have met. There were a number in that crowd killed and more wounded; one or more were killed riding in an omnibus several squares from the opera house.[15] I found my way to my hotel, as did my friends a few hours later. They said the riot inside the theatre was terrible; bags of gunpowder were thrown from the galleries on the chandeliers, but fortunately none exploded. Dynamite was happily unknown at that time.

IX

At breakfast the following morning Hancock proposed that we call and pay our respects to the Commander-in-Chief of the Army, General Winfield Scott. The general received us very graciously and said as we were about to take our leave, "Young gentlemen, I want you to dine with me at six o'clock, sharp, mind." An invitation to dine with General Scott was looked upon as a British subject regards an order to dine with Her Majesty. At six o'clock "sharp" we were on hand. There was but one other invited guest, a professor of Columbia College. After the soup was served, a shad was placed on the table. As soon as the General saw the shad he turned to his waiter and said, "James, what has become of the shad I purchased in market this morning?" James replied, "That is the shad General." "This is *not* the shad I selected this morning, sir; what has become of that fine shad?" James insisted that the shad before the General was the identical shad the General had purchased and he, James, had brought home from the market. The general was equally positive that another, inferior, shad had been substituted. This was kept up so long that I feared the shad would get cold before we were helped.

James was told in an angry tone to bring in the potatoes. The General said, "Gentlemen, I wish to call your attention to the potatoes I will give you; they are the finest potatoes in the United States, and were sent to me by a friend residing in New Jersey where they are raised." General Scott had the happy faculty of believing that anything he had on his table was the best in the world. Hancock, on the other hand, never knew, I believe, when satisfying his hunger, whether he was eating fish, flesh or fowl. The "best potatoes in the world," fortunately, were handed me last.

As soon as Hancock got his potatoes on his plate, he commenced to mash them; the General turned around and said, "My God, my young friend, do you mash your potatoes? you can't tell the taste of a potato when mashed." Hancock replied, "I like my potatoes mashed," and continued to mash them. I saw how the General manipulated his potato and tried to imitate him; he was pleased to notice me and said, "Oh, I see you know how to eat a potato." "Yes, General," I answered, "I cannot tell the taste of a potato when mashed." "Quite right, quite right," replied the General. Hancock caught my eye and looked as though he would like to annihilate me.

Before dinner was over the professor excused himself as he had to deliver a lecture to his class. The General said when dinner was over, "Young gentlemen, we will have a game of whist, and I will play dummy." Our hearts, figuratively speaking, sank in our boots; we had formed our plans to visit some of our sweethearts and have a good time. However, there was no escape for us; we returned to the parlor and cards were procured. Neither Hancock nor I knew anything about playing whist. General Scott prided himself on his knowledge and skill at the game—we were better at draw poker. The General said, "I presume you both play a good game of whist." I said, "I do not, General, but Mr. Hancock plays a beautiful game." Hancock gave me another withering look. General Scott said, "Well, we will see." The cards ran overwhelmingly in our favor; we beat the General four straight games. He got very angry, pitched into my friend, and told him he knew nothing in the world about whist. I suppose he let me off because I could not tell the taste of a potato when mashed. I recollected Mrs. Scott's definition of *ennui,* "a tallow candle, a game of whist, and General Scott." We all but the tallow candle, and I wished for that.

Hancock was requested to ring a bell near him. The unfortunate James appeared. General Scott pitched into James most

unmercifully; he said to him, "Look at that fire, sir, why did
you not attend to it?" There was nothing the matter with the
fire that we could see. "Fix it at once, sir," said the General,
"and you stand there, sir, until I tell you to go." Poor James!
Luck now changed, and the General won two straight games.
A girl was never happier with a new dress, or dusky maiden
with a pair of new red shoes, than the General was now. He
turned to James and in the mildest and most affable manner
said, "Now, James, you may go and bring up the *petite supe.*"
The *petite supe* ended, and so did the game of whist. It was
too late to make our contemplated visits. As soon as the door
was closed by James, Hancock turned on me and said, "Heth,
what made you make such a d—— fool of yourself at dinner,
saying you could not tell the true taste of a potato when mashed;
you always mash your potatoes." "I deny the allegation and
defy the allegator," I said. For nearly thirty years I never failed
to tell the potato episode on my friend.

After ordering some clothes in New York we left for
Philadelphia where I was to remain a day in order to consult
Doctor Chapman,[1] at that time ranking as the first physician
in the United States. Doctor Chapman was a great friend of
my father. When my father was ill on one occasion, without
being sent for the Doctor came all the way to Blackheath to
see him, and, my father thought, saved his life. After a
thorough diagnosis of my disease he said, "Stop taking
medicine; go home; put yourself under the care of your mother
and sisters; try and see if you can digest a small piece of rare
beefsteak, or a mutton chop cooked rare. Tell your mother to
make for you some of that delicious calf's foot jelly she gave
me when I was at Blackheath. As soon as the White Sulphur
opens, join your friend Jack Miller, hunt when strong enough;
keep regular hours, and don't drink too many juleps; take the
water at regular intervals, and you will get well." I followed
Doctor Chapman's instructions and immediately improved.

We arrived in Washington and spent a few days in the capital. I had so far regained my health that, after thanking my dear friend Hancock for his kindness, said, "Old fellow, I would be much pleased if you would accompany me to my home in Richmond and be my guest while there, but I know you have other engagements. I can get home all right now. Besides," I said, "you wish your leave extended and I strongly suspect General Scott will not extend it after the gastronomic faux pas you committed, mashing your potatoes."

Leaving Washington about the middle of May, I reached home the same day. My mother and sisters were, of course, delighted to see me and at once took me under their sheltering wings and most tender care. Each wanted to send off at once for a different doctor; each had discovered the very remedy I required to make me well. I pulled out my memorandum book and read what Doctor Chapman advised. My mother, as well as my eldest sister present, who had been educated and lived in Philadelphia three years, were firm believers in Doctor Chapman. When I came to the prescription of calf's foot jelly I saw a smile of pleasure on my mother's face, and I knew Doctor Chapman had won the day. There is nothing which pleases a Virginia housewife (General Scott once corrected an officer for saying housewife, "No, sir, say huz-wif") more than to praise her pickles, jellies, cakes, breads, etc. Yes, there is one thing she enjoys more, and that is to see you eat them until you are ready to burst—that is the greatest compliment you can pay her.

Doctor Chapman handed me, as I bade him good bye, three five-dollar gold pieces, requesting me to deliver them to his niece who was visiting her relatives in Richmond. The day of arriving in Richmond I saw Miss Chapman and handed her the money. Of course I fell in love with Miss Chapman; ·all men who saw her fell in love with her, and I was keenly bitten by the epidemic—she was the Recamier of America.

When the White Sulphur opened, I hastened to accept an invitation I had received from my friend Jack Miller to spend the summer with him at the White Sulphur and get well, as he said. There was no railroad at that time to the White Sulphur, so I went by "the raging canal," to Lynchburg, and thence by stage to the Springs. My friend was delighted to see me; his cottage and that of his bachelor uncle, Bedford Caldwell, were on a hill in the rear of Mr. Caldwell's residence, surrounded by a beautiful grove of trees; they contained four spacious rooms, and from them was a view of the grounds and walks below. We could see the visitors as they went to the hotel for their meals; at the same time we were as secluded as if we had been on the mountain five miles distant. We took our meals at Mr. Caldwell's, Jack's grandfather, not more than one hundred yards from our cottage, and better beef and mutton I never ate. My only indulgence in the way of strong drink was a glass of brandy and water before dinner, and a glass of fine Madeira at dinner from Mr. Caldwell's private cellar.

The glorious air of the White Sulphur, generous food, the water and exercise, soon told on me, and I was in a fair way to regain my wonted health. Jack Miller proposed a deer hunt; I acquiesced. I was anxious to try my new Purdy gun my father brought me from London. A party was readily made up; the drive was on the Greenbriar Mountain; my stand on the bank of the Greenbriar River. Soon I heard the hounds open; they came nearer and nearer, and I had the pleasure of seeing a fine buck, bound down the mountain and come within forty yards of me. As he was about to plunge into the river, I fired and he fell dead in his tracks. My gun had behaved to my entire satisfaction; nine of the eleven buckshot had struck the deer. I remained in the mountains till some time in October, hunting deer and the mountain pheasant, which last were plentiful. We made trips at intervals to the Warm, the Salt, the Sweet, and the Hot Springs. A most agreeable summer it was.

I bade adieu to my friend and made a visit to my uncle, Mr. Richard Cunningham,[2] who owned a beautiful estate in Culpepper county, on the Rappahannock River five miles from Brandy Station; his place, and the surrounding country, was destined to become historic ground. Many battles were fought ten years later over these hills and dales; those incidents of a fractricidal war will be told later. Mr. Cunningham, who married my father's sister, having no children, at my father's death adopted a young sister and my youngest brother; he gave them all the advantages that a good education could provide, and he and my aunt were father and mother to those soon to be orphans. I had now so far regained my health that I was able to enjoy the good things which his ample and hospitable table afforded. I remember his Surchal and Bual wines, esteemed in that day among the best in Virginia. The partridge shooting around Elk Wood (the name of my uncle's estate) was superb. I have from boyhood been an enthusiast in hunting game of all kinds. My people were before me, and my father was quoted as the best shot in Virginia, as my uncle was after him. I never attained any skill in the use of the shotgun, but enjoyed the sport just as much as if I could bag my fifty and sixty a day and not miss a shot.

Before I left Richmond for the Springs, my sister was married to Julian Harrison,[3] who owned a splendid estate on the upper James River, known as Elk Hill. My mother's home in Richmond adjoined that of John Y. Mason,[4] who was Secretary of the Navy under President Tyler; in 1853 he was appointed Minister to France, and reappointed by President Buchanan to the same position. The judge was a most genial, agreeable and learned gentleman. On one occasion he was standing beside the Emperor Napoleon at some grand reception when a tall, fine-looking negro, as black as charcoal, representing some country as ambassador, passed by. The Emperor was a great friend of Judge Mason; he turned to him and said, "What do you think of him?'' referring to the negro ambassador. The judge replied, ''I think in my State, Virginia, he would bring at least fifteen hundred dollars.''

I passed a delightful winter in Richmond.[5] Judge Mason had lovely daughters, very bright and agreeable. Miss Fannie had many in love with her, among whom was a favorite cousin of mine; this I presume, saved me from contracting the epidemic.[6] One of his young daughters, Miss Mary Ann, a child then probably ten years old, was exceedingly bright and quick at repartee. My cousin and I used to tease this child in order to hear her give us ''Rolands'' for our ''Olivers,'' and her ''Rolands'' were always better than our ''Olivers.''

X

I was so well in the spring that I reported for duty[1] and was ordered to Governor's Island, reporting to my old friend Major Cady.[2] In July 1850, I was ordered to Fort Leavenworth, where my company was about to start to build a new post on the Arkansas River and on the trail leading from Fort Leavenworth to Santa Fe, New Mexico. It was not safe to travel in the Indian country without a pretty strong party. Some two hundred recruits were to be taken to New Mexico. I was detained in order that I might avail myself of this escort. The officers accompanying these recruits were the following: First Lieutenants and Brevet Captains R. S. Ewell,[3] Abraham Buford,[4] First Lieutenant Alfred Pleasanton,[5] Second Lieutenants J. P. Holliday,[6] Thomas Bingham,[7] and the writer. Captain Ewell was sick from the same disease from which I had previously recovered, and remained in an ambulance as long as I was with the column. The command fell to Brevet Captain Buford. Buford was the most accomplished swearer I had ever seen up to that time—I had not met General Harney. Lieutenant Bingham had just been graduated from West Point and assigned to the Second Dragoons. Bingham had been informed that the Second Dragoons were hard drinkers, and that he would not be favorably received in the regiment until he could drink a gallon of whiskey each day. He devoted most of his time to the accomplishment of this very undesirable feat; he succeeded, and died early.

Captain Buford was a Kentuckian and devoted to blooded horses and racing. He had with him two blooded horses, one from the Woodpecker[8] strain, and a sorrel mare, a beauty, with all the marks of a race horse. I was told that Abe Buford cleared by Venus ten thousand dollars. We struck the buffalo in abundance at the big bend of the Arkansas; this was my first sight of buffalo. Abe ordered his boy in charge of his racers to saddle the Woodpecker horse. Abe weighed, I should think, about two hundred pounds, possibly more. He mounted his horse, went after a buffalo, but his weight was too great and he failed to overtake the herd. We were all laughing at his failure when he returned to the column. He got mad and ordered his boy to saddle Venus. He mounted Venus and made for a cow buffalo. Venus carried him over the ground as if he did not weigh more than fifty pounds, ran near the cow, and then shied off as she got the scent of the buffalo. Abe found it impossible to approach near enough to enable him to get a shot.

I determined now to try my luck; I ran after a band, say five hundred in number, and when abreast of them, commenced firing my six-shooter indiscriminately into the herd. I think the shots were delivered at a distance of forty or fifty yards. Accidentally one shot told, and a buffalo fell. On examination I found I had killed a cow. I went to our camp and reported the result of my run. Abe Buford and Pleasanton pooh poohed at my having killed a cow. They had been once before on the plains and hunted buffalo. I told them to let me have a wagon and some men and to come with me and I would show them that I had killed a cow. This was agreed to, the cow was found, butchered and brought in. I was quite a hero. Buford and Pleasanton when scouting for Indians had each killed a buffalo but never a buffalo cow. The cow was much fleeter than the bull and when pursued by the hunter separates itself from the herd. It was necessary to be on quite a fleet horse to overtake her. My cow fed the entire party, officers and men, and was pronounced very fine, though six months later I would not have touched it as food.

The post my company was to build was on the Arkansas River[9] in the center of what was known as the great southern buffalo herd. There were in 1850 two distinct buffalo herds. One ranged north of the Missouri River and into Canada—this was the northern herd; the second, or southern, ranged from the Missouri south into Texas. It was my fortune to spend something over three years at this post, and although there was not a house within two hundred and fifty miles, my sojourn at this "sod fort" was by all odds the happiest three years of my army life. The object in building the post was to keep the road open from Leavenworth to Santa Fe by clearing it of depredating Indians, to serve as a resting place for officers and soldiers going from Mexico to the United States, also to protect the monthly mail going from the States to Santa Fe.

Buffalo were in sight of my post ten months in the year. From September to March we never killed a beef; I supplied my post with buffalo meat which at that season was far superior to beef. The travel across the plains over the Santa Fe and the Salt Lake trails commences when the grass is sufficiently advanced in the spring to afford food for animals, that is, about the middle of May, and ceases after October as there is little or no fuel to be found on the plains, and blizzards often occur. During the months that travel is feasible buffalo meat is very different; the meat of the bull is always tough, and never fat. The cows drop their calves in May and wean them in September. For five months the meat of the cow is indifferent, very poor. The soldiers of my company became so fond of buffalo that they asked for it all the year round. I did not have it on my table from May to September, preferring antelope, and, still better, deer.

During my sojourn on the plains at Fort Atkinson, and subsequently at Fort Kearny, I killed over one thousand buffalo. I became a buffalo fiend. I never enjoyed any sport as much as I did killing them. From constant practice with Colt's army six-shooter, large size, I became an expert in the use of the pistol on horseback. This training saved my life in two Indian fights. When on foot, and shooting at a mark, either with a pistol or with a rifle, I never met a man that could not beat me easily; but on horseback at full or half speed I was, as General Maury would say, "facile princeps." I would take no aim, but drop my pistol, pull the trigger, and the ball would generally go where I looked. I have killed jack rabbits running, with my six shooter; a wolf I hardly ever missed.

In hunting buffalo successfully there are two essentials: first, a horse sufficiently fleet to overtake your cow, and who will not shy when you approach her and he gets the odor of the buffalo; second, to be perfectly cool and not draw your pistol from your holster until you are within a few strides of her side, then shoot her behind the left fore shoulder; your ball will enter her lungs, and in thirty seconds you will see the blood gushing from her nostrils. If you want more meat, you can turn from her and select another cow for your bag. After your run you will find the cows you have shot, and from whose nostrils you have seen the blood gush, dead, within a few hundred yards from where you delivered your shot. Rarely did I fire at a cow more than once.

I made with the Indians who frequented our post many surrounds (as they termed them) of buffalo. One or two hundred Indians mounted on their fleet buffalo ponies would approach a band of say, a thousand buffalo, the wind blowing from the buffalo to them; a line would be formed, the Indians being fifty or seventy-five yards apart; now they would start, twenty men, more or less, from each flank of the line, who would make a circuit around the herd. As soon as the buffalo got the scent of these, they would commence to move off; the line would now move rapidly on the herd, some to the right others to the left, close in on the buffalo and do their work. The Indians used no firearms in killing buffalo, only the bow and arrow. I have seen an entire band of buffalo exterminated in a surround. The buffalo apparently became bewildered and would run in a circle, meeting as they did their pursuers in every direction they would turn. The Indians would take all the meat from the carcass, leaving only the bones. The hide was carefully taken off to be converted into the buffalo robe of commerce by the overworked squaws. The tongues they cared nothing for.

I would ride around when the Indians were butchering and bargain for the tongues; six tongues for a small cup of sugar was the bargain. These tongues I would throw into barrels of brine strong enough to float a potato, keep them there three weeks, then hang them up and smoke them. When dry I would box them up and send them to friends in Virginia, New York and elsewhere. Buffalo tongues cured in this way were highly prized being richer than beef tongues. I cured one year over fifteen hundred tongues.

Colonel E. V. Sumner[10] had preceded our command several weeks; he located the post, Fort Atkinson, on the bank of the Arkansas River. It was a rectangular structure, built of sods,

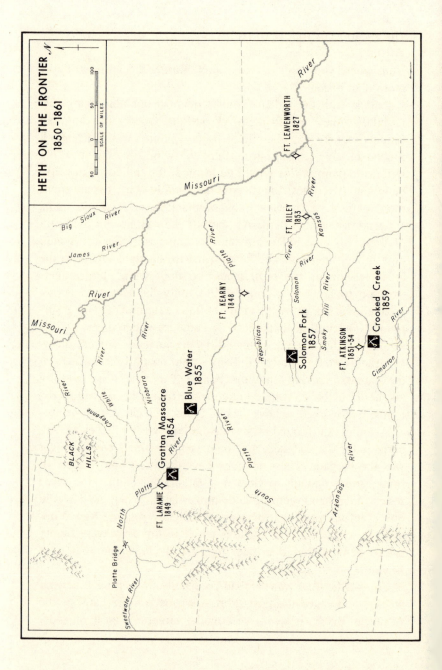

HETH ON THE FRONTIER
1850-1861

N

SCALE OF MILES

FT. LEAVENWORTH
1827

Missouri

FT. RILEY
1853

Big Sioux River

James River

River

Missouri

Platte River

FT. KEARNY
1848

Kansas River

Solomon Fork
1857

Crooked Creek
1859

Cimarron River

Smoky Hill River

Solomon River

Republican River

FT. ATKINSON
1851-54

Blue Water
1855

Niobrara River

White River

Cheyenne River

Grattan Massacre
1854

BLACK HILLS

North Platte River

FT. LARAMIE
1849

Platte River

South Platte River

Kansas River

Arkansas River

Platte Bridge

Sweetwater River

four feet thick at the bottom, six feet high, and two feet thick at the top. A similar wall, parallel to the outer, was built thirty feet from the outside wall. In this wall I left apertures for doors and windows. Two difficult problems had to be solved—where to procure fuel for the winter, and where to get saw logs to protect us from the winter snows and blizzards. Every available tree that we knew of, that would turn out fifty feet of lumber, had been utilized. The six-mule teams I had were kept constantly going to a creek some fifteen miles distant to bring in such fuel as could be obtained; three and four days were necessarily consumed in getting loads.

I determined to explore the country south of the Arkansas River. With an escort of ten men and rations for a week I started out, travelling due south. I found about thirty miles from my post a creek which had some very good timber on it. I hurried back to my command. The problem now to be solved was how to get these logs to my post. Firewood was as necessary to procure as logs for lumber. Fortunately a freighter with twelve wagons loaded with supplies for the troops arrived. His name was Alexander Majors. Majors was a very religious man and a teetotaler; he paid his ox-drivers five dollars a month more than any other freighter on the condition that they refrain from swearing and drinking while in his employ. He would not travel on Sunday and held religious services in his camp.[11] At that time he could neither read nor write; his great object, he said, was to reform the morals of the road.

I informed Majors that I wished him to take his twelve wagons and go to the creek I had found and get me twelve good loads of saw logs. He refused, saying it was then late in the summer, that every day was precious to him, and if he were caught in a snow storm he would lose all his oxen. I replied, "It is better that you lose your oxen than that I lose my company," and that I would be compelled to impress his wagons and teams into service, and that he would be well paid.

Seeing that there was no escape he left at daybreak the following morning, and in four days returned with a good lot of saw
logs. I told him to make out his bill. He made it out for twelve
hundred dollars; I added three hundred to it. He was satisfied,
and reached his home in Independence, Mo., without losing an
ox.

I wrote to Major E. A. Ogden,[12] the quartermaster at Fort
Leavenworth, commending Majors very highly and requesting
him to send all supplies for my post by him. Majors told me
in after years, when a member of the great freighting firm of
Russel, Majors and Wadell[13] that I had given him his start in
life. He was reported then to have made a million and a half.
His firm supplied General Albert Sydney Johnston's[14] army in
Utah with all supplies for that army sent from Leavenworth.

When I reached my company, I found that, there being no
commissioned officer with it, Colonel Sumner had assigned
Lieutenant Albert Magilton[15] to command it until I arrived.
Magilton was from Philadelphia; when appointed a cadet at
West Point he and his brothers were members of a circus. His
brother became famous as a man-monkey. Lieutenant Magilton
in my estimation was the meanest human being I ever encountered. Magilton wore no socks for nine months in the year, and
whenever I saw him he wore a red flannel shirt which I believe
he wore until it was ready to drop from his person. He was
a great smoker, but was never known to purchase ten cents'
worth of tobacco; he would frequent the quarters of his brother
officers who had smoking tobacco, fill his pipe, smoke it and
before leaving refill it, and surreptitiously take a handful of
tobacco, and if he saw he was detected he would say, "I take
this for future reference."

But what disgusted me with this born black guard, was this:
One day he asked me how much money I thought he had saved
since he graduated, I replied, "I hope a great deal." He said,
"I have saved up, counting interest, three thousand dollars."

I said, "Go ahead, and you will be very rich." He then said this which disgusted me immeasurably: "I wish you to tell me if you don't think I have done right. My father is a carpenter and lives in Philadelphia. I gave him the money I had saved and instructed him to build as many small cheap houses as he could with it, and rent them; he built five houses, rented four and lives in one himself, and has not paid me a cent of rent. I am going to stop that; I won't stand it. Don't you think I am right?" I was too mad to answer at once, but asked if he had paid his father for the time and trouble he gave in building his houses. He said, "No, of course not, and I would not pay him a d----d cent." I turned on him and said, "Magilton, you are the veriest whelp in the shape of a man I ever met, to turn your mother and father into the street, who nursed you, who fed and clothed you, until unfortunately you were sent to West Point." I left him. Magilton was ordered to join his company. I completed covering the quarters and laid in hay though very late in the summer; still it was better than nothing, and fuel enough to carry us through the winter.

Before leaving Fort Leavenworth to join my company a gentleman named Samuel Mason asked me to appoint him sutler at the post I was to build; he informed me that he had three wagons loaded with supplies soldiers needed, and was ready to start with Brevet Captain Ewell's command. Mr. Mason's wife was a sister of Lieutenant Alexander Dyer[16] of the Ordnance Corps. I promised Mason to appoint him sutler on my arrival at the new post. Mason did not cross the plains with us but left his sutler's outfit in charge of his brother-in-law, Randolph Harrison Dyer.[17] The name at once attracted me as "Randolph Harrison," was and is today, one of the best known in the State of Virginia. Harry Dyer, as he was called, and I became warm friends, which friendship continued until his death a few years since. He came from good old Virginia stock and had all the noble qualities which go to make up a good man. Harry Dyer and I messed together when crossing the plains and continued to do so as long as we were at Fort Atkinson. The only commissioned officer other than myself at the post was an assistant surgeon, named Longworthy;[18] we did not invite him to join our mess.

We were now as comfortably housed as sod walls and dirt floors could make us. I do not think we had a chair at the post; stools with three wooden legs were our seats. Our tables were made of lumber from dry goods boxes, as were the coffins in which we buried our dead. I was young and did not mind roughing it. I was happy hunting buffalo, wolves, and jack rabbits; this was varied by a not infrequent scout after thieving Indians. Thirty or forty good cavalry horses were furnished by the Government which were used in these scouts and fights when we were fortunate enough to overhaul the rascals.

Sometime in November Captain and Brevet Lieutenant Colonel William Hoffman[19] and his wife and child arrived. Hoffman was near promotion as a major and did not relish bringing his family to this place, and I did not blame him. The Indian tribes that came to our post were the the Cheyennes, Arapahoes, Kiowas, Prairie Apaches, and occasionally, bands of Sioux.

The first Indians to visit our post were the Kiowas, who up to that time had never shaken hands with the whites. Sugar, coffee, flour and rice were issued to them. The Kiowas thought we intended to poison them. They kept the provisions three days before they touched an ounce. They made medicine over the issues, moving round the food on all fours and making a noise supposed to be such as a grizzly bear makes; this was interrupted at intervals, and they would seat themselves in a circle around the pile and pass the pipe, keeping this up for an hour or more. The Chief of the Kiowas, who was also their great medicine man, led in these incantations. Tohausen[20] proved a good friend, and saved my life and the lives of thirty odd soldiers the following year, as will be told at the proper time. The Kiowas left and went south.

In October five Cheyennes came and asked permission to spend the winter at the post. They had their lodge, or tepee, with them; permission was granted. The party consisted of two men and their squaws and one boy. Carviano and Montawona[21] were the names of the men. I gave them some sugar, and coffee and flour, and we became good friends; they accompanied me in all my buffalo hunts during the winter, and my success as a hunter I attribute to their instructions. I was particularly benefited in their pointing out to me how to select from a band the fattest cows. The hero in a buffalo hunt was not he who killed the most buffalo but he who killed the fattest buffalo.

The millions of buffalo roaming over the plains in 1850 have all disappeared. As soon as the railroads to the Pacific were constructed, thousands of men swarmed into the buffalo ranges with long range rifles carrying a ball of heavy calibre, shot them down by the thousands for their hides, tongues, or bones; again, these buffalo hunters would hunt regardless of seasons; large bands would be put in motion when the cows were dropping their calves; the calves, or many of them, would be separated from their mothers and be destroyed by the wolves or die from want of nourishment.

It seems to have been a great shame that the monarch of the plains should have been sacrificed to ruthless gain; but there is another view to take of this entire destruction of the buffalo. Their disappearance *settled the Indian problem,* and has saved thousands of lives and much expenditure of money. So long as buffalo were abundant there were no people on earth more independent than the Indians of the plains. The buffalo was his Commissary and Quartermaster's Department, furnishing him food and clothing. The skin made his tepee; the sinews furnished him with strings for his bows and thread; the hides, converted by the squaw into the buffalo robes of commerce, were exchanged for powder, lead, guns, blankets, red and blue cloth, paints, and other articles they desired. They were the happiest people, and as I have before said, the most independent.

Now all is changed; the Indians must remain on the reservation allotted to them or starve. Until he becomes self sustaining by tilling the ground, the Government furnishes him with food and clothing. The Indians, especially the older Indians who nomadically roamed over the plains, are not happy. To be confined to a few thousand acres of land, and not permitted to leave it, is like chaining the eagle. The Indian man in his nomadic state did no work; he supplied his family with buffalo meat and went to war; his wife, or wives, pitched and struck his lodge, brought all the wood and water and did the cooking. Frequently they had to go one, two, or three miles for wood; large bundles, corded with a rawhide lariat, would be placed on her back and so packed to the tepee. The Indian after reaching his tepee with a pack animal loaded with buffalo would at once dismount, enter his lodge, throw himself on his bed of buffalo robes, light his pipe, and sing one of his songs without meaning and void of tune.

The Indian man doing no work was weak, the muscles of his body were undeveloped. It is but natural when the Government officers say to him, "Here is your piece of land; cultivate it and be self sustaining," that the Indians should fail to make good crops. The Indian man who brought to his lodge a pail of water from a stream flowing within a few feet of his tepee would be disgraced doing squaw work and his wives would be insulted by being told that they had a squaw for a husband.

I have often watched the squaws unpack the animals loaded with buffalo meat. As soon as the unpacking commenced, the squaws would be beset by all the papooses who could toddle and make their demands; when the livers were found the squaw would cut off a piece as large as her hand, toss it to a papoose, who would at once proceed to devour the raw liver and apparently enjoy it as much as a white child would a piece of cake. When butchering buffalo, I have often seen Indians cut off a pound or so of liver, put some of the contents of the gall bladder on it, and apparently greatly relish the luncheon. I tried a little of this once, but could not eat it. It was seldom a buffalo cow was killed that was not with calf. The Indians seemed especially to enjoy the feet of the fetus; he has often told me that to him, it was the sweetest part of the buffalo; of course it was eaten raw. I was never induced to try this tid bit.

The hardest work the squaw did and that which told on her most, was preparing the green buffalo hide for commerce. A stake is driven in the ground with a foot or eighteen inches above the ground; the raw hide is placed over this; when armed with an iron with a round handle, but flattened and serrated at one end, she strikes the inside of the green robe and removes all superfluous pelt; it is then stretched on an upright frame and exposed to the sun to dry. The next process is the most laborious of all; the dried hide is placed on the ground, and the squaw, standing on the hide, provided with her dubbing iron, (the handle of which is part of an elk's horn bent at one end very much like an adze; the bent edge is strongly lashed to a piece of iron, or steel, say four inches broad and sharpened). With this one strikes the hide, taking off shavings of pelt, until it is reduced to the proper thinness.

The next process is to place in a camp kettle buffalo brains and ingredients from the stomach, and boil the same for an hour or so. The skin is now laid on the ground, hair side down, and the mixture in the kettle, by using the long hair on the buffalo bull as a mop, is rubbed over the hide to soften it. Again it is put on the frame and exposed to the sun, that the greasing process might be absorbed.

A cord of buffalo sinew is now tied to a pole and set firmly in the ground, having a loop; through this loop portions of the hide would be run and with both hands and with all her strength she hauls with one hand and then with the other, until the robe is sufficiently pliant for commerce; then, after being trimmed around the edges, it is ready for market.

XI

The hard work done by the Indian women made them prematurely old—a squaw at thirty-five appeared to be sixty; they have but few children. Having lived for years among the Indians, if I were asked to name the most characteristic difference between the civilized mind and the Indian, I should say, the manner in which women are treated. The women are simply beasts of burden and slaves. The muscles of the women are better developed than those of the men, and I enjoyed on several occasions seeing a young woman, a squaw, administer to her husband a sound thrashing, which I have no doubt he richly deserved. I spent a great deal of time when among the Indians in their lodges observing their peculiar customs. I was thrown in with so many different tribes that I made no attempt to learn any one language but confined myself to learning the common language used by all Indians on the plains, the sign language. This I knew and had no difficulty in communicating my wishes to any tribe and understanding theirs. From the Rio Grande to the Canadian frontier I could easily converse with any Indian I encountered.

The wives of an Indian do not live in peace and harmony; not infrequently a regular set-to would occur. The husband, if present, wrapped his head in a blanket, said nothing, and let them fight it out, or he would make a bolt for the door of his lodge and seek peace in that of a friend.

The Indians of the plains of 1850 believed in a Good Spirit, and a Bad Spirit. They were both to be propitiated in the same manner, *through the pipe.* When he smoked, the first puff of smoke he blew upwards, that for the good diety; the second was blown towards the earth, that for evil spirits; the third he blew in his hand and rubbed his hand on his body.

Smoking the pipe was to the Indian worship of some kind. When smoking each Indian would exhibit what he termed his particular medicine. One would refuse to smoke until he had ascertained that all composing the ring of smokers had nothing metallic on them—a knife, a watch, a bunch of keys, all had to be laid aside; another would hold in his hands some long grass, with which during the smoke he would constantly brush the ground immediately in front of him; another would provide himself with a small piece of dried chip and when the pipe came to him he would pinch off a piece and crumble it into the pipe. We would laugh to ourselves over their incantations, but I believe they were as sacred to the Indian as the wafer when blessed is to the devout Catholic.

The winter of 1850-1 passed without incidents worth mentioning; hunting buffalo and shooting wolves at night were our principal amusements. The sutler's store was only a few rods from my quarters; Harry Dyer was my constant companion. There were two windows at the end of the store opposite the door. A fore-quarter of buffalo would be picketed about twenty paces from these windows, the lights extinguished in the store; soon the wolves would appear, scenting the meat. When twenty or more were tugging at the meat, we would fire our double-barrel shotguns into the crowd, bringing down sometimes half a dozen and wounding many more. This could be repeated every half hour during the night. Where buffalo existed in the numbers they did around our post, thousands and tens of thousands of wolves were found who fed upon the dead and dying buffalo. The small coyote, the red wolf, and the large white wolf were in abundance. Each year I remained at Fort Atkinson we bagged over five hundred wolves.

Colonel E. V. Sumner, Second Dragoons, passed Fort Atkinson during the summer of 1851 with a large command en route to New Mexico. There were several officers accompanying this column with their families. Colonel Sumner encamped near our post. The ladies of his command came to our post to visit Mrs. Hoffman, the wife of Colonel Hoffman. An ambulance which had brought two ladies to visit Mrs. Hoffman was standing in front of her door; there were many Cheyenne Indians at the time camped near the post, two squaws being near the ambulance. When Mrs. Thompson came out and was about to enter the ambulance, one of the squaws, astonished at the smallness of her waist, raised her hands, bringing the thumbs and forefingers of each hand near together, approached Mrs. Thompson's waist. Mrs. Thompson turned her head, and, mistaking the squaw for a man and supposing he intended to embrace her, gave a shriek. Her husband[1] came up just then; he was drunk; he seized the ambulance whip and, seeing a Cheyenne Chief near the ambulance, thought he was the offender and struck him several blows with the whip. This would have disgraced the chief forever unless atoned for.

Colonel Sumner left the day following. In the meantime things were becoming quite lively in the Cheyenne camp. The Cheyenne chief said he would kill the first white man he met; the Cheyenne were much excited. Colonel Hoffman wrote a note to Colonel Sumner and informed him that he had probably left on his (Hoffman's) hands an Indian war, and requested that he return and settle the trouble one of his command had caused.

Colonel Sumner had reached the Cimarron, a tributary of the Arkansas; he countermarched and returned to the post. A big pow-wow was the result. The chief told Colonel Sumner he wanted him to put handcuffs on Captain Thompson and tie him behind a wagon and make him march in that way to New Mexico. The Colonel positively refused this mode of settling the trouble. Finally, the offended dignity of the Indian was healed by giving him a horse, three or four blankets, some red and blue cloth, a sack of sugar, and a half sack of coffee.[2] Colonel Sumner resumed his march and no further trouble arose from this drunken freak of a man. Colonel Hoffman soon after was ordered to the recruiting service.

Lieutenant Simon B. Buckner was ordered to command the fort. The change was one we all enjoyed. Buckner I had known as a cadet at West Point; he was greatly beloved in the regiment, was an accomplished officer and gentleman. We have been friends for over fifty years.

About this time I received a letter from my mother, informing me that my brother John,[3] some six or eight years my junior, was threatened with pulmonary disease. I at once wrote him, sending the means, and told him to come to me. We were in a high and dry atmosphere, where little rain fell; one could sleep out without shelter, and his blankets in the morning would be as free from moisture as though he had slept in the New York Hotel. I had often heard the old trappers extol the climate as the best in the world for consumptives; they say people living in these plains never die; sometimes they dry up. My brother joined me; I gave him two good buffalo ponies and told him to live in the open air and hunt buffalo, wolves, jack rabbits; and under my tuition he soon became as expert a buffalo hunter as myself. John Heth was very popular; he became interested in the sutler's business with Henry Dyer and this continued until the breaking out of the Civil War.

Captain and Brevet Major Robert H. Chilton,[4] First Dragoons, was stationed with his family at Fort Leavenworth; he was a Virginian and married Miss Mason, a niece of the celebrated George Mason of Gunston Hall, the author of the Bill of Rights. The Major took a great fancy to me and I was his devoted friend. Every summer the Major with his company made us a visit to help us out in the event of Indian troubles. He brought me the first trip he made, two beautiful greyhounds, a male and female. "Fly" and "Flirt" became widely known in the army. "Flirt," the female, was the most beautifully formed animal I ever looked at, and the fleetest. I never knew "Flirt" to fail picking up a jack rabbit within five hundred yards, after it jumped from its bed. In that distance, five hundred yards, she would gain at least seventy-five yards on "Fly," her brother. Nothing I had on the plains gave me as much pleasure as these two dogs, for all of which I was indebted to my good friend, Major Chilton. One of his daughters was the loveliest girl at seventeen I ever looked at. She is still a beautiful woman, and married my friend General Peyton Wise, of Richmond, Va. The second daughter, also beautiful, married a Mr. Maverick of Texas.

"Flirt" had no trouble in overhauling an antelope, the fleetest animal on the plains, but for some reason she would never take hold of them. The beautiful race we would enjoy, but sometimes regretted missing antelope for supper, especially when buffalo were not fit to eat.

Just before Colonel Hoffman was ordered on the recruiting service, three men from Santa Fe, en route to the States, came to the post stripped of everything, horses, blankets, arms and provisions; they had been overhauled by a band of Pawnee Indians on the Arkansas, above our post, and robbed. Hoffman ordered me to take thirty men and punish those Indians; I invited my Cheyenne friends to accompany me. The Cheyennes and Pawnees were sworn enemies; in fact the Pawnees were the Bedouins of the plains; their hands were against all men. I left the post about dark, expecting to reach the supposed camp

of the Pawnees about daybreak, and to pitch into them as soon
as it was light enough to see.

We reached the Pawnees about two hours before daylight,
dismounted and waited for day.[5] They were on an island located
on the further side of the river. The water in the river was not
over a foot deep anywhere; we mounted and went at a rapid
pace to the island. The Pawnees came to meet us in a body;
I made signs to them to surrender. The reply was a volley; no
one was hit. I ordered the men to charge. I had previously
instructed them, in the event of a fight, that two should keep
together, as I knew the Indians would scatter. In a few minutes
several Pawnees were killed, and they scattered like a flock of
partridges. I saw one making off toward the sandhills, and I
went after him; when within five or six paces of him he halted
and turned on me, and adjusted an arrow. I noticed then a soldier had followed me and when the Indian halted he jumped
from his horse and brought his musket to bear on the Indian.
The Indian first evidently thought to shoot me, but seeing the
soldier he thought him the more dangerous of the two and shot
him. Casey's gun missed fire—Casey was the soldier's name.
At the moment the Indian fired at Casey,[6] I fired at the Indian
and my ball went through his head; he fell dead. The Indian's
arrow struck Casey just below the navel; he lived only a few
days. A number escaped when we first charged them.

I saw the finest looking Indian I had ever beheld standing
on the bank of the island; he had been shot twice, once in the
groin, and an arm was broken by a rifle ball. Knowing he could
not escape, he commenced singing a war song, drew his knife
and plunged it into his chest until he fell. I now got my
wounded over the river, and dispatched a courier for the fort
for an ambulance and the doctor. I looked around for my
Cheyennes and found them where the fight took place. They
had scalped the dead Pawnees, of course, and were just about

to scalp the Indian who had plunged his knife in his own body. The Cheyennes were proceeding very leisurely with their work. The entire scalp was taken from the Indian's head, together with the ears. They skinned it all around, then in front far enough back to enable them to get a good hold with both hands, then with his feet on the shoulders of the dead Indian, he gave a sudden and strong pull, and the scalp came off, making the same sound as a whip when cracked.

While waiting for the arrival of the doctor and ambulances, I witnessed a strange piece of Indian incantation. The Indians seated themselves around a buffalo wallow; in the buffalo region you can scarcely go a hundred yards without running across a wallow. As its name implies, it is where the buffalo wallows to scratch himself and rub off the winter hair from his body. They are always circular, about a foot deep in the center, and say eight or ten feet in diameter. Seated around the wallow, the Indians had drawn a circle in its center and placed in quincunx order the trimmings of the fleshy parts of the scalp of their victims. A dried buffalo's head was near the circle, and on the horns were strung the ears, also the surplus hair they had cut off when preparing the scalp for future use. All being ready, they shuffled around the wallow on their hands and knees; this done three times, they stood upright and bowed three times to the four points of the compass, then seated themselves on the ground. The pipe was now produced and I was invited to smoke, but, noticing that I had metal buttons on my trousers, I was not permitted to participate in these incantatory proceedings. The first smoke inhaled was blown upwards to the good spirit, the second to the earth to the evil spirit, then to the four points of the compass. During this the oldest Indian repeated a dirge, a prayer which he explained meant that he asked the good spirit and the evil spirit to always give them plenty of their enemies' scalps, and that they might never lose their own.

The doctor and the ambulance arrived and we soon reached our sod home.

On one occasion I was returning from a hunt and when near the Arkansas River I noticed something moving in a patch of long grass. I took it to be a wolf and told the soldier nearest me, who was a fine shot, to fire. The soldier dismounted, aimed his rifle, and was about to fire, when I saw a small hand raised. Fortunately his rifle missed fire. I ran to the high grass and found a child about three years old. We carried the infant to the fort. I gave it to one of the camp women to take care of, who had an infant of her own. I sent my interpreter after the Indians, who had been encamped near the place I found the child, and they were informed of the find. The Indians hastened to the fort, made medicine, that is, howled, and went through their incantations for a couple of days, named the boy for me, calling it by my Indian name, Yo-ba-ma-etz. Before leaving the fort the mother brought the child to the doctor, saying that the white woman's milk had made her baby sick. The doctor gave her some medicine with directions how to administer it. I saw her give the child one dose, then, stripping the body of its scanty attire, she poured out what remained in the vial in her hand and rubbed it on the child's body, supposing it would be equally efficacious applied externally.

The Kiowa Indians made annual raids into Arizona and across the Rio Grande into Mexico, their object being to steal horses and capture Mexican girls.[7] A Mexican woman, then about twenty-five years old, who was with the Kiowas, having a baby four years old, came to the sutler's store and besought Mr. Mason, our sutler, to buy her. Mason was a kindhearted old gentleman and could not refuse her appeal after listening to her sad story. Her mother, her sister and herself were captured by the Indians five years before. Her mother was old, and after the first day when the Indians were rapidly getting away, they knocked the mother in the head, killing her. Her sister gave birth to an infant, and the second day then proceeded to treat her and her new-born infant in the same cruel manner. Louise, the youngest, was taken by one of the Indians as his wife; he had two or three other wives. Unfortunately, or fortunately, for Louise, her husband some six months before was killed in a battle with the Pawnees. The three wives treated her abominably, took from her everything she had, and not only treated her badly but maltreated her child; her life was not endurable. Mason struck a bargain with the Indian having charge of Louise and gave one hundred dollars in Indian goods for the woman and her child. Louise proved to be a good laundress, and after a while a fair plain cook. The child, which I called Kiowa, after her tribe, was a bright little girl and spent as much of her time in my quarters as I would permit. Candy was the first inducement. She became very fond of me as I did of her. I taught her the Lord's Prayer, "Now I lay me down to sleep," etc. The soldiers were very kind to her, but they taught her to curse horribly. The Kiowas when encamped near the fort stole little Kiowa twice; this created as much excitement as if they had carried off a white child. I had no trouble in having her returned. I would send for old Tohausen and very soon the child was sent back. To prevent trouble when the Kiowa Indians were around, I had an iron picket pin driven in the ground half way between the door of my quarters and the guard house, tied a good strong cord about sixty feet in length to Kiowa's ankle and fastened the other end securely to the picket pin, and gave orders to the sergeant of the guard not to permit any Indian to approach her. She soon got accustomed to being picketed out; she knew she would get candy for not crying. After this I had no further trouble on this score.

XII

Simon Buckner was an enthusiast on Shakespeare. A play would be selected and the several parts assigned to our messmates, and the play would be read. This and whist were our chief amusements during the winter evenings; there was no gambling at our post and only very moderate drinking. Every night after reading Shakespeare, or playing whist, we adjourned to the sutler's store to roast buffalo marrow bones upon the stove, spreading the marrow on toast; this with a glass of Scotch whiskey was a feast for the gods.

I had hunted buffalo so much with the Indians, who, as I have said, used only the bow and arrow in their hunts, and it seemed so easy to kill buffalo in that manner that I determined to try that method of hunting. I found it the most difficult job I had ever undertaken. After many trials, and shooting away a hundred or more arrows, I at last succeeded in locating one in the right spot and brought down my cow. I was now content. This feat was soon known to all at the post; the soldiers of my company were very proud of their lieutenant's prowess as a buffalo hunter; they told soldiers passing the post, en route to New Mexico, and soldiers en route to the States, that their lieutenant would mount a horse bare back, and with his bow and arrows kill more buffalo in a single run than the most expert Indian hunter could kill in two. I was asked when I reached my home in Richmond, Va., if this story was correct, that I had hunted buffalo on a horse, without a saddle or bridle, only a lariat in the horse's mouth, shooting them with arrows and clad only in a breechcloth similar to that worn by the Indians.

Lieutenant Robert Johnston,[1] First Dragoons, stationed in New Mexico, was ordered to my post one summer to render assistance should trouble arise with the Indians. Johnston's company, and some thirty men from my own, were scouting after Pawnees when we neared the Smokey Hill Fork (a stream which, uniting with the Republican Fork, forms the Kansas or Kaw River). We saw a band of antelope feeding in the river bottom; they winded us and ran toward the column. I have said before that I have never met any one who could not easily beat me shooting a rifle, or pistol on foot. As the antelope approached us I said to Johnston, "You see that buck leading the band, well, when they get within one or two hundred yards from us and see us, they will halt and remain still for ten or fifteen seconds; I will knock that buck's eyes out."

I borrowed the sergeant's rifle, dismounted, and the band halted as I knew they would. I fired, and the leader, the buck, fell in his tracks. I handed the sergeant his rifle and said, "Sergeant, you will find I hit him in his right eye." The sergeant galloped off; on his return he said, "Lieutenant, you made a center shot, you hit him in his right eye." I do not think I could have duplicated that shot once in ten thousand times, and then it would have been an accident. My men told Johnston's dragoons that they had seen me do the same thing a hundred times, only this difference: the antelope would be running at full speed when I knocked out their eyes. So reputations are sometimes made; this feat spread far and wide, and I was spoken of as the finest rifle shot in the army.

The sport that gave me great enjoyment was coursing the jack rabbits with my greyhounds. On one occasion Simon Buckner and I were coursing rabbits, I was much absorbed in the chase, when my buffalo mare put her foot in a badger hole, fell, and threw me over her head. I struck the ground with my left shoulder. As I fell I heard something snap with quite a noise; it proved to be the crupper to my saddle. I was dazed by the fall. Buckner asked me if I were hurt. I told him I thought I was shot, mistaking the noise made by the snapping of the crupper to my saddle for a pistol shot. It was eighteen months before

I fully recovered the use of my left arm; this was the only accident that happened to me in all my runs.

The Indian when hunting, or in battle, holds his bow in his left hand; in the same hand and along the back of the bow he grasps three or four arrows; his quiver is in front of him; he can discharge his arrows as fast as a soldier can his pistol and with far greater accuracy. I asked an Indian when hunting one day, if their ponies often fell with them and how they managed to keep them from stepping into prairie dog holes. The Indian replied that was not his business; the pony's business is to look out where he steps. Sometimes they have falls and it often happens that Indians have been killed, generally from falling on their arrows. Many years before 1850 the Indians, of some tribes, used poisoned arrows, but finding that accidentally many were pricked with their own and died, they gave up this practice. I could not learn what poison their ancestors used, but I presume that of the rattlesnake.

For miles above and below my post there was one continuous prairie dog town, many of them abandoned towns. The prairie dog in shape is not unlike the guinea pig; its color is a reddish brown; it lives on the roots of grasses around its hole; in time the grass is all killed; he then seeks greener pastures and makes a new home.

Rattlesnakes were galore around Fort Atkinson; I never rode out in the summer, fall, or spring, that I did not run across from one to a dozen; they were often killed on the post. The stuler found one curled up on a dry goods box in his store, but I only recall one man, a herder, being bitten by a snake. A copious supply of whiskey speedily eradicated the effect of the poison. I would frequently dismount and try to get a rattler to strike, using the wiping stick of my rifle to provoke him. I never succeeded in obtaining a strike but once, then he missed the stick, and I saw distinctly two jets of an orange colored fluid come from his fangs. The fangs are hollow and rest on sacs about the size of a pea; when the snake strikes, the mechanical motion causes the poison to flow into the fangs.

The Indian ponies are sometimes struck by this reptile; the pony is tied up, and if bitten on the nose, as was the one I saw, the nose is thoroughly scarified, powder well-rubbed into the wounds thus produced, and touched off with a hot coal. It appears to be an efficacious treatment. I tried it on one of my horses that had been bitten by a snake, and he was soon all right.

The traveller over the plains is often mistaken in supposing that the prairie dog, the prairie owl, a small bird, and the rattle snake live in the same hole. I was once riding rapidly through a prairie dog town. I got very near a prairie dog before he saw me; his hole was only a few yards off. As my mare cleared the hole the prairie dog came out under her feet; this was such an unusual occurrence that I held up and examined the hole. Coiled up in the mouth of the hole was a large rattlesnake; the prairie dog evidently preferred risking the horse and myself to the snake. To satisfy [myself] I cut open several snakes; in one I found a young prairie dog and a young owl; this satisfied me that the prairie dog, the snake and the owl did not constitute the happy family many supposed. I have often seen the prairie dog cooked and tasted it, but I never enjoyed the food; it had a strong earthy taste—to me very unpleasant; others seemed to like it.

During the summer of 1852 a party from New Mexico en route to the States reported to Captain Buckner, our commanding officer, that they found on the Cimarron the body of a white man, who had evidently been killed by Indians. An investigation satisfied Buckner that the white man had been killed by a Kiowa Indian. Captain Buckner ordered me to take some thirty men and two pieces of cannon, visit the Kiowa village, and bring the offender to the fort. The Indians were encamped on the opposite side of the river a mile or two from the fort.

I crossed over the river and struck the lower part of the Indian village. The old chief in charge here was much excited and very angry that I should come to his village prepared for war. I asked him to send for Tohausen, the head chief and my friend; he did so, but the news of my arrival had spread through the village and every man at once prepared for a fight. The sand hills were here only about one hundred yards from the river. They came in squads of ten to fifty and soon numbered five hundred strong and surrounded my force of thirty men. Just then old Tohausen arrived; he was quiet, and talked peace, but said, "Yo-ba-ma-etz, you had better take your men back to the fort; there is still a small road open for you across the river."

The river was nowhere over a foot deep. I thought Tohausen and demanded that the offender be given up; he was always believed that any indiscretion on my part at that time would have resulted in the extermination of my entire party, just as Lieutenant Grattan[2] and his thirty men were massacred below Fort Laramie in 1854. I recrossed the river; not a shot was fired.

Captain Buckner, my commanding officer, approved of my course on hearing a statement of the facts. Buckner sent for Tohausen and demended that the offender be given up; he was brought down on a sick bed, and after a while was released. This affair became known throughout New Mexico and at other military posts, and I am happy to say my course was favorably commented upon.

We received our mails at Fort Atkinson, more frequently called, in derision, "Fort Sod," by sending an ambulance to Fort Leavenworth the first of every month with our monthly returns and reports; the ambulance returning brought the mail that had accumulated at Leavenworth. I was sent to Fort Leavenworth during the summer on some duty, I think, to get a supply of horses and mules; I enjoyed the trip. It gave me an opportunity of seeing my friends the Chiltons, with whom

I generally stopped, and other friends of the Sixth Infantry, my regiment, stationed at Leavenworth.

I found there on this occasion Brevet Captain Mansfield Lovell, 4th Artillery. Lovell during the Mexican war was aide-de-camp to General Quitman. The war ended, General Quitman presented Lovell with a magnificent Woodpecker colt, the finest specimen of a cavalry horse I ever saw. Lovell had received orders to go to New York or Newport;[3] he could not take his horse with him, but he sold him to me at what I thought a reasonable price, $200 in gold, saying, "Heth, I let you have 'Bill' because you know a good horse and will treat him well." I had some recruits to take out to my company, also a number of horses and mules.

Lovell had been on the plains the year before, and had killed a buffalo bull, riding "Bill." After killing the bull he jumped "Bill" back and forth over the dead buffalo, so "Bill" was not frightened by the smell of buffalo. I anticipated sport after reaching my fort. I gave "Bill," the morning we crossed the Little Arkansas, to a Dutchman to lead, cautioning him not to fasten the halter to his saddle, but to hold it in his hand; as soon as my back was turned he fastened the halter to a ring in his saddle, riding behind a portable forge. The tail gate of the forge dropped off, the Dutchman's horse became frightened, shied, and threw the Dutchman. "Bill" and the horse took a turn at full speed on the prairie; something tripped both at the same instant, both fell and snapped their left fore legs short off below the knee. The hind part of the hoof of "Bill's" foreleg was turned to the front, and the bones protruded beyond the skin. There was but one thing to do—I ordered a soldier to shoot both animals.

New Mexico, when we took possession of the country during the Mexican war, was in a very bad condition religiously and morally. The priests said they had a dispensation from the Holy Father to take a wife but not to marry; many had families; they owned the principal gambling establishments as well as the best breed of game chickens in the territory, and were always ready for a bet and a battle. New Mexico had now passed into the hands of the United States, and the Church authorities in the States determined to put an end to these proceedings on the part of the New Mexican priests.

A pious, good, holy Bishop was sent to New Mexico to regulate matters. I travelled across the plains with Bishop Lamy,[4] who had with him a number of sisters, nuns, to assist him in his work of reformation. The Bishop succeeded in reforming the priests. The following summer the Bishop passed our fort with a priest and half a dozen Mexican boys who were to be sent to Rome to be educated for the church and then return to New Mexico. The Bishop stopped with us two days, and requested permission to celebrate mass, which was of course granted.

I turned over to him my quarters and the post carpenters to make the necessary preparations for the celebration. While this work was going on in my quarters, I went to the sutler's store and found there the priest the Bishop had brought with him. Harry Dyer, our sutler, called me aside and said, "You see that fellow? I have bet at his monte bank in Santa Fe a hundred times and have had many a fight with his chickens. He is, or was, a hard case; since he has been in the store he has taken two or three pretty stiff drinks and he wants another; ask him to take a drink." I did so, and he took what was called on the plains a "sockdolager," about half a tumbler, or more, of whiskey. Harry filled two quart bottles with whiskey which he, the priest, had purchased. Presently the Bishop sent for the priest to assist him at mass; he put his bottles of whiskey in the pocket of his coat. I noticed that an inch or two of the necks of the bottles protruded. During the celebration of mass we could hear the necks of these bottles clinking against each other, which excited our risibilities.

Mass over, Louise, our laundress and cook, came to the Bishop and requested him to baptise her child, the Kiowa; at a certain time in the ceremony the Bishop turned to me and asked "What name?" I said, "Kiowa." The Bishop hesitated for a moment and said, "I know of no saint by that name." I replied, "Well, call her anything, call her for her mother, Louise"; so the Kiowa was called. The good Bishop apologized for not being able fully to complete the baptismal ceremony, not having, as he said, the holy oils with him, but promised on his return to have them and finish up matters. But alas! when the holy man returned the Kiowa had gone, I believe to heaven. She died after a short illness of hydrocephalus, water on the brain, the doctor said. I was much distressed at the death of this child; I had become devotedly attached to her, and made my plans for having her educated when she attained the proper age.

XIII

During the summer of 1852 I was sent to St. Louis to purchase supplies with which to build a new fort. For some reason that I never understood, the Department Quartermaster was much opposed to building a new fort on the Arkansas River and threw many obstacles in the way. General Clarke, who commanded the department, had his headquarters at Jefferson Barracks, ten miles below St. Louis; the headquarters of the Sixth Infantry was also there.

Hancock was adjutant to the regiment. He had married Miss

Russell, the lady who threw the glove from her window when we serenaded her some two years previous. Hancock was married when I was on sick leave in Richmond, the winter of 1849-50. He wrote me of his proposed marriage and asked me to be one of his groomsmen; it was not convenient for me to accept, so, much to my regret, I missed seeing my friend married to the most beautiful girl in the West. I spent much of my time at the barracks with Hancock.

When in St. Louis I had much leisure time awaiting the authorities in Washington to decide some, I thought, absurd point raised by the Department Quartermaster. Lieutenant and Brevet Captain Ulysses S. Grant, Fourth Infantry, was in St. Louis at this time on leave; his station was Detroit, Mich.; he brought his wife on, to be with her mother during her confinement. Grant I had known in the City of Mexico; we took quite a fancy to each other; I found him a most genial and pleasant companion. He never tired listening to my buffalo hunts, my wolf hunts, and coursing jack rabbits. I would listen to his natural boasting about his wonderful boy baby,[1] the like of which never had been seen before, and about a pony[2] he had brought with him from Detroit, with which he had won many races pacing on the ice.

At that time the only way to reach Jefferson Barracks from St. Louis was by stage, which left the city daily at ten o'clock. I had occasion to go to the Barracks on business, and missed the stage. I met Grant and complained about my hard luck; he said, "I will drive you down to the barracks this evening with my fast horse." I consented, on the condition that he would dine with me at the Planters' House and have his buggy and fast pony there after dinner, which was agreed to. I saw in front of the hotel a buggy with (I thought) a rat of a pony attached to it, and when Grant came out I asked him if that was his fast pacer. He said "Yes." I told him I had half a dozen ponies on the Arkansas River that could beat that thing. He said, "Get in and I will show you what she can do when we get out of the city limits."

The pony was going along at a jog trot; I continued to tease him; he suddenly pulled the reins, hit the pony with his whip, and she broke into a pace or rack. I had never before been behind anything with so much speed. The street made quite a sharp bend, and we ran into a cow. I was thrown on the sidewalk between two baskets of cranberries. Grant struck the curbstone with his shoulder and was knocked senseless and taken to an apothecary shop, where he soon recovered, and no bones were broken. Some one caught the pony and brought it back. The shafts were broken, also the harness. I said, "We must give up our trip to the barracks." Grant said, "No, the arsenal is only a few hundred yards from here, we will lead the pony down there and make those ordnance fellows fix the buggy and harness." We did so; the damage being repaired we drove to the barracks, and I transacted my business, after which we returned to the city. What further relates to this episode will be told when I tell what occurred at Appomattox, April 9, 1865.

News was received from the plains that the Indians were becoming very restless and threatening. The Superintendent of Indian affairs, residing in St. Louis, requested General Clarke to order me to Washington to inform General Scott of the condition of affairs. The order was given, and I arrived in Washington just after General Scott had been nominated for President by the Whig party. When I reported he appeared to be in a bad humor. He said, "Why did General Clarke order you to Washington?" I replied, "I suppose to represent to you the condition of affairs on the Arkansas River, and ask you to send additional troops to that point. We are now surrounded by six tribes of Indians, the Comanches, Kiowas, Cheyennes, Arapahoes, Prairie Apaches, and some Sioux, numbering, I think, quite three thousand warriors. They are there to receive their annuities by appointment of Major Fitzpatrick, their agent, and are not peaceably inclined."[3]

Just then a politician came in; he was received, of course, most graciously. He said, "General, I heard John Minor Botts[4] make a speech last night; he eulogized you in the most glowing terms and carried away his audience." "Oh!" said the General, "Botts is a fine fellow; tell him when I am President I shall not forget him;" and then said, "Gentlemen, I can count on my election with the same certainty that I can count the fingers on my hand and the toes on my feet." I thought to myself you had better wait until the votes are counted. General Scott received forty-two electoral votes against two hundred and fifty-four given Pierce. What a disappointment it must have been to the old General.

Being so near my home I determined to run down and see my sister and my sweetheart. I found that both were then on a visit to Shirley, Mr. Hill Carter's estate,[5] below Richmond on the James River. I took the first boat and landed at Shirley, where I had often visited before. I spent two days there most delightfully, and then hurried back to St. Louis.

I found Grant still there; he insisted on my seeing the wonderful boy. I went with him to his father-in-law's, Mr. Dent's. As soon as we entered the house Grant stopped at the foot of the steps and called to the nurse to bring the baby down to the parlor; soon the baby appeared. I was at a loss to know what was expected of me, so I took the baby from the nurse. I was lavish in my encomiums of the youngster; it *was* a splendid looking child. I suppose I had the baby about ten minutes when Mrs. Grant came in; she hastened to where I was and promptly relieved me from playing nurse. When Grant was President, I went one day to the White House to pay my respects to Mrs. Grant and the President. Mrs. Grant said, "Do you remember when we first met?" I said, "I presume it must have been in St. Louis before you were married." She said,

"No, it was not; the first time we met you were holding my baby, and if you had held it five minutes longer as you were holding it when I came into the parlor, I should have had no baby."

General Clarke thought I had better hasten back to my post and I was of the same opinion. I took the first boat up the river to Leavenworth, and then hurried to my post. I overtook Major Fitzpatrick, the Indian agent, en route to Fort Atkinson to distribute to the Indians their annuities. The Major was then quite sixty years old; he had been among the Indians for forty years, first employed by the American Fur Company. He spoke Cheyenne very well, and the sign language perfectly. He was very popular with the Indians. They were much pleased on seeing their agent, knowing now that their goods were close at hand. The goods were distributed and the Indians were happy.[6] The bottoms of the river were covered with teepees for ten or fifteen miles below the fort and the same distance above. I think they must have had eighty or ninety thousand head of ponies and mules.

I noticed that at least four out of five of their mules and ponies were branded with a Mexican brand; these animals had been stolen from the Mexicans during their raids across the Rio Grande. The Indians soon started in search of buffalo. The Comanches and Kiowas informed us that they would shake hands, and be at peace with the whites who travelled the roads we were on, but intended to fight the whites in Texas. This was an anomalous condition of affairs, the Government issuing guns, powder and lead to the Indians on the Arkansas River, with which to kill our soldiers and people in Texas. Within two or three months after receiving their annuities at Fort Atkinson, on the Arkansas, we would hear of a fight somewhere south of us. On several occasions Indians wounded by our soldiers in Texas came to the fort to be cared for by our surgeons, and many wearing army overcoats.

During the winter of 1852-3, two U. S. trains of twenty wagons each started very late in the season, loaded with supplies of clothing principally, for the troops in New Mexico. These trains were caught in a terrible blizzard above the fort, and lost so many oxen that the wagon masters in charge determined it was best to lay over until spring. The wagons were corralled on the banks of the river and the oxen herded in the islands near by. I felt anxious about the government supplies, and rode to where the wagons were corralled. I found all right, and rode on to the bluffs. The river bottom was here quite two miles wide; it was early in March, and the wind was blowing from the northwest at a fearful rate; I would say from forty to fifty miles an hour.

On reaching the bluffs, I noticed smoke to the northwest; it was approaching me rapidly; there was little to burn on the plains except dried buffalo chips. There was scarcely a square yard where there was not to be found from one to a half dozen of this fuel of the plains. The air was filled with burning chips, falling to the ground; others would be ignited, taken up by the wind and carried before it, so the fire was kept up. I put my horse at full speed for the wagon corral; when I reached there, the wagon sheets were in full blaze, the men working like beavers to save provisions and their personal belongings, but in less than half an hour the wagons and their contents were consumed. I was glad that I witnessed the destruction of the Government property, inasmuch as I was able in my report to exonerate the wagon masters and teamsters from all blame. I happened to have on my buffalo robe overcoat, and by turning up my collar was protected; my horse was somewhat scorched.

I broke up a piece of ground near my fort and planted corn. Twelve months after, I found the grains of corn as well preserved as though they had been in a barn; no rain fell for eighteen months. The following summer and fall we had, for that country, a good deal of rain, which gave us the only good shooting we had during our sojourn at Fort Atkinson. The buffalo wallows were filled with water, and a long grass similar to broom sedge sprung up around the edges of the wallows. The ducks that breed in the far north were now seeking warmer climes with their broods and would rest for a while in the wallows and feed. The duck and mallard and the blue winged teal were in abundance, and occasionally the canvas-back duck. Dismounting when we saw a wallow and approaching cautiously, the long grass concealed us, and when within ten or twelve paces of the wallow, a duck and mallard, sometimes two pair, would rise and give us a beautiful double shot. We would frequently bring in a bag of twenty mallards and twice as many teal in a day's shooting; the mallard and teal were as fine as any I have ever eaten. My men got thoroughly tired of ducks and were clamorous for buffalo.

As I have said before, all officers from the States going to New Mexico to join their regiments, as well as those returning to the States, passed Fort Atkinson, and usually spent two or three days at the fort, resting their animals, so I became as well posted as to what was going on in that country as if I had been stationed there. When a new officer, or a distinguished citizen, arrived in Santa Fe, his arrival would be honored by a Mexican baile, or ball. There was stationed in Santa Fe a young officer, very much liked, very wild, and full of fun. He bore the not very polite or well-sounding sobriquet among his friends, of "Hell Roaring" Jackson.[7] Jackson said he was determined to institute reformations at these bailes, so he sent around a circular, informing the Mexican girls that they would not be admitted to the bailes unless they wore stockings, and that he proposed to inspect them to see that this order was carried out. I learned it did not create any great disturbance among the New Mexican senoritas.

From the following story told me, I should judge that these Mexican bailes were very unlike the balls given by the select

four hundred of New York. In fact, I should say they must
have been decidedly promiscuous. Two miners came to one of
them; one knew a Mexican damsel and asked her to accompany
him to the baile, and she consented. She was a splendid dancer;
her friend could not dance but his miner friend was a noted
terpsichorist. He asked him to dance with his girl, and they
took a turn; he asked his senorita how she liked his friend as
a partner. She said, "He dances beautifully, but he smells
bad." This he repeated to his friend, who said, "Well, I took
a bath and changed my clothes before coming here, that is, all
but my socks." "Why did you not change your socks?" was
the inquiry. "Well," he replied, "I did not have a clean pair
of socks and no money to buy a new pair." "How long have
you been wearing those socks?" "About seven weeks." "Why,
that is what she complains of; here is fifty cents, go and
purchase a new pair and put them on." He soon reappeared
and said he had bought a new pair of socks and put them on.
"I will see my girl and tell her that now you are all right, then
you dance with her." He did so. The senorita sat down, and
her sweetheart asked her what was the trouble. She said, "He
smells worse than ever." On inquiring, it was found that he
had thrust the seven weeks socks in his bosom, separated only
by the fellow's vest from the senorita.

XIV

When I look back on the trips we took during the winter
to Crooked Creek[1]—Harry Dyer, Dr. Ridgeley,[2] John Heth and
I—it makes my mouth water now. We killed, en route to the

creek, a fine cow, and, selecting a place for our tent under the sheltering bank of the creek, we built a big fire of dry cottonwood logs in front of the tent, and broiled on the coals or on our gridirons the choice fat morsels of the cow; and of course we were never without something to drink. The great difference between the flesh of the buffalo and that of good beef is that one is more digestible than the other and you can eat much more buffalo than beef. An Indian when hungry will eat pounds of buffalo, but if he eats the white man's buffalo (beef) in the same quantity he is sure to be made sick.

The time was approaching when Fort Atkinson was to be abandoned. Dear Simon B. Buckner had been ordered east, and Brevet Major Edward Johnson was promoted to Captain of "D" Company. Three or four months after Johnson joined us, we were ordered to Fort Riley, a new fort, to be built at the junction of the Smokey Hill Fork and the Republican Fork, forming the Kaw or Kansas River. As we abandoned this (to others) miserable pile of sods, where I had passed so many pleasant years, where every sand hill, every hollow, and I was about to say every buffalo wallow, had an association very pleasant to me, connected with them, I felt that I was parting with dear friends forever. No more such buffalo hunts, such wolf hunts, such coursing of jack rabbits again. I felt as though I would like to be buried on the bluff by my little Kiowa. Nothing of interest occurred on our march; after passing Council Grove and leaving the plains, striking the prairie country where the grass was long, we had splendid prairie chicken shooting. It was late in August and the young birds were delicious eating, but I could not but compare this sport with that I had left behind me.

On my arrival at Fort Riley[3] I was immediately appointed Post Quartermaster and set to work building quarters according to plans furnished from Washington. I built two sets of stone quarters for the men, and I think three sets for the officers. A bridge was erected over the Blue River, where all our supplies from Fort Leavenworth had to cross, and another over the Republican Fork to reach the timber in the forks of these rivers.

When this fort (Riley) was first located, the number of wild turkeys in the timber was so numerous that it would appear like exaggeration to attempt to enumerate them. I killed six in half an hour; the combined weight, I remember, was something under ninety pounds. Before winter set in, quarters sufficient for the soldiers and officers were completed. The chimneys smoked horribly although we had employed the best masons to be had in Cincinnati to do the work. Major Cady (grand old "grandpa" Cady) was in command. Cady was a great theorizer; he worked out a plan, mathematically, for a chimney that was sure to draw well; we were to have no more smoking chimneys. Captain Ned Johnson, who was much of a wag and delighted in teasing Major Cady, covered the top of the chimney with boards; the result can be imagined. An investigation showed the cause. The only remark Cady made was, "That was that d----d fellow Johnson's work, I know."

Work was stopped on account of the cold weather, and having little to do, I made up a select party to go on a buffalo hunt. We went up the Smokey Hill Fork five or six days' journey and then struck south, striking Pawnee Fork some ten miles above its mouth, where we found buffalo in abundance. I killed a couple of fat cows, and we feasted. The weather was delightful; we remained on Pawnee Fork four or five days, loaded our wagons with fat buffalo meat, and started home. The weather favored us; it was cold enough to preserve our meat. We got it to the fort in excellent condition, and distributed it among our friends; they pronounced it the best meat they had ever tasted. It was in fine condition and killed at the right season.

In the spring I received a letter from Hancock informing me that Captain Wharton[4] of the Sixth, stationed at Fort Kearny on the Platte River, had been detailed on the recruiting service, and if I wished, General Clarke would transfer me to Wharton's company, and I would be in command of the fort. Of course I accepted the transfer, and the order was issued. Then en route to Kearny, I overtook Colonel Steptoe's[5] command en route to California, but as Steptoe was travelling slowly, I pushed on. Captain Wharton was still there, and I took my meals with the Whartons. His wife was the lady who, in the early seventies, was tried at Annapolis, Md. for poisoning Captain Ketchum,[6] of the Sixth Infantry. As I happened to mess with the Whartons until they left Kearny for the States, I was summoned as a witness on this celebrated case.[7] The object in summoning me was to trace Mrs. Wharton from the time she married until the alleged poisoning, and I happened to be the only person available who saw her at Fort Kearny. My testimony was all in her favor.

The latter part of the summer of 1854, buffalo were reported to have been seen a few miles south of the fort.[8] Dr. Alexander[9] and I determined to investigate, and on reaching the sand hills we dismounted and proceeded to reconnoiter; we saw half a dozen bulls feeding in the bottom 200 yards from the top of the sand ridges. I noticed one young bull in the bunch. He had shed his winter coat, but there was, however, a bunch of old hair about three inches in diameter adhering to his side just behind his left fore shoulder. I pointed this out to Dr. Alexander and told him I would kill that bull, and would, as rapidly as possible, empty the six barrels of my pistol, aiming at the bunch of hair. This I did; the bull fell, and on examination we found the six bullets had either passed through the bunch of hair or on the edge of it.

While butchering the buffalo I noticed what I supposed to be columns of smoke arising south of us. The Indians (Sioux) were at that time on the war path, and I supposed the smoke was caused by their fires; the clouds of smoke gradually approached us when to my astonishment what I supposed to be smoke turned out to be clouds of grasshoppers; the atmosphere presented the same appearance that it does in a heavy snow storm. One of the soldiers who was assisting in butchering the bull said, "Lieutenant, we must hurry up or those grasshoppers will eat up all our meat before we get it home." On returning I witnessed what I never saw before, an antelope fast asleep. Doctor Alexander and I, on foot, got within ten paces of the antelope before he heard us; we both fired, and he fell in his tracks. I thought then, and still think, he must have been old and deaf.

I took great pride in my company garden. I had two and a half acres in potatoes, beautiful looking, also corn, tomatoes, melons, etc. When I reached my post my garden was totally covered with grasshoppers, and by sunset every vestige of green had disappeared; the potato patch had the appearance of having been burnt over, the stems looking as though they had been carefully scraped with a knife. We were compelled to close our windows and doors; but before doing so, thousands of these insects had found their way inside the houses, and the walls were covered with them. On the second day after they had devoured everything a grasshopper could eat, a well-drilled army receiving an order to march could not have obeyed the command with more precision than the grasshoppers did; by some instinct they all rose together and took flight in a northerly direction.

Fort Laramie is located on the Laramie River, three hundred and fifty miles west of Fort Kearny,[10] in what was then the Sioux country. Lieutenant Grattan with thirty men was sent out to bring to the post of Laramie an Indian who had committed some depredation. The Indian belonged to the Broule [sic] band of Sioux, who were encamped ten miles below Fort Laramie on the Platte River. Grattan demanded the offender; his demand was refused. He ordered his men to fire on the Indians. As well as we could learn no Indian was killed. In ten minutes Grattan and his entire command were wiped out. The Sioux had Grattan in the same situation as did the Kiowas have me in 1852 on the Arkansas River. This brought about the Sioux war which ended in the battle of Blue Water the following year, of which I shall have occasion to speak hereafter.

The Sioux made several raids on my mule herd at Fort Kearny, and succeeded in getting some half dozen mules. I was returning from pursuing one of these raiding parties and had occasion to cross the Platte River. On a wooded island in the river I found three old Pawnee Indian women who had been abandoned by their people. They left them with a buffalo robe apiece and a small supply of provisions. The Cheyennes, in close pursuit of the Pawnees, came across these old squaws and proceeded to scalp them. Two were dead, the other still alive; I buried the dead and put the living squaw in an ambulance, but she died before reaching my post. I have already said that one of the most marked traits of difference between the civilized mind and the savage is the way in which they treat their women; a second special difference is the way they treat their old and helpless.

The Pawnee Indians lived on the Platte some one hundred and fifty miles below Fort Kearny; they were friendly to the whites traveling the trail that passed the fort, leading to California, but they could not help stealing anything they saw around the post, and they were frequent visitors, the women being the greatest thieves. When caught stealing they would be taken to the guard house where I had a half dozen barrels with a hole large enough to get their heads through but the bottom of the barrels and one hole on each side large enough for their arms to go through; the word "thief" was conspicuously printed on the barrels. This barrel shirt was slipped over their heads and they would be made to march on mark time, under charge of a sentinel in front of the guard house. I found it had a good effect.

Nothing of interest happened during the winter. In the spring[11] General Clarke appointed me regimental quartermaster with orders to report at Jefferson Barracks on the arrival of Captain Wharton. In the meantime I received an invitation from General Harney to serve on his staff during his campaign against the Sioux, who were to be punished for the Grattan massacre. I consulted General Clarke before accepting General Harney's invitation. General Clarke advised me by all means to accept. I went to Fort Leavenworth to join General Harney, who was then in St. Louis making preparations for his campaign.

When I reached Leavenworth the orderly of General Philip St. George Cooke[12] informed me that the colonel wished to see me at once—I was not to stop to change my clothes. I went to the colonel's office and he said, "Here is a communication of some importance for you. I have been directed to hand it to you." I opened it and was as much astonished at the contents of the letter as if it had been a notification that I was then and there to be shot. It informed me that the President had appointed me a Captain in the Tenth Regiment of Infantry,[13] one of the four new regiments Congress had authorized during the winter. I thought for a moment and then handed the paper to Colonel Cooke, saying, "Colonel, this is all a hoax; this trick was played by Hancock and others." The Colonel said, "No, this is genuine." I looked at the document again and said, "This orders me to Washington, must I go?" "Well," said the colonel, "I should think you have been in the army long enough to know that you must obey orders; I know from other sources that you have been appointed a Captain in the Tenth Infantry."

I went to St. Louis, saw General Harney, had a long talk with him about Indian matters, ran down to Jefferson Barracks and saw the Hancocks. Hancock was much disappointed at not being promoted, and I thought he deserved promotion much more than I did, for he had a gallant Mexican war record, which should have counted in his favor. With the exception of myself, Mexican service seems to have been the guide of the Secretary of War and the President in making the higher promotions from the army to the new regiments.

On reaching Washington I went to the Adjutant-General's office, saw Colonel S. Cooper,[14] whom I knew, and handed him my letter of appointment, asking if it was all right. He replied, "Yes, you have been appointed a captain in the Tenth Regiment of Infantry." I said, "Colonel, thinking it useless, I was not an applicant for promotion, as I had no political influence to urge it; how was it I was appointed a captain? To whom do I owe the favor?" Colonel Cooper replied, "Political influence did not have much weight in the selection of officers of the army to these new regiments; in fact, I think it was detrimental in many instances. You owe your promotion to the Secretary of War, do you know him?" I replied, "I do not even know the name of the Secretary of War; he does not know me, nor do I know him." The Colonel said, "Come with me and I will introduce you to the Secretary." I was introduced to Mr. Jefferson Davis, Secretary of War. I thanked the Secretary and told him how agreeably surprised I was. He said, "I was sorry not to be able to appoint you to one of the cavalry regiments." I told him the appointment in an infantry regiment suited me quite as well. The Secretary was then pleased to say, "I think, Captain, you have fairly earned your promotion. You have been in the Indian country four years; you have kept your routes open; you have had several Indian fights and have done well. I understand you are a wonderful buffalo hunter and a fine horseman, and that you have killed buffalo riding bareback with a bow and arrow. And, by the way, I received a letter this morning from General Harney, who requests that I order your company to join him in the expedition against the Sioux. Would you like to do so?'' I replied that I should be delighted to go on the expedition. "Well," said the Secretary, "I will have to mount your company." This pleased me still more, "Go to Governor's Island, New York Harbor; there are some three hundred or more recruits there, and select eighty-four men. Don't be in a hurry making your selections. The men you choose should not weight over 130 or 140 pounds, preferably lighter, and should not be over five feet eight or nine inches in height. You want young, athletic fellows. When you have selected your men, telegraph your first lieutenant to come to Governor's Island and conduct them to Fort Leavenworth; you go to St. Louis. Grimsley[15] will be directed to furnish you with equipment; then purchase your horses; the quartermaster at Fort Leavenworth will be directed to pay for them." I left Washington that evening for New York, and took three days selecting my eighty-four men, managing to get a splendid lot.

I telegraphed my first lieutenant, hurried to St. Louis, saw my friend Grimsley with whom I had had dealings before, and secured the equipment for my company. On arriving at Leavenworth I secured the services of my friend Harry Dyer and Mr. Mason, my old sutlers on the Arkansas, to assist me in purchasing horses, and this was soon accomplished. On arriving at Leavenworth from the plains, I had left there my noted buffalo horse, "Old Rom." I receipted for him again.

The few days at Leavenworth enabled me to drill my men a little and get them in some shape. My lieutenants were First Lieutenant N. A. M. Dudley[16] and Second Lieutenant James Deshler.[17] Dudley's sobriquet in the army was the "Great North American Dudley." Deshler, a fine officer was killed on the Confederate side at Chickamauga, commanding a brigade.

General Harney's command left Fort Leavenworth early in August;[18] after passing Fort Kearny we struck buffalo. General Harney was very anxious for a supply of buffalo meat for the command. I told him he should have it. I borrowed a six shooter; I had one of my own, and was starting out to make my run, when Captain Van Vliet,[19] quartermaster of our command, rode up to me and said every one was anxious for a buffalo, and he feared if I made a run I would therefore interfere with Tesson who would kill all that was wanted. I replied, "You will see that I will kill three cows to Tesson's[20] one."

Tesson used a double-barrelled shot gun, I an army six shooter. Tesson shot to the left, I to the right, hence he rode on the right of the band, I on the left. I was fortunate in finding a bunch of fat cows. I shot seven times, using, of course, my second pistol for the seventh shot. The run over; I found six of my cows, identified by the shot entering the left side of the animals. I was anxious to find my seventh cow. I looked around and saw Tesson near a cow, both standing still. I rode up; Tesson fired; the cow fell on the left side. I said, "Tesson, help me to turn this cow over." He did so, and there was behind her left fore shoulder the hole made by the bullet of my pistol. He said, "Yes, this is your cow by all the rules governing buffalo hunters." I had killed seven cows; Tesson had killed none.

This feat of mine spread over the entire command. A few days since (October, 1897), when on Pennsylvania Avenue, I met a soldier who was present when I killed the seven cows, and as I was hobbling along he said, "General, do you think you could kill seven cows in a run as you did in 1855?" I said, "I believe if I were on the plains and saw a fine band of cows I would be fool enough to try, and probably break my neck." This was my last buffalo hunt, I never tried to kill more buffalo than was wanted. I was ever anxious to save my horse.

XV

General Harney was a singular man; if he liked you, all that you did pleased him; if not, the reverse. He was a great friend of mine; for several days when with him, he alluded to the manner I doubled those cows and said they were the fattest and best he had ever eaten.

The command reached the North Platte, passing through Ash Hollow, and encamped a short distance above on the river bank.[1] The Brule band of Indians, who had massacred Grattan and his command the previous year, were encamped on the Blue Water, some two miles from us. I was sitting with General Harney in front of his tent; about sunset Col. P. St. George Cooke reported to General Harney for orders for the following day. To my astonishment the General said, "We will continue our march up the river." Colonel Cooke left. General Harney turned to me, (General Harney was the greatest swearer I ever heard; he used to say that there was but one man in the army that could beat him and that was his brother, the Doctor) and said, "I wonder what those damned Indians will say of my not attacking them." I replied, "I know exactly; they will say they came where they now are, and offered to give the big White Chief, the Hornet, as they call you, a fight, but that you tucked your tail between your legs and ran away." The General rose from his seat and said, "G—— d—— them, will they say that, Captain?" I replied, "That is precisely what they will say."

The General, with his stentorian voice cried out, "Colonel Cooke, Colonel Cooke." The Colonel turned, Harney beckoned him to return; the General said, "Colonel Cooke, I intend to attack those damned red skins in the morning. I wish you to take your cavalry (Cooke was in immediate command of all the mounted force of the army present) and make a circuit; get on the far side of the village; conceal your force among the hills; start at two o'clock to-night; I will move on their village so as to reach it by light, with the infantry and artillery; they will break and run towards you, don't let a d——d one escape.''

My company, being mounted, was under the command of Colonel Cooke. I went to Colonel Cooke's tent. He said "What did you say to Harney that made him change his plans so suddenly." I told him what was said. Colonel Cooke replied, "He is not fit to command; of course he should attack; these are the very fellows we are looking for, and another such opportunity will never occur again."

We, the mounted force, were in position at day break; Harney advanced; the Indians fled abandoning their camp and many ponies. Their camp was destroyed and ponies secured. The Indians ran towards the cavalry, we attacked them; about two hundred bucks fled across the Blue Water. Colonel Cooke ordered Captain A. P. Howe, Fourth Artillery, (whose company was serving as cavalry) and mine to charge the flying Indians. I charged across the Blue Water and got into a pretty hot, running fight. Howe, when he reached the Blue Water, deliberately halted to water his horses he said; and when he came to where I was the fight was over.[2] I was very much vexed, as I had suffered on account of Howe's stopping in the charge to water his horses. I reported this to General Harney. He cursed Howe black and blue, and said, "He is not worth the powder and lead it would take to kill him; he is as damned a coward as was his brother Marshal Saxe Howe, whom I have often court-martialed, and I shall put charges against this fellow."[3]

When we reached Fort Laramie a court was ordered for A. P. Howe's trial; I was a member of the court. When the court assembled, I was about to arise and request I might be excused from serving on Howe's trial as I did not think, with my feelings, I could do him justice. Before doing so the President of the Court said the court could not try Captain Howe as it was not a legal court; the same officer who ordered the court had preferred the charges, so Howe was not tried and dismissed from the service as he deserved.

During the war General Edward Johnson met Howe in the Allegheny Mountains, and Johnson gave him a good thrashing; after the war Johnson was summoned as a witness before a court in Washington, I think in Wirz's trial.[4] Howe was a member of the court; when Johnson was about being sworn, Howe arose and said, "I object to that man's giving any evidence before this court, as he was guilty of treason; he fired on loyal men under my command during the war." Howe was very generally disliked by his army associates.

After the battle of Blue Water, Sept. 3, 1855, the papers reported me killed. I had been shot through with six arrows,—any one would have done the work. My classmates in New York, at the suggestion of my friend and classmate Lieutenant Julian McAllister, met and drew up resolutions which were published in the daily papers. It is a very pleasant thing to be *killed,* if you live to read the nice things your friends say about you. I believe my dear wife has several obituaries of mine which my grandchildren may like to read.

From the *Evening Post*:

Captain Henry Heth, of the 10th Infantry, who was reported in the journals of the 1st instant as killed in the battle fought between General Harney's command and the Sioux Indians at "Ash Hollow," graduated from the Military Academy in 1847, beloved by his classmates and respected by his professors. Soon after receiving his commission as brevet second lieutenant he sought the enemy in Mexico and served well as a subaltern in the 1st Infantry. He was promoted to the 6th Regiment, and selected

by General Clarke as his aide-de-camp in his expedition
to Cuernavaca. On the declaration of peace his orders
assigned him to frontier duty, and for two years he served
as the only officer with his company in the heart of the
Indian territory. While there he contributed greatly to the
safety and comfort of those travellers who passed in the
vicinity of his post and completed the defences at Fort
Atkinson.

He remained in command of his post for a long period
and braved all danger which the small number of his garrison, in comparison with the bands of hostile Indians in
its neighborhood, rendered more eminent from day to day.
His orders required him to make frequent excursions to
keep the roads free from Indians committing depredations
and murders. The energy which he exhibited and the success which he gained while contending with these difficulties elicited the praise of his regiment and department;
every one admired his bravery, judgment, and, above all,
the aptitude he displayed in acquiring a thorough knowledge of the Indian character.

Devotion to his profession rendered the most arduous
duties acceptable, and his watchfulness and vigor insured
the safety of many a traveller. Emigrants have shared his
flask, been cheered at his table and sheltered by his
rooftree, leaving with him their blessings in return for his
kindness and feeling, their drooping courage revived by his
kind hospitality. Others who were sick and dying received
the tenderest care at his hands, and when the final moment
arrived, and their thoughts sought their far distant homes,
they found in their desert one possessing a woman's sensi-
bility and refined feeling to bear their last farewell to the
loved ones at home. Disease, contracted in Mexico, finally

drove him to his home for rest and medical aid, but he hardly allowed himself to recover before he was reported in the field, performing services of so distinguished a character that the appointment of regimental quartermaster was offered to him on the 13th of September, 1853.

When General Harney was ordered on his present expedition against the Indians, he selected Captain Heth as his aide-de-camp, although personally unacquainted with him, trusting entirely to his reputation and his peculiar fitness for the duty, which all conceded he possessed. On the third of March last the President commissioned several army officers in the new regiments with advanced grades. These officers were selected for distinguished service. Captain Heth was one of them, and was ordered to form a mixed corps of his company of recruits and a party of friendly Indians to serve as his scout. Six months of his captaincy has hardly passed away, and he has already demonstrated the justness of the executive in selecting him for promotion, and proved that the pride we felt in possessing such a friend was legitimate. As an officer he possessed qualities which were beyond cavil; and as a man, he was one of the very few who with truth could adopt the motto:
"Sans peur et sans reproche."

Although perfect as a soldier, he was far more to be admired in the dear relationship of friend and companion.
"None knew him but to love him,
None named him but to praise."

He was the defender of the absent, the weak and the persecuted, and could appreciate the sorrows of a child mourning her dead bird, as well as sympathize with the grief which causes the strong heart of man to break. It is proposed by some of his classmates that the class of forty-seven subscribe for the purpose of having the remains transferred from their prairie grave to the West Point cemetery, and of erecting a suitable monument to his memory. We also suggest, on account of his early death, brilliant success and endearing qualities, that his classmates should wear the usual badge of mourning thirty days.

"NOUS NOUS SOUTENONS."

MEDITATION

LINES TO THE DEPARTED HENRY HETH, OF THE TENTH INFANTRY

Thou, too, are gone to give an account, in simple words, of thy short life.

Called to the other world of happiness and purity, thou wilt find a place more suited to thy kindly nature;

For, though a soldier's life had been thy destiny on earth, and nobly didst thou fill the rank of officer—

Yet such a gentle spirit and a sympathetic feeling seemed rather to fit thee for a gentler sphere.

A studious scholar at the noble *Point* thou didst give promise of a fair career; and oft surrounded by thy young companions, didst beguile their leisure hours by some pleasing narrative.

But as length the time arrived when class-mates separate, and each to his apportioned garrison goes forth;

Then, with a cheerful manly courage, to the distant West thou journeyed on through dead of Winter—

Sent forth to drive the red man from his bloody war
path.
This thou didst, and bravely, too, likewise giving kind
assistance unto weary emigrants.
At length, however, in a hostile struggle, the "pale-face
officer" is killed,
And like some beauteous, healthy plant, fresh in all the
vigor of its youth, nipped in the bud by some unlooked
for tempest,
Thou didst yield thy youthful frame to God,
And the white *Heath* sunk to mother earth from whence
it sprung
But shall thy class-mate leave thy bones to prairie-soil,
to waste away, like those of some lost traveler?

General Harney remained only a few days at Fort Laramie;
he, with the greater portion of his command marched north to
the Missouri River and wintered at Fort Pierre, an old Indian
trading post established by the American Fur Company. My
company and Howe's were left at Fort Laramie to winter.
Nothing of note occurred at Laramie during the winter of
1855-56. It was the most severe season that I ever felt in the
West. I, as well as my men, lived in the tepees we had captured
from the Sioux, and found them quite comfortable. Lieutenant
E. McK. Hudson[5] and I formed a mess. Hudson was a man
of fine taste and fond of good living. The snow was from two
to three feet deep on a level, and the mercury was often below
zero. Antelope in great flocks were on the Platte River two
miles from the post; they had broken through the snow paths
to the river to get water. The antelope lived on the sage brush.
By concealing yourself under the bank of the river, usually
about three feet high, where one of these antelope paths struck
the river, you could shoot antelope all day, but the flesh was

not edible, it tasted exactly like chewing sage brush. We tried it every conceivable way, boiled, roasted, corned, in stews, highly seasoned, but there was no way of disguising the powerful flavor of the sage.

My recollection is that on account of the deep snows and severity of the winter we were without mails for four months. I was seated in my tepee one night reading—the mercury was below zero, when two young officers came in and said something very disagreeable had just happened. They were engaged in a game of draw poker in the sutler's store, when an altercation occurred between Lieutenant Hardcastle[6] of the Sixth, and Mr. Tutt, the sutler's clerk, over the game, and Tutt slapped Hardcastle's face. Hardcastle left the store at once, and promptly challenged Tutt to fight him the next morning at sunrise. Tutt accepted the challenge and the duel was to take place on the Platte River, rifles the weapons. They said they knew but little about such things and asked me to come with them and see that matters were properly conducted. I told them I would be on hand.

Thinking over the matter, I thought I could arrange it so that it would be impossible for either of the principals to be hurt. We had to walk three-quarters of a mile to reach the grounds selected; it was intensely cold, and the snow was from two to three feet deep. Fifty yards were paced off and the principals took their places. I purposely delayed matters as long as possible, the principals holding their rifles, and I felt certain that their fingers would soon freeze, which they did. The word "Fire!" was given. Tutt shot in the air. Hardcastle fired at Tutt. I saw where his ball struck in the snow—it did not come within fifteen feet of Tutt. The affair was pronounced honorably settled, and I believe the belligerents shook hands, Tutt apologizing. Hardcastle was as game a fellow as I ever saw.

Early in the spring General Harney ordered me to proceed to the Platte Bridge, some 120 miles above Fort Laramie, and prevent its being destroyed by the Indians. The California Trail crossed the Platte River over the bridge; if burned by the Indians, it would interfere seriously with the travel of emigrants. Just before leaving Fort Leavenworth mail was received from the States. Hancock wrote me and sent a copy of the "London Illustrated News," containing an account of a school of rifle practice Lord Hardinge[7] had established at Hythe in England with drawings illustrating his methods. I was much pleased with the account of this school of practice and determined, with some changes, to try it. I found by keeping an accurate account of each shot fired, that my men in six weeks time improved seventy-five per cent in accuracy of fire. I thought this was worth being known, so I prepared a pamphlet giving the details and drawings of the tripods, sand bags, targets, etc., and was ready to send it to the Adjutant General by the next mail. The mail by which it was to be sent brought a circular from General Scott, directing all officers having independent commands to forward through their commanders their views as to the best method of obtaining greater accuracy of fire in the army. My views on this subject were sent to General Harney instead of to Washington.[8]

In the latter part of the summer of 1856 my company was ordered to march across the country, viz, from Fort Pierre to Fort Snelling, on the Mississippi River, a long, tedious march;[9] three hundred miles of the distance had never been travelled by troops. A few days before leaving Platte Bridge, a hunter visited my camp, who had just crossed the Black Hills; he informed me that the hills were filled with grizzly bear. For years I had listened to the stories of such men as Kit Carson, Bill Bent, and other *mountain men,* as they were called, relating their encounters with grizzly bear, and their hairbreadth escapes. One old and noted bear hunter showed me his arm and shoulder, which had been terribly "chawed up" by a grizzly. I made up my mind to let grizzly bear severely alone.

The desire to have a shot at the monarch of wild animals on this continent was great; the opportunity might never occur again. All wild, as well as domestic, animals, it is said, flee from the scent of the grizzly bear. I was informed that one stroke of a grizzly's paw would tear out two or three ribs of a buffalo, which they at times lay in wait for. Sanders, my hunter, and I started at daybreak, crossed the Black Hills, and saw numerous spoor of the grizzly, but no bear. On reaching the southern base of the Hills we found a cool, limpid stream, the banks of which were covered with willow and a few scattering hackberry and cottonwood trees.

We had not breakfasted. I told my companion that we would now breakfast and let our animals graze. I directed him to go down the creek and collect wood, while I would start the fire and get the water for our coffee. The fire was started. Sanders[10] came running to me, saying, "Captain, here comes up the creek the damnest biggest grizzly I ever saw; get your rifle." We concealed ourselves under the bank of the creek. The bear, a monster, before arriving opposite to us, changed his course and went directly from us. I said to my companion, "I will fire first; if I hit him, he will stop and you, being a good shot, will have a better opportunity to kill him." I fired; the bear gave a terrific growl, wheeled around, and struck his hind quarter with his paw. My hunter had a splendid chance. He fired, and, though a fine rifle shot, he failed to touch the bear, who now made for me. Dropping our rifles we ran for a hackberry tree a few paces distant, and no two men ever climbed a tree faster. We were out of the bear's reach when he arrived under the tree. The brute was furious; he pawed the ground, bit the trunk of the tree and demolished a few square yards of willows. While this was going on the grass around our fire became ignited and we saw our saddles and blankets being destroyed. After venting his rage on the bark of our tree and the willow brush, we were delighted to see the huge beast walk off leisurely and disappear.

I had enough of grizzly bear hunting. Repairing our saddles as best we could, we resumed our hunt, not for bear, but for deer and antelope. About sunset we saw an antelope feeding. I told my hunter to kill it as we needed fresh meat for our supper. When about one hundred and fifty yards from the antelope, the hunter fired. I saw where the ball from his rifle struck the ground one hundred yards beyond, knocking up the dust. The antelope bounded off, ran quite one hundred yards and fell; while butchering, the hunter showed me the heart of the antelope. The rifle ball had literally split the heart in half. When crossing the Black Hills to rejoin my company we saw much bear spoor. I had lost all interest in hunting grizzly bear. I got out of the bear country as rapidly as possible and joined my command.

We got through to Snelling without any incidents worth mentioning. I rested three days at Fort Ridgely, where I found Captain Barnard E. Bee of my regiment, and was his guest. I was always a great admirer of Bee; he was as gallant a soldier as ever drew a sword, and a splendid man in every respect. I met him first at West Point as a cadet, and we were warm friends. Bee was mortally wounded in the first battle of the war, the first Manassas, or Bull Run; had Bee lived he would have made a great name for himself, and attained the highest rank in the army. At one time during the battle, when his brigade wavered, he went in front of it and said, "Look, men, at Jackson's brigade; they are standing like a stone wall," hence Jackson's sobriquet of "Stonewall," was thus obtained.

On arriving at Fort Snelling, my horses were sold. Major E. R. Canby, 10th Infantry, was in command.[11] Major Canby was, I think, the most accomplished and best informed officer I ever met, only excelled by that prince of soldiers, Lieutenant Colonel

C. F. Smith,[12] the model soldier of our army and Lieutenant Colonel of the 10th Infantry.

When I was on my cadet furlough, I visited my numerous relations on the James River. When seated on the back porch of my uncle's house at Orapax on the James River, a troop of children came out to play; they were led by a girl some nine or ten years old; my attention was attracted by the long, blue, home-knit stockings she wore. I could not suppress a smile whenever I looked at the stockings. The wearer of these stockings was destined, twelve years later, to become my wife; and I may be pardoned for saying old Virginia never produced a more complete specimen of woman and finer character than Miss "Teny" Selden, now Mrs. Henry Heth. As a Christian wife and mother, and doer of good works, she has rarely been equalled, never surpassed. She has now been my helpmate for forty years; whenever I have failed it has been when I went contrary to her advice. We are now both old, and must in the course of nature soon pass away; but as age creeps on, my love for her increases as my dependence upon her becomes greater. No man was ever happier in his marital relations than I.

When I passed through Washington en route to Richmond, I called to see the Secretary of War, John B. Floyd. Floyd prided himself on his skill as a rifle shot. I told him of the brochure I had prepared to increase accuracy of fire in our army, and the results I had attached. He said, "As soon as your leave expires report to me, and I will place you on special duty to draw up a system of target practice for the army."

After I had regained my health in 1850, and was about to go west, I was requested by my uncle to escort his daughter, my cousin, to our relative Mrs. Lavinia Randolph Deas,[13] residing at Saugerties, N. Y. I think when travelling with a person you have the best opportunity of learning the person's character and peculiarities; whether this be true or not, I know when I bade my charming cousin good-bye, I was as much smitten as I could be with a child of fourteen.

Having determined to secure a wife, if possible, before returning to my regiment, my thoughts constantly turned to my favorite cousin whose charms were the themes of many officers who had met her while visiting Virginia. The first question asked was, "Have you been to Norwood? Have you seen Miss 'Teny' Selden?"[14] I speedily visited the old family seat on the James River and at once contracted the epidemic which had proved fatal to so many others. In a week we became engaged. I confess I never felt secure until the knot was tied. Virginia girls of that day were natural-born flirts; the Virginia belles had so many admirers that they could not concentrate their affections. I know my securing this James River belle caused many a heart to ache.

The 7th of April, 1857, was a day never to be forgotten by all assembled. Five of my groomsmen were officers of the army, A. P. Hill, E. D. Blake,[15] John C. Kelton,[16] Robert Johnston,[17] and John Pegram,[18] most of whom became general officers during the Civil War. My uncle, Miles Carey Selden, had the reputation of being one of the best and most accomplished providers among the planters of old Virginia. His mutton, beef and hams were noted far and wide; his cellar of choice old wines which had been buried during the Revolution and the War of 1812, attested its age. The beautiful old silver, rare china and glass, the house adorned with plants from the well-kept hothouses, made the wedding not only the finest I had ever seen, but a scene of brilliancy and enjoyment seldom equalled, never surpassed.

The festivities lasted a week, the bridesmaids and groomsmen remaining with us during that time. After this we visited relatives in Richmond and on the James River, where we were regally entertained. We then went north, stopping several days in Washington. I saw the Secretary of War and told him my leave of absence would expire in a short time, and that I was ready to commence work on a system of target practice for the army.[19] The order was issued and all the papers called for in General Scott's order, directing officers to give their views to the best method of attaining accuracy of fire, were turned over to me.

During President Pierce's administration, the company representing Sharp's breech-loading gun succeeded in having a bill reported appropriating $100,000 to purchase the Sharp's breech-loading gun, claiming it was the best gun for military purposes that had been invented. Someone proposed, on the third reading of the bill, that Sharp's name be stricken out, and the best breech-loading gun for military purposes be inserted; this was done.

The Secretary of War told me one evening that he had been down to the Washington Arsenal testing a breech-loading gun, and in his opinion it was the best gun he had ever tried; and he added, "I intend to order a board of officers to assemble at West Point to test the various breech-loading guns, and have told the inventors that the decision of this board would be final." The Board met,[20] all the different breech-loading guns were presented for trial. When the vote was taken it was unanimous in favor of Burnside's gun. Burnside had resigned from the army[21] and borrowed quite a large sum of money to enable him to perfect his gun; now he could easily repay it.

Seeing an opportunity to visit New England, where these guns were manufactured, the Board applied to the Secretary of War for permission to visit the different manufactories and see their capacity for doing work. Permission was granted. We visited Colt's works at Hartford where we were entertained in a royal manner, also Providence, R. I., where Burnside had his workshop; here we were entertained at one of the famous Rhode Island clambakes. My wife could not be persuaded to "taste of a clam.'' The clambake was at the famous Pop-a-squash, where it was said King Philip, the Indian chief, during his war, concealed his papooses and squaws.

Burnside in high spirits accompanied us to Washington. I went directly on to Virginia, and, leaving my wife at her father's, returned to Washington. Burnside and I occupied a room opposite Willard's hotel. On my return I found Burnside very much depressed; he said that there was a screw loose somewhere, that he had not received the award, but would find out where the trouble was that night. About one o'clock Burnside returned to our room. I was awake, and he said, "Heth, I am a ruined man; the man I met said I could get the contract if I would pay $5,000, otherwise nothing. I refused." I jumped out of my bed, seized his hand, and said, "Old fellow, you have done exactly right. I only wish you had knocked the damned scoundrel down."

Burnside left Washington, went home, called his creditors together, made a fair statement to them, made over to them his patent and all he possessed, sold his uniform coat, sword and pistols, and with the proceeds went to Illinois and joined our friend George B. McClellan who was vice-president of a railroad then being built in Illinois.[22] He secured an appointment under McClellan, and in a short time became treasurer of the road. He was in this position when the Civil War broke out. The appropriation for the best breech-loading gun for military purposes was divided up among the numerous applicants. The Secretary of War is reported to have said that he would arm the army with bows and arrows before he would arm it with Burnside's gun.

Passing through Washington en route to Virginia, I got all the reports that had been made relating to increased accuracy of fire in the army. On reaching home I went to work on my system of target practice. I first looked over the reports of officers on this subject. My report was missing. I came to the conclusion that the officer to whom it was sent (the Department Commander) did not think it worthy of transmittal. On close examination, I found my report "verbatim et literatim," with all drawings attached, but sent under another name than my own.[23] I was much disgusted at this theft, but for reasons resolved to defer action. The war prevented my preferring charges, and now the maxim "de mortuis nil nisi bonum" had best be followed. I found drawing up a system of target practice a more difficult undertaking than I supposed; in the spring I completed my work. It was approved by the Secretary of War, and put in practice.[24] Since my system was adopted, others more elaborate and better have been proposed, and are now in use. The great improvement in firearms necessitated a change.

I reported for duty and was ordered to Fort Leavenworth to join a column en route for Utah, where my regiment was stationed. An order had been issued prohibiting women from going to Utah, as trouble was expected; so my wife was left at her comfortable home in Virginia. When the column left Fort Leavenworth I was assigned to the command of some two hundred recruits. I appointed Lieutenant W. H. F. Lee adjutant of the battalion, and his cousin, Louis Marshall,[25] quartermaster. Marshall, Lee and I were messmates on this long march. Lieutenant Lee showed many of the good qualities which make a good soldier, doubtless inherited from the great soldier, his father, General R. E. Lee.

When I bade the Secretary of War adieu in Washington he said, "Next spring I intend to order you to West Point as commandant of cadets. How will you like the detail?" I said nothing could please me more, but the detail was never made; why, I can't say.

When we reached Utah, I found the greater portion of my regiment, the 10th Infantry, stationed at Camp Floyd, forty miles south of Salt Lake City, Lieutenant-Colonel C. F. Smith commanding the regiment, General Albert S. Johnston com-

manding the department. Adobe quarters were being erected,
and by November were ready for occupation. Colonel Smith,
the best disciplinarian and instructor of tactics in the army, soon
had the regiment in splendid drill and discipline. The expedition
under General Johnston was sent to Utah to enforce the laws
of the United States, and to protect the emigrants to California
who had to pass through Utah en route to the gold fields.[26]
The Mormons, then as now, each year sent to the States and
to England a number of their shrewdest men to make converts
to their so-called religion, who would be collected on the Missouri River near Independence, Mo., and then divided into.
parties, say of one hundred to one hundred and fifty. Twenty
or twenty-five ox wagons were assigned to each squad, and
under dignitaries of the Mormon Church were conducted to Salt
Lake and there distributed to different parts of the territory.

The unmarried girls would be assigned to Mormon men,
many of whom had already two or more wives. I was assured
by reliable men, who were in positions to know, that most of
the girls who were thus brought to Utah became mothers soon
after arriving.

Two years before the Sidney Johnston expedition started for
Utah, a Mormon bishop and apostle, Pratt by name, was sent
to New England on a proselyting mission; the rascal became
the intimate of a family, seduced the wife of his host, and persuaded her to elope with him, their destination being Salt Lake
City. The husband went in pursuit, and finally tracked them
to Arkansas, where in some western town in that state the
bishop had bought an outfit, wagon and horses, and started for
Utah. The injured husband had no difficulty in securing the services of a number of Arkansas boys; pursuit was made, the
culprit overtaken, and then the husband killed this miserable
bishop and apostle, rescuing his faithless wife from worse than
death.[27] This was duly reported to Brigham Young by Mormon
spies.

The following year a party of well-to-do people in Texas determined to go to California via Utah.[28] It was said to have been the wealthiest emigration party that had ever crossed the plains. They passed through the town where the outraged husband the year before had secured his squad to guide and assist him in recovering his wife. It was reported, or said to have been reported, to Brigham Young, that this very wealthy emigrant train was made up from the inhabitants of the town in Arkansas that had assisted in the shooting of their sainted Bishop Pratt. On reaching Utah these people were nearly out of supplies; they had expected to purchase food there. Brigham issued orders to his people not to sell to these starving emigrants an ounce of food. Progress was slow. They reached a place called Mountain Meadows.[29] Brigham issued orders to kill the entire party, except children too small to give evidence, who might be spared to be adopted into Mormon families. Major John D. Lee, a bishop in the Mormon church, was designated as commander of the force which was to exterminate these poor men, women and children.

On September 12, 1857, just after breaking camp, Lee[30] attacked the emigrants, who, returning the fire, rapidly corraled their wagons, thus affording some protection for the women and children. After a siege of four days, Lee sent in a flag of truce, informing the emigrants that the Indians who were attacking them were afraid to let them pass on with their arms; if they would lay down their arms and march out, that he would guarantee them protection. Foolishly they did so. When the last one had reached a point some two hundred yards from their corral the Mormons shot down the band of emigrants,[31] sparing about eleven infants.

Mountain Meadows was visited by a party of persons from Camp Floyd, and wagons filled with skulls and bones brought away. Every skull I examined has a bullet hole in it. Long tufts of hair were found hanging to the sage brush. A part of Brigham

Young's booty was a fine carriage and a piano. It appears that the apostle and bishop, John D. Lee, was an especial favorite of Brigham Young, but he forfeited in some way Czar Brigham's good graces, and Brigham had Lee turned over to the Courts, tried and executed for this Mountain Meadow outrage. This did not occur until twenty years after the massacre.[32] The real instigator and culprit was permitted to die peaceably in his murderous and polygamous bed. I look upon Brigham Young as one of the shrewdest and most sagacious men this country has produced, and I feel certain it has never, and God grant may never, produce as bad a man again.

XVI

The United States Judges were now to hold their courts. Judge Cradlebaugh[1] held his court in Provo.[2] My company was selected to accompany the judge to Provo, protect the court, and take charge of prisoners. Judge Cradlebaugh was a bold, fearless man, and as far as I could see, a just and good judge. It was soon evident that the juries did not determine the guilt or innocence of prisoners from the evidence given, nor did they pay any attention to the judge's instructions, but implicitly followed the instructions received from Salt Lake City, in other words, from Brigham Young.

Several persons were turned over to me for safe keeping; the Mormons of Provo commenced to stone my sentinels at night. I issued a proclamation warning the Mormons if this was continued, my guards had received instructions to fire upon the parties thus offending.[3] A few paces from my encampment stood an abandoned stone building with a cellar below it. It was occupied by one or more of the officers of my company and others of my command. The Mormons threw into the cellar, bags of gunpowder and attempted to explode the same, but failed. The situation was becoming very hazardous, and the facts were reported to headquarters by Judge Cradlebaugh and myself. General Johnston sent down Major G. R. Paul[4] with eight companies of the 7th Infantry, one of artillery, and one company of cavalry, with orders to encamp near Provo, but not to enter the town unless called upon by me to do so. Judge Cradlebaugh, much disgusted, adjourned his court, and the troops returned to Camp Floyd. I was much complimented on my return by my superiors and others with my management of affairs when at Provo. Holding United States courts in Utah was a travesty on justice. President Buchanan said no blood would be shed during his administration. Brigham Young, who was kept well posted, knew this and acted accordingly.

The Mormon Church was thus organized: Brigham Young, President, styled, "Trust and Trustee of the Church of Jesus Christ of the Latter Day Saints." His counsellors were Orson Pratt,[5] Orson Hyde,[6] Heber G. Kimball[7] and twelve apostles; they resided in Salt Lake City. The territory was divided into districts, in each of which a bishop presided, assisted by a number of retainers, whose duty it was to make domiciliary visits every week to each home in his precinct, and forward weekly reports to his bishop as to the loyalty of the occupants and especially whether or not they had paid their tithes to the church.

These reports were forwarded by the bishops to Salt Lake and inspected by Young. Young had in his employ some seventy-five men called Danites,[8] the most hardened and bloodiest cutthroats in the community, and when any assassination was ordered these men were employed.

The tithes exacted from all in the community were one-tenth of everything raised, even one-tenth of the eggs. No excuse would be taken for failure to pay into the tithing house in Salt Lake this tax; thus Brigham Young soon became enormously wealthy. His bank account in London was said to have been very large, also in other cities abroad. If a family became dissatisfied and wished to leave the territory, they would first be warned; if they persisted their cattle would be killed and their house burned; then if they attempted to leave, they would be permitted to go a certain distance in the mountains, and the Danites would be upon them and exterminate every soul, not sparing infants. Brigham Young exercised as much power in Utah as ever Czar of Russia, or Sultan of Turkey, exercises in their dominions.[9]

Governor Cummings[10] wrote to General Johnston, complaining, among other things, that I had not reported to him my arrival at Provo. General Johnston replied, "I beg most respectfully to suggest that, under the circumstances, there would have been a manifest impropriety in Captain Heth's reporting to you; such an act would be an acknowledgement of military supremacy in you which does not exist." General Johnston by his instructions was equally bound to respond to the call of the judiciary for troops as to that of the executive.

General Johnston was anxious to be relieved from the command of the Department of Utah, and had so expressed himself to the authorities in Washington. On February 29, 1860, he was relieved and turned over the command to Colonel C. F. Smith. This placed me as senior captain present, in command of the regiment at all parades, reviews, and drills. General Johnston left Camp Floyd in the early spring of 1860, carrying with him the love and affection of every officer and soldier. On the day he left the troops were drawn up in the road he passed, and I do not believe there was a dry eye in that line. General Johnston, as we all know, fell in the hour of his signal victory at Shiloh. Had he lived, many believe there would have been no battle the day following April the 7th. The command of the

Department of Utah could not have fallen to a better soldier than C. F. Smith; everything moved on smoothly and well.

When I was in Utah, Captain Henry Burton[11] of the English Army visited Salt Lake. I called on him and invited him to make me a visit at Camp Floyd; he did so and remained with me two weeks. Captain Burton was the same who, disguised as a Musselman doctor, made the trip to Mecca and kissed the sacred black rock; had his nationality been detected he would have met certain death. He lived in Persia two years, studying the habits, customs and language of the Mohammedans, preparing himself for this perilous undertaking. The Mohammedans, he told me, believed that if a Christian ever touched the sacred black rock, Mohammedanism was doomed. He, with Speke and Grant, were the first African explorers; he contracted a fever when in Africa, and was traveling to rid his system of its effects. Burton was a wonderful linguist; he spoke every European language and many others. I found Captain Burton a most enjoyable companion. He was anxious to secure some Indian trinkets, and especially an Indian scalp. I happened to have what he wanted, and gave him my collection. He said he promised his sweetheart in England to bring her an Indian scalp. I received one or two letters from him after his return to England, but the war put an end to our correspondence; he is now dead.

To show the great interest the American people take in a prize fight I must relate what occurred on the route between Independence and Camp Floyd, when Mr. Lincoln was elected President. The pony express bringing the news of the election brought also the result of the celebrated prize fight in England between Heenan and Sayers. The first question put to the rider of the pony when en route was, "Who won the fight?"[12] The next was, "Who is elected President?"

In October, 1860, I received news of the illness of my child, whom I had never seen. I applied for a short leave, which was granted.[13]   Little did I think then that the next time I met my regiment and my company in which I took so much pride we would be on opposite sides on the field of battle. Colonel Alexander,[14] the colonel of my splendid regiment, was stationed at Fort Laramie, but now at Camp Floyd on a court martial, and was about to return to his post. Colonel Crossman,[15] chief quartermaster of the Department of Utah, was to leave for the States. I was offered a seat in their ambulance, which I readily accepted. The journey was made in about twenty-five days. When I reached Fort Leavenworth every one was talking about war, war. I ridiculed the idea of war; I was a strong Union man, and believed war was an impossibility.

When passing through St. Louis, I found at the Planters' House a captain of my regiment, Captain John Dunovant[16] of South Carolina, with a broken leg. Dunovant was saturated with the war fever; he was going to South Carolina, and if no other State seceded South Carolina would, and go to war if no other State did. I told Dunovant that in that event we would dig South Carolina up and throw her into the ocean. As I went east, war talk increased, and I became uneasy. A convention met in Richmond, strongly union in sentiment, but when the governor was called upon for 75,000 men, the convention suddenly changed its views and Virginia seceded.

I had made up my mind that, in the event of my state, Virginia, seceding, I would cast my fortune with her. No act of my life cost me more bitter pangs than mailing my resignation as a captain in the United States Army,[17] separating myself from those I loved, bidding adieu to my splendid company, my pride, and the finest regiment in the army.

When Virginia seceded, April 18, 1861, so far as I know there happened to be but four officers of the United States Army in the State—Colonel Robert E. Lee, Major Robert Garnett,[18] Lieutenant Edwin I. Harvey,[19] and myself. I reported to Governor Letcher for duty.[20] An expedition under Brigadier-General

*Courtesy of the U. S. Military
Academy Archives and Special
Collections, West Point*

Henry Heth

William Taliaferro[21] was organized to go to Norfolk, Va., and if possible capture the navy yard across the river. General Taliaferro appointed me his adjutant general, Harvey his commissary general. Nothing resulted from this wild scheme. The officer in charge of the navy yard burnt the United States vessels at the yard, attempted to blow up the dry dock but failed, and abandoned the yard. Colonel R. E. Lee, on his arrival in Richmond, was appointed Commander-in-Chief of the Virginia forces, and when the Confederate government moved to Richmond, he was appointed a general in the Confederate Army.

John B. Floyd[22] and Henry Wise[23] were appointed brigadier generals in the Confederate Army. Each of these gentlemen had occupied prominent positions; each had been governor of his State; Floyd was Mr. Buchanan's Secretary of War; Wise had been minister to one of the South American States and a prominent member of Congress from Virginia. Floyd and Wise were rival politicians, and hated each other as only rival politicians can. One of the most farcical and ridiculous campaigns that occurred during our Civil War, or in any war, I believe, I shall now attempt to describe, but I must confess it would require one more skilled in word painting than I to adequately relate what happened.

XVII

General Floyd applied for permission to go to West Virginia, *his country,* as he called it, and raise an army. He requested Mr. Davis to order me to assist him in organizing this force.

I was so ordered.[1] Wytheville was General Floyd's headquarters. I had conceived an idea that a man who had been Secretary of War knew everything pertaining to military matters. I soon discovered that my chief was as incapacitated for the work he had undertaken as I would have been to lead an Italian opera. As companies reported for duty I mustered them into the service, taught them, or tried to teach them, how to make out their muster rolls, issued to them tents, knapsacks, etc. Night schools for the officers were organized, and tactics given them to study, but I found that some could not read, so schools were abandoned. When ten companies reported, a regiment was formed, and it received its number from Richmond. While this was going on, the commissary, quartermaster, ordnance and medical departments had to be organized; it will be readily seen that I had no time to play. I had no one to assist me.

In the meantime General Wise was organizing his army in eastern Virginia, and obtained permission to make a campaign in West Virginia. When General Floyd heard this he was simply furious, and cursed Wise a hundred times a day: "G—— d—— him, why does he come to *my country*? Why does he not stay in the east and defend *his own country,* Accomac and Southampton; there is where he belongs. I don't want the d—— rascal here, I will not stand it." Wise, when en route to Western Virginia, I was told, stopped at every cross road and made a speech, saying "Come and join me; bring a musket; if you have no musket bring a rifle; if no rifle, a shotgun; if no shotgun, a pistol; no pistol, a gate hinge; no gate hinge, by G—— bring an India rubber shoe, but come." Wise went booming down the turnpike leading to Gauley bridge, and then down the Kanawha River.

General McClellan was at that time organizing troops in Ohio; hearing of Wise's approach to the Ohio, he sent a few regiments to meet him; at Scarey Creek[2] Wise engaged this Federal force and was defeated. He retreated by the same road he had advanced on, burnt the bridge over the Gauley, and reached the White Sulphur Springs, where Floyd found him when he passed that point. General Wise sent word to General Floyd as he passed the Springs, asking him to come and see him. Floyd complied; he went to General Wise's quarters.[3] After the usual formalities had been observed, General Wise stood up, placed his hands on the back of his chair and made a speech. I think he spoke a couple of hours; he reviewed the history of the United States from its discovery, the Revolutionary War, the Mexican War, the causes which led to the present troubles, his march down the Kanawha River, the affair at Scarey Creek, and his retreat to the White Sulphur. Floyd listened patiently. General Wise, before taking his seat, asked General Floyd where he was going. Floyd replied, "Down that road,"[4] pointing to the road on which Wise had retreated. Said Wise, "What are you going to do, Floyd?" "Fight," answered Floyd, intimating that that was what Wise had failed to do. If a look could kill, Floyd would have been annihilated, for I never saw greater hatred condensed in a look before or since. Floyd arose, bowed, and left.

Floyd now moved in the direction of Gauley Bridge, crossed Sewell Mountain,[5] turned to the right, struck the Gauley River at Carnifix Ferry, crossed by means of a rope ferry, and went into camp. He had not been here many days when a Federal regiment, the 7th West Virginia, commanded by Colonel Tyler,[6] afterwards General Tyler, encamped within a half mile of Floyd's command; no two companies were within a quarter of a mile of the other. Floyd asked me what he should do. "Do," I said. "There is but one thing for you to do, attack them at daylight tomorrow morning."

I was ordered to attack, and fell upon those isolated companies; they could make but feeble resistance; many were killed and wounded, and more captured.[7] Those who escaped probably found their way to the Ohio River. General Rosecrans,[8] on hearing of the disaster that had befallen the 7th West Virginia, started with about 9,000 men to punish Floyd. General Wise, in the meantime, left the White Sulphur and advanced to a point near Hawk's Nest,[9] some twenty miles from Carnifix Ferry. General Wise had on his staff two newspaper editors, Floyd the same number on his staff. Floyd was the ranking brigadier general. He sent orders to General Wise to join him. Wise refused, or failed, to comply. Floyd asked me what he should do. I said, "When a junior refuses to obey the orders of his superior, there is but one course to pursue, arrest him and order him to Richmond." "Oh, no," said Floyd, "that would never do; I would get both of his newspapers down on me."

Rosecrans was drawing nearer and nearer. I took the precaution to throw a temporary bridge across the Gauley River at the rope ferry. As soon as Rosecrans arrived opposite us, he threw forward a strong skirmish line and made a forced reconnaissance; soon pretty sharp fighting resulted.[10] Floyd received a gunshot wound in the fleshy part of his arm. Both Floyd and Wise were brave men, and their hearts were thoroughly in the cause they were contending for, but unfortunately they were politicians whose hatred for each other was of long standing. I saw General Floyd and told him that Rosecrans was in command and that he had three men to his one; that it was true his right rested on the precipitous banks of the Gauley, but there was a half mile between his left and the river; that he had not enough men to fill up this gap; that the best thing he could do would be to recross the Gauley on the improvised bridge I had constructed. Floyd swore he would be d—— if he would ever surrender a foot of his country to the d—— thieving Yankees. In an hour he changed his mind and told me to cross with the command.[11] This was done that night, and by daybreak the last man and wagon was safely over. Within half an hour after effecting the crossing, the end of the bridge on Rosecrans' side gave way, and the current swung the bridge around to our side; our end was then cut, and the bridge was carried rapidly down the river.

We reached Sewell Mountain in a few days. General Wise, knowing that Floyd had fallen back, and that Rosecrans was about to reinforce Cox,[12] the Federal commander at Gauley Bridge, thought it best to fall back also. We found him on the east side of Sewell Mountain. General Floyd halted his commands on the top of the mountain and called a council of war.[13] The question to be decided was, whether it was best to make a stand and fight on Sewell Mountain, or fall back some twelve miles to a point called Muddy Creek and fight there. Floyd contended that Muddy Creek was the place to receive the attack of Rosecrans. Wise, of course, took the opposite view and was for fighting at Sewell Mountain. The council determined on Muddy Creek. Floyd issued orders to this effect. After the council had adjourned, General Wise got on his horse and rode to his command, where he struck the first detachment, halted, raised himself in his stirrups, and in a stentorian voice called out, "Who is retreating now? Who is retreating now?" He rode slowly on, and seeing another group of his men, he repeated the same to them. Presently, his entire command had assembled and he said, "Men, who is retreating now? John B. Floyd, G—— d—— him, the bullet-hit son of a b——, he is retreating now."

Floyd moved his command to Muddy Creek.[14] Wise would not budge, but remained at Sewell Mountain. Soon Mr. Davis was advised of the condition of things in West Virginia. He sent General R. E. Lee to look into matters and to straighten them out. General Lee,[15] on his arrival, made a thorough examination of both Sewell Mountain and Muddy Creek, and ordered Floyd to Sewell Mountain; this, of course, was a great feather in the cap of Wise and his people. If you will look up

the Richmond *Examiner* and other papers published about that
time, you will find General Lee the best-abused man of that
day.

John M. Daniel[16] was one of Floyd's staff, and editor of the
Richmond *Examiner*. He said to me one day that it was a d——
shame for Davis to send Lee to supersede a man like Floyd;
that Lee was no more to be compared to Floyd than the moon
was to the sun; that Floyd had forgotten more about strategy,
grand tactics, and handling troops on the field of battle, than
Lee ever knew or ever would know. I asked this solon where
Floyd had acquired his great military knowledge. He replied,
"Has he not been Secretary of War, and a great military
student? It would have done very well to have sent Lee to report
to Floyd to dig ditches where Floyd wanted them."

Rosecrans advanced as far as Sewell Mountain, but did not
attack, slight skirmishing being the only result. The roads were
in a dreadful condition, the bottoms appeared to have dropped
out. General Lee obtained his supplies from Jackson River, one
hundred miles from Sewell Mountain and only half loads could
be hauled. General Rosecrans, seeing that nothing was to be
gained by remaining at Sewell Mountain, fell back to Gauley
Bridge. Floyd requested General Lee to permit him to cross
New River and march to Cotton Hill,[17] which overlooked
Rosecrans' encampment, and *destroy the Federal Army*. The
New River and the Gauley River united at Cotton Hill and
formed the Kanawha River.

I had a long talk with General Lee and expressed to him my
views as to Floyd's ability to exercise an independent command.
I told him if Floyd was given an independent command, it
would be merely a question of time when it would be captured;
that I did not think the Confederacy could afford to lose three
or four thousand men, simply to gratify the ambition of a politician who was as incapable of taking care of his men or fighting
them, as a baby. When I had this conversation with the General,

it was raining; the next morning it was a bright, beautiful day. I met the General at breakfast. He said, "Well, Colonel, I hope as this is a bright day you take a less gloomy view of matters than you did last night when we parted." I replied, "No, General, I am of the same opinion still; I have seen too much incompetency in General Floyd during the past four months to cause me to change my views."

Floyd crossed New River and camped at the base of Cotton Hill. From Cotton Hill, extending along New River, there is a precipitous range of mountains; the distance between the base of the mountain and the river is from a half to a quarter of a mile. The banks of the river are perpendicular and from 80 to 100 feet high, and the river runs like a mountain torrent. The mountain I have mentioned, about five or six miles from Cotton Hill, slopes down to almost nothing, and is here only two or three hundred yards from the river bank. If I have made myself clear as to the situation of mountain and river, it will be seen with a force in Floyd's front marching over Cotton Hill and another marching behind the mountain to where it slopes down into the river, Floyd would have been caught in as complete a cul-de-sac as man or nature could have constructed.

I told General Floyd that his position was faulty, that he could not subsist his command where he was, that the roads were becoming worse and worse each day, that he was hauling his provisions 100 miles.[18] I could see that he was not gaining anything by remaining where he was; that General Rosecrans could drive him away whenever he chose to do so. "Let him dare cross the river, and not a d—— Yankee will ever recross it; I will never yield a foot of *my country* to the rascals." I then added, "General Rosecrans will capture you and your entire command." Floyd said, "No, sir, I will die before I will be captured. Do you know what they say they will do with me if captured? They say they will put me in an iron cage, haul me around their d—— country and exhibit me as if I were a

wild beast." Very soon after this conversation, General Rosecrans crossed the Kanawha with a large force,[19] large compared
to Floyd's, sending another force under General Benham behind
the mountain to come in and form across the mouth of the cul-
de-sac.

I was skirmishing with Rosecran's advance, when Floyd,
much excited, rode up to me and said a country girl had just
ridden in and informed him of the approach of Benham's force.
"By G——d, they will get in my rear; I shall be attacked in
front and rear; what must I do?" I think visions of the iron
cage were very vivid then. I said, "General, leave me with
one regiment and a battery of artillery, and a dozen cavalry;
take the rest of your command and if the mouth of the sac is
occupied, cut your way through; let me take care of myself;
I will delay Rosecrans in every way I can by causing him to
form line of battle; you may thus save a portion of your command, and yourself from being caged." Floyd followed my
advice. Benham, I was informed, came within a quarter of a
mile, or half mile, of the mouth of the cul-de-sac, and for
reasons best known to himself came no farther. Rosecrans we
understood, preferred charges against him.[20] Floyd was thus
enabled to escape without receiving a shot. As soon as he was
safe, he sent word to me of his escape and directed me to follow, which I was not slow to do. I got through all right with
the loss of only a few men when skirmishing with Rosecrans.

About twelve o'clock at night I reached Floyd's camp; it was
raining hard. Floyd had burnt his tents in order to lighten his
wagons. Rosecrans was in pursuit. I reported to Floyd; we had
a conversation about the condition of affairs; he said, "This
is fast becoming a rout; I tell you what I will do; I will have
the command assembled and make them a speech and tell them
that reinforcements are coming to join me." I said, "General,
I would not disturb the men, they have had a hard day's march,
let them sleep; and especially I would not tell them that rein-

forcements were coming to assist you, they would soon find out
that it was not true, and their confidence in you would be
destroyed." "But," said Floyd, "they like to hear me speak."
I said, "Yes, but now I think they would prefer sleeping. Give
orders for the command to move at three o'clock—it is now
twelve—make your speech when they are assembled, or when
on the march tomorrow. Leave me here and I will do all in
my power to detain Rosecrans, who is pushing on after you."
This he agreed to. Rosecrans continued the pursuit two days
and then gave it up. Floyd's command became badly scattered,
the men leaving and going to their homes.

XVIII

On arriving at a point near Dublin Depot, on the railroad,
I received a dispatch to report to President Davis in Richmond.[1]
I reported to the President, who said, "Young man, how much
rank can you stand?" I replied, "Mr. President, you must be
the judge of that." "Well," he said, "I will make you a Major-
General and send you to the Trans-Mississippi; Price[2] and
McCulloch[3] are fighting each other over there harder than they
are fighting the enemy."

This announcement was anything but pleasant. It so happened
that a kind Providence, in this event, came to my assistance
as it did again later on. When it became known that I was to
be sent to the Trans-Mississippi Department, the friends of Price
and McCulloch were loud in their objections. They said, "It
is a shame to send a boy out west to supersede old veterans
such as Price and McCulloch." It was taken up in the Confeder-

ate Senate, as it was in the lower house. When I thought the propitious time had arrived, I called on the Secretary of War, Mr. Benjamin, and told him I did not think I was the person to send to command across the Mississippi; that he had doubtless read all that had been said; that, when I reached there they would both unite and fight me; that I would find myself between the upper and nether mill stone; that these men would never second me in my efforts to beat the enemy, and I felt sure I would be compelled to relieve both and order them to Richmond; send an older man, one who had not been discussed.[4] Mr. Benjamin said, "We cannot make you a major-general in the event of your not going to the Trans-Mississippi Department." I said, "That is all right." I was made in a few days a brigadier-general and ordered to West Virginia.[5]

Before dismissing the Floyd-Wise campaign, I must relate an incident that occurred at the interview between President Davis and General Wise. When Wise called to see Mr. Davis in Richmond, Mr. Davis said, I presume in a playful way, "General Wise, I think I will have to shoot you." General Wise started from his seat and said, "Mr. President, shoot me, that is all right, but for God's sake let me see you hang that d—— rascal Floyd first." The mistake was, and I think their most ardent admirers will acknowledge, that those two men, Floyd and Wise, were out of place as general officers, exercising independent commands, and it was a mistake in ever bringing them together, where cooperation is expected. As well might peace and harmony and concert of action have been expected if you threw a game cock into another game cock's yard. But if the Confederate government made this mistake, it was equally so on the Federal side, Banks and Butler to offset Floyd and Wise. General Grant captured Floyd's command at Fort Donnelson in 1862. Floyd escaped on a steamer, thus preventing the Federals from hauling him around the country and exhibiting him in an iron cage. Following is a letter from Floyd to the President:

HEADQUARTERS
ARMY OF THE KANAWHA,
Camp Sewell, September 15, 1861

His Excellency Jefferson Davis,
President Confederate State of America.

Dear Sir:

Amidst the multiplicity of your trials and vexations I had
hoped that no ground of annoyance from this quarter of
the country should be superadded to your burden. In this,
however, I regret to say I find myself mistaken. Things
have assumed a complexion here which require your
prompt and immediate action. The petty jealousy of
General Wise; his utter ignorance of all military rule and
discipline; the peculiar contrariness of his character and
disposition, are beginning to produce rapidly a disorganiza-
tion which will prove fatal to the interests of the army if
not arrested at once. He obeys no order without cavil, and
does not hesitate to disregard a positive and peremptory
order, upon the most frivolous pretext, as you will see from
the official correspondence I have transmitted to the
Department. The obvious and probably the proper course
for me to pursue would have been instantly to have arrested
General Wise and sent him to Richmond. This, however,
would not have cured the evil, for he has around him a
set of men extremely like himself, and the demoralization
of his corps I incline to think is complete. But such a
course, whilst it could not have arrested the evil of which
I complain, would certainly have been productive of others
more annoying and as much to be regretted, if not more

than those I desire to be remedied. Upon his arrest and trial parties necessarily could be made to divide, and the enemies of your government and of the country attempting stealthily to organize, and who will organize before very long, would seize upon such an incident to shape, if possible public opinion, or direct public sentiment and sympathy. Besides, it would tend to distract public attention from the great and absorbing subject of the war to the insignificant affairs of individual disputes. This course I have decided to pursue will, I think, result in an active and clamorous support of you and your measures by that gentleman and his friends, because his transfer from the line by a simple order will save him from the pains and penalties of being cashiered, which would be his inevitable fate if charges were preferred against him, and in that event his whole influence would be lent to any opposition, however unscrupulous. It is impossible for me to conduct a campaign with General Wise attached to my command. His presence with my force is almost as injurious as if he were in the camp of the enemy with his whole command. He is perpetually attempting to justify his own former blunders by inducing me to repeat the same. He was bitterly opposed to my crossing the river and declared even to my teamsters that I would be cut all to pieces. On both occasions when he knew I was to fight, he refused to come to my assistance; but worst of all is the spirit of antipathy and dislike which he attempts to engender in the minds of his officers and men toward everybody under my command. I hope you will pardon me for making a suggestion by which these difficulties can be most easily obviated and the public interest in this quarter best promoted. It would be to order General Wise with his legion to service either with Beauregard or Magruder.

John B. Floyd.

I cannot remember whether it was on this visit to Richmond, or the year following, I had occasion to call on Mr. Davis at his private residence, and was conducted to his private office. After transacting my business I got up to go. Mr. Davis said, "Don't go, I want to talk to you." After a while I again made a movement to go; he said, "Sit down; I have a letter I wish you to read." He handed me a letter, which was quite lengthy. I read it, and when returning it I asked him if he had answered it. He said, "Yes, here is a copy of my reply." The reply was short and forcible. The letter to President Davis was from General Joseph E. Johnston, and it was a scorcher complaining of the injustice done him by not making him the senior General in the Confederate Army, but the fourth in rank.[6] We talked for some time, when Mr. Davis was called out of his office by a servant; he remained out half an hour; on returning I thought he was very nervous. I had looked at my watch when he was absent and found it to be two o'clock. I bade him good night and left. The next day I learned why Mr. Davis kept me so long in his office the night before. The present Miss Winnie,[7] I think, came into the world that night. Mr. Davis wanted some one to keep him company.

I appointed as my staff, Randolph H. Finney,[8] adjutant general, Miles C. Selden[9] and Stockton Heth,[10] aides. My headquarters was at Lewisburg, W. Va. I got some 2500 or 3000 men together, and organized them into regiments and battalions. The Federals had thrown a force forward as far south as Giles Court House; this was uncomfortably near our railroad, and I determined to attack them. This I did early in May 1862,[11] and drove this force away after a short engagement. The Federal commander was Colonel Hayes, afterwards President Hayes. President Hayes, it will be remembered, removed, during his administration, the Federal army from the Southern states. The people in Richmond, where I was living at the time, were much rejoiced at this. They appointed a committee of three to visit

Washington and request the President and his Cabinet to visit Richmond[12] as the guests of the city. I was one of this committee. We opened communication with the Postmaster General, General Key,[13] and the day was fixed for our visit to Washington. We met General Key. When en route to the White House, the General asked me if I had ever met the President; I told him I had not, that I called on him once and he refused to see me. "How was that?" asked the Postmaster General. I related to him my visit to Giles Court House in 1862 and the result of that fight. After transacting our business General Key said, "Mr. President, General Heth says he called to see you once and you refused to see him." The President said, "How was that, General?" I replied, "General Key alludes to that little episode of the war, when, in May 1862, I called to see you at Giles Court House." "Oh," said the President, "that was a funny affair; your men threw some shells over where I was." "Yes," I said, "I sent you my cards." The President said, "I was mounted at the time, and one of your shells burst near my horse; a piece of it struck me in the leg, cutting a round piece out of my pants and stocking knit drawers and carrying away about two or three ounces of flesh. I scarcely felt it at the time, or when retreating, but when I dismounted my leg gave way completely; and although I received several much more serious wounds during the war, none have given me the trouble that your shell gave me." I told the President I was glad it was no worse. President Hayes—then, I think, a colonel—was badly wounded at the battle of South Mountain, September 14, 1862.[14]

When I left Lewisburg, the Federals advanced and occupied that town. I determined to attack them and did so, but a panic seized upon my raw troops, and I met with signal disaster.[15] Colonel George Crook commanded the Federal troops on this occasion. Crook was a splendid officer, and afterwards became a major general in the United States Army.

Hearing that General Kirby Smith was preparing to invade Kentucky, and being anxious to participate in this invasion, I applied to join him; this was granted.[16] When ready to commence the invasion, Smith with 6000 men turned Cumberland Gap, then held by General Morgan of the Federal Army,[17] and entered Kentucky. I was left with about 4000 to bring up and guard the trains.

Near Richmond, Ky., Smith found the Federals 10,000 strong under General Nelson, known as "Bull" Nelson, who was afterwards killed by General Jefferson D. Davis in the Galt House in Louisville.[18] Smith at once attacked this force, attacking Nelson's center, sending a brigade under Brigadier General Smith[19] to attack Nelson's left flank. The Federals gave way, formed again a half mile from the first position, were attacked, gave way the second time, formed the third time, and were again attacked. Brigadier General Smith with his brigade on this occasion succeeded in getting well in rear of Nelson's troops, who were routed, leaving 2,500 men killed or wounded on the field. Smith captured 7,000 prisoners; a few of Nelson's men escaped in small squads and reached the Ohio River.[20] It is true Nelson's force was composed of raw men who had never heard a hostile shot fired.

I have always considered the battle of Richmond, Ky., the most complete victory of the war. Kirby Smith hurried on to Lexington, Ky.,[21] leaving me at Richmond to parole the prisoners. This occupied about twenty-four hours. I then hurried to Lexington, where I found any number of Kentucky politicians who were there, as they said, to reorganize the state government. I had a long talk with Kirby Smith, saying to him, "I presume, for good reasons, we have never been able to reap the fruits of our victories," and that I felt certain he could capture either Louisville or Cincinnati; that there was no force at present in either of those cities. He agreed with me but said the politicians told him his presence was necessary in Lexington to assist in organizing the State Government. I told him I was convinced that the capture of Cincinnati would do more towards organizing the state government than his presence in Lexington. Finally I said, "If you cannot go and take Cincinnati or Louisville, let me go and take one of the two places." Smith replied, "I will let you know tonight what I will do."

About midnight he came to my room and said I might take such and such brigades and make a *demonstration* on Cincinnati. I started promptly with about 6000 men and several batteries of artillery.[22] I sent a number of spies ahead. I marched from twenty to twenty-five miles a day. I found that there was no need for spies; half a dozen or more men met me each day, just from Cincinnati, representing that the utmost panic prevailed in that city; there was no organized force there. The authorities were impressing the lawyers, the doctors, and shopkeepers to defend the city; some had guns, some pistols, they had some cannons but no ammunition, and on the improvised breastworks, wooden logs were painted black and put up; and that at the first shot fired they would break for the river. I was furnished with what was said to be a complete inventory of the government stores and property in the city. I sent General Smith each day two or more dispatches giving him this information; finally, Smith gave me permission to attack.

On reaching the vicinity of Newport a force was discovered. I threw out some skirmishers; before the skirmish line fired a dozen shots this force broke and ran, throwing away knapsacks, guns, and all impedimenta. I was forming my line for an attack, when up rode a courier, and handed me a dispatch; it was a lengthy epistle from General Smith, recalling the permission given, and positively ordering that no attack be made on Cincinnati;[23] winding up his dispatch he added, "Cincinnati and Louisville will fall like ripe apples into our hands as soon as the great battle between Bragg[24] and Buell[25] is fought."

It had been agreed upon that when Smith with his army

invaded Kentucky, Bragg, who was opposed to Buell in Tennessee, should get ahead of Buell and enter Kentucky; this he successfully accomplished, General Smith wrote to Bragg asking him if he did not wish him to bring his army to his assistance; this after Bragg had reached the blue grass, or fertile, region of Kentucky. Bragg said, "No;" that when Buell came in striking distance, he would crush him like an eggshell. Smith handed me this note to read. A short time after, Smith received a second note from Bragg in which he said if Buell attacked him his army would be destroyed. Smith handed me this note. What had happened? Buell certainly had received no reinforcements; we were not wise enough to solve the riddle. I said, "Can he be crazy? Has he lost his mind?" Bragg was on the road Buell had to follow to reach Louisville; he drew back from the road, permitting Buell to pass on without firing a shot.[26] I marched my command to a point near Lexington and went into camp.

When General E. K. Smith invaded Kentucky, General G. W. Morgan of the Federal army occupied the strong position of Cumberland Gap. General Carter L. Stevenson was in his front to prevent a further movement on the part of Morgan into Tennessee. After the battle of Richmond, Ky., General Morgan evacuated Cumberland Gap; this relieved General Stevenson who joined General Smith. Morgan moved in a northeasterly direction to the Ohio River; Smith started for Mount Sterling to intercept Morgan.[27] Morgan passed to the east of Mount Sterling, before Smith reached that town. Bragg and Smith now went to Frankfort, Ky.

In the meantime, Buell having recruited and refitted his army at Louisville, moved out the day Governor Hawes was inaugurated, to find Bragg.[28] Bragg moved in the direction of Perryville, where he fought Buell, after detaching a division of his army on some wild goose chase, and without the assistance of Smith, whom Bragg should have had in supporting distance. After the battle of Perryville, Bragg hastily left Kentucky.

As far as I can judge, Bragg's management of this campaign was as faulty and badly-managed as any military operation of the war. Smith's army arrived at Perryville the night of the battle; he proposed to General Bragg to unite the two forces and attack Buell. Bragg refused to attack, telling Smith he could attack him with his force if he chose to do so, but he (Bragg) would not participate in the battle.

In discussing Bragg's course in Kentucky,[29] General Smith and I came to the conclusion that General Bragg had lost his mind, and Smith said he would so state in his report to Mr. Davis. After preparing his report he gave it to me to read. I said, "You have not stated that you thought Bragg has lost his mind." "No, I have not; I think it would be better of you to state that to the President when you go to Richmond." I told Mr. Davis what conclusion General Smith and I had formed in Kentucky after witnessing Bragg's incompetency in this campaign. There was no man in either of the contending armies who was General Bragg's superior as an organizer and a disciplinarian, but when he was in the presence of an enemy he lost his head.

XIX

On reaching Tennessee I received orders to report to General R. E. Lee.[1] I was delighted to be ordered to General Lee's army to serve with the forces defending my native state. General E. Kirby Smith was a splendid officer. In his first battle, Manassas, or Bull Run, he displayed much ability and was badly wounded.[2] In the battle of Richmond, Ky., he displayed strategy and tactical ability. It was the most decisive battle of the war. Had General Smith been Bragg's senior, I believed at the time, and have never had reason to change my mind, he would have destroyed Buell's army, and the winter of 1862-3 would have found the Confederates still in Kentucky with the ranks greatly increased.

I reported to General Lee in March, 1863, and was assigned to Brigadier General A. P. Hill's division, near Moss Neck[3] on the Rappahannock. When I reported to General Lee, there were quite a number of officers near his tent. On the opposite side of the Rappahannock some military display was going on, a review perhaps. An officer, said, "I wish I could throw a hundred shells among them and kill them all." "Oh no," said General Lee, "do not wish that, wish that they were all at their homes with their friends and that they would stay there."

General Hooker, with an army of 120,000 strong, lay on the opposite side of the Rappahannock. Hooker commenced to move the latter part of April, and crossed the Rapidan at the fords above Fredericksburg.[4] General Lee met Hooker's advance May 1, 1862, and drove it back to Chancellorsville. On reconnoitering Hooker's position, General Lee found it too strong to attack in front; he ordered Jackson, with the three divisions, to move around Hooker's front and attack his right flank.[5]

Jackson's movement was reported to some officers of the XI Corps., but it appears no preparation was made to receive his attack.[6] The XI Corps was encamped in woods and an open field, around Melzy Chancellor's house. Jackson formed his attacking force in three lines: first, Rhode's [sic] division; second, Colston's division; and third, A. P. Hill's division forming the rear line.[7] The first line, Rhode's, was in five hundred yards of the field occupied by a portion of the XI Corps. Jackson passed through the woods like a tornado and fell upon the XI Corps, which was totally unprepared for resistance; many of

the Federals had not time to take their guns from the stacks.
Rhodes alone swept them back pell mell.[8] When my brigade
reached the cleared field, not a Federal soldier was to be seen.
I passed over a line of muskets stacked; this line of muskets
was, I think, two hundred yards in length. I saw fifty or more
camp fires burning, with camp kettles filled with meat being
cooked, and thirty or forty beeves in the various stages of being
butchered.

A man has recently published an account of the battle of
Chancellorsville in defense of the XI Corps, which, in my opinion, does the XI Corps, or the rank and file of this corps, signal
injustice. The blame for this disaster should be laid upon the
officers who received information of Jackson's approach and
failed to report the same to their superiors. The men of the XI
Corps were in no wise to blame; unarmed men cannot contend
against armed men.

Hill's division did not fire a shot in this attack;[9] it passed
on and occupied a line of abandoned breastworks, in the woods,
I think about half a mile, more or less, from the Chancellorsville
Tavern.[10] The left of the division rested behind these works
which terminated on the Plank Road.

In order to understand *how* the battle of the 3rd of May was
won, it will be necessary to refer to an incident which occurred
on the morning of the 2nd of May. After General Jackson's
infantry had passed the furnace,[11] his artillery and ammunition
wagons when passing the same point were attacked. Word was
sent to Jackson, and he ordered A. P. Hill, whose division was
the rear one of his command, to send a brigade to repel the
force attacking his artillery. General Archer's brigade brought
up Hill's rear. He ordered Archer to countermarch and go to
the assistance of the artillery. Jackson continued his movement
and attacked as previously described. Night came on; both
Federals and Confederates were in much confusion and much
excited. Skirmish lines were being established and considerable

firing occurred. As a general thing, the firing was done by the Federals, firing into their own troops, and the Confederates firing into each other, each mistaking the other in the dark for the enemy. It was thus Stonewall Jackson was wounded by his own men, and A. P. Hill was disabled.[12]

Hill wounded, the command of his division devolved upon me. Archer's brigade arrived, and I told him to march his brigade down the breastworks we occupied, and prolong the line. On reaching the right of the division and attempting to prolong the line, he found that the Federals occupied the ground he should have occupied. Resting the left of his brigade on the right of the division, he threw his right back, his position being nearly at right angles to the division.[13] I received orders to attack at seven o'clock in the morning. I sent word to Archer shortly before seven o'clock to swing around and form on my right. When Archer commenced to swing around, he struck the Federals in his front, and drove them. Seeing what was going on in Archer's front, I gave the order to move forward, moving parallel to the Plank Road. I reached the open field in front of Chancellorsville Tavern; two or three hundred yards from the edge of the woods bordering on the field I found some thirty pieces of Federal artillery posted, supported by infantry. Artillery and infantry opened on my command. The division could not stand this tremendous fire, and was driven back into the woods it had passed through. Rhodes's division came up and met with the same fate; then followed Colston's division, with no better success. The trouble under which the Confederates were laboring just then was that they could find no open space where their artillery could be effectively used.

I now return to Archer. He drove the enemy before him, and came to an open field where he found a battery of artillery. He captured the battery. Here was a place for our artillery;[14] soon some thirty Confederate guns were assembled in this field, having an enfilade fire on the Federal artillery that had played havoc with Jackson's three divisions,[15] also a direct enfilade fire on Hancock's lines.[16] The Federal artillery was soon hopelessly demoralized, guns dismounted, horses killed. The Federal artillery withdrew to the woods behind Chancellorsville Tavern, as did Hancock's lines. Jackson's infantry having nothing now to oppose it, occupied the field in front of the tavern.[17] The following morning it was found that General Hooker had recrossed the river with his entire force and occupied his old position opposite Fredericksburg.[18] General Lee resumed his position opposite Hooker. I have not attempted to describe the battle of Chancellorsville, but simply to show how the accidental sending back of Archer's brigade of Hill's division enabled the Confederates to obtain a position for their artillery, and by so doing to win the battle.

After the battle of Chancellorsville, the Army of Northern Virginia was reorganized. Three Corps were formed, commanded by Longstreet, Ewell and Hill, A. P.[19] I was promoted to a major general and given a division in A. P. Hill's corps.[20] My division was composed of the brigades of Pettigrew, Davis, Archer and Brockenbrough.[21]

General Lee determined to invade Pennsylvania. Ewell's corps, the II, crossed the Potomac first; Hill's followed Ewell; Longstreet followed Hill.[22] The cavalry was to have followed Longstreet and keep on the right flank of the army, watch the enemy, collect supplies, and give General Lee information of the movements of the enemy. This order was modified, General Lee permitting Stuart to drop down the Potomac, strike the enemy a blow, then cross the Potomac and get into position. When General Stuart attempted to cross the Potomac, he found General Hancock of the Union Army crossing the river at the point where he expected to cross; this compelled Stuart to cross lower down. When he struck west to get in position, he found the Union forces in his way, and was compelled to make a long detour in order to avoid them.

I shall not attempt to give a description of the battle of Gettysburg, only so much of it as I saw and participated in. On
June the 29th, I reached Cashtown, eight miles from Gettysburg.[23] My division was the leading division of the III Corps.
My men were sadly in want of shoes. I heard that a large supply
of shoes were stored in Gettysburg. On the morning of the 30th
of June, I ordered General Pettigrew to march to Gettysburg
and secure these shoes. Pettigrew reached a point near Gettysburg, but did not attempt to enter the town, and countermarched, reaching Cashtown the evening of the 30th of June.
He reported that he had not gone to Gettysburg; that there was
evidently a cavalry force occupying the town, the strength of
which he could not tell; that some of his men reported the beat
of drums (indicating infantry) on the further side of the town;
that if he entered the town his men when searching for shoes
would have become scattered, and if there was a large force
there, it might have proved disastrous to his command. Under
the circumstances he deemed it prudent to return and not carry
out my orders. General Hill rode up just then, and I directed
General Pettigrew to repeat to Hill what he had told me. Hill
said, as I had done, that he did not believe that there was any
force at Gettysburg, except possibly a small cavalry vidette. I
said to Hill, "If there is no objection, I will march my division
to-morrow, go to Gettysburg and secure those shoes." Hill
replied, "Do so."

The next morning, July 1, 1863, I moved out at five
o'clock.[24] On reaching the range of hills which overlook Willoughby Run[25] I placed a couple of batteries in position and
ordered the battalion commander, Colonel W. J. Pegram, to fire
at the woods in his front for half an hour and see if he could
get a response, but no response was obtained. My infantry
arrived. I placed Davis's and Archer's brigades in line, the right
of Davis's and the left of Archer's resting on the road leading
to Gettysburg, and ordered them to move forward and occupy

the town. These brigades soon became engaged with General Buford's dismounted cavalry,[26] the cavalry were driven. General Reynolds arrived on the field with the head of his corps; Davis and Archer were now attacked by Reynolds and driven back with some loss. General Archer was captured, and General Reynolds was killed.[27]

When encamped at Cashtown, I told my quartermaster if he captured any hats to bring me one, as mine was in a dilapidated condition. He brought me a box containing some dozen felt hats. I tried them on and found all too large. My clerk said, "General, I think I can fix one to fit you." He doubled up a dozen or more sheets of foolscap paper and placed the paper between the leather and the felt of the hat; by this means I was able to wear it. I mention this as I am confidently of the belief that my life was saved by this paper in my hat.

I now formed my division along Willoughby Run, in the McPherson or Reynolds woods, as it is now sometimes called. The engagement of Davis and Archer gave General Lee the first intimation that there was an infantry force within thirty miles of him. I saw General Lee several times between the 27th and 30th of June. The first thing he would say showed his anxiety about his cavalry. "Have you heard anything about my cavalry? I hope no disaster has overtaken my cavalry." The last time I saw him before the first of July he said, "Any news to give me about General Stuart? Well, General Heth, if General Hooker does not find us, we must find him." He had not learned that Hooker had been relieved by General Meade.[28] He was not aware that the Union army had crossed the Potomac until the morning of the 29th of June; the eyes and ears of his army were absent.

Had General Lee known that the Federal army was moving on Gettysburg he would have had there, on the 1st of July, his entire army; who can doubt the result? I have said my division lay along Willoughby Run in line of battle. General Ewell,

who had advanced as far as York, Pa., was ordered to
Cashtown. Rhodes, commanding a division, was on a road
north of Gettysburg, and en route to Cashtown, when he heard
my guns. He faced to the left and was approaching the position
I occupied when he struck Reynold's troops and the right flank
of the XI Corps.

Hearing the heavy firing on my left I rode where I had first
placed my artillery in position and found there Generals Lee
and Hill. I told General Lee that as Rhodes appeared to be heavily engaged, I thought I had better go in. He replied, "I do
not wish to bring on a general engagement to-day; Longstreet
is not up." I returned to my division; soon I went again where
I had left General Lee and told him that I believed they were
withdrawing troops from my front and pushing them against
Rhodes, and again requested permission to attack. The General
said, "Wait awhile and I will send you word when to go in."
I returned to my division, and very soon an aide came to me
with orders to attack.

I struck the Iron Brigade and had a desperate fight. I lost
2300 men in thirty minutes. I was struck by a minie ball on
the head which passed through my hat and the paper my clerk
had placed there, broke the outer coating of my skull and
cracked the inner coating, and I fell senseless. Pettigrew was
wounded also.

Colonel Fox,[29] in a treatise of regimental losses in the American Civil War, pp. 555-6, says:

> The severity of the losses among the Confederates and
> the heroic persistency with which they would stand before
> the enemy's musketry, becomes apparent in studying the
> official returns of the various regiments. At Gettysburg the
> 26th North Carolina[30] regiment of Pettigrew's brigade,
> Heth's division, went into action with an effective strength
> which is stated in the regimental official report as over 800

men. They sustained a loss, according to Surgeon General Guild's[31] report, of 86 killed and 502 wounded, total 588. This loss occurred mostly in the first day's fight. The quartermaster of the 26th, who made the official report on July 4th,[32] states that there were only 216 left for duty after the fight on the 1st instant. The regiment then participated in Pickett's charge on the third day of the battle in which it attacked the position held by Smyth's brigade, Hay's division, Second Corps.[33] On the following morning it mustered only 80 men for duty. The missing ones having fallen in the final and unsuccessful charge. In the battle of the first day, Captain Tuttle's company[34] went into action with three officers and 84 men; all the officers and 83 men were killed or wounded. On the same day and in the same brigade (Pettigrew's), Company C of the 11th North Carolina, lost two officers killed and 34 out of 38 men killed or wounded. Captain Bird[35] of this company, with the four remaining men, participated in the charge on the 3d of July and then the flag bearer was shot and the captain brought out the flag himself. This loss of the 26th North Carolina at Gettysburg was the severest regimental loss during the war.[36]

I remained insensible for some hours. When I regained consciousness I directed my ambulance driver to take me to a point where I found Generals Lee and Hill; both of these officers seemed nervously awaiting an attack to be made by General Longstreet on our extreme right. When Longstreet opened, I arose and looked out of my ambulance; the sun presented the red appearance it frequently does an hour or two before setting. General Hill was near my ambulance when Longstreet's attack commenced. I recollect saying to him "If this attack could not have been made sooner it should not have been made now, for if Longstreet gains a victory he will not be able to reap its legitimate fruits; night will soon put an end to the fighting and we shall find the Federals entrenched tomorrow morning, in probably as strong or stronger position, and we will be compelled to go over the same thing again.''

The battles of July 1st and 2d at Gettysburg were victories for the Confederates; the attack on Cemetery Ridge, made by Pickett's division and my own, assisted by two brigades of Pender's division under General Trimble, was a failure on the part of the Confederates, and properly claimed as a victory by the Federals. The real victory of the Federals at Gettysburg was the fact that General Lee thought it wise to recross the Potomac. His losses had been severe in each of the three days' battles; he could expect no reenforcements, while the Union army could be increased indefinitely.

As I did not participate in, and saw nothing of, the fighting on July 2d and 3d, I shall attempt no description of these battles. When I resumed command of my division after July 3d, I heard that General Longstreet said that if Heth's division had done as well as Pickett's the Cemetery Ridge would have been carried.[37] A short time since I asked General Longstreet if he had said this, he replied, ''No, and I never thought it.'' I quote from a letter of Longstreet's to me, ''that your division, with bloody noses after its severe fight of the 1st, was put in to do a great part in the assault of the 3d, was a serious error, and events doubly show that your division should not have been ordered as a part of a column to march a mile under concentrating fires and carry positions held by veterans of four times our numbers, very strongly posted.[38]

I have been frequently requested by officers and soldiers of my division to write an account of the Battle of Gettysburg. I have never done so and do not propose to do so. In writing of the war I made it a rule not to attempt to give an account of what I did not see myself. The statements made by others who participated in the battles of the 2d and 3d of July, 1863,

I cannot affirm or deny. I was rendered unconscious, as I have stated, early in my attack on the Iron Brigade in McPherson Woods on the 1st of July. No encomium of mine can add to the heroic gallantry of my division at Gettyburg on the 1st of July, 1863. Its severe and (I believe) scarcely paralleled losses on that day attest, better than eulogies, its fighting qualities.[39] It never halted in this charge until, I am informed, it was ordered to do so, and the McPherson Woods had been cleared of as fine a body of men as was in the Federal army.

On the 4th, orders were received to retire; we took up the line of march to Hagerstown, reaching there July 7th, and remaining until the 13th. On the night of the 13th we moved in the direction of our pontoon at Falling Waters. This was the most uncomfortable night I passed during the war; it rained incessantly; the roads were eight or ten inches deep in mud and water.

My command brought up the rear of the army; we were compelled to halt every half mile; the road was blocked by wagons, artillery, etc., in our front. On one occasion we were detained two hours; as soon as we were halted the men sought the best shelter they could find,—houses, barns, fencecorners, and dropped to sleep. This could not be prevented as the night was as dark as Erebus, and the rain fell in torrents. A number of men were thus left behind when the march was resumed. About daybreak quite a body of Confederate cavalry passed my command, going in the opposite direction. We reached the heights bordering on the Potomac, where I was directed to halt until everything had passed.[40]

Epaulments had been thrown up for artillery on either side of the road. The men lay down and went to sleep. There was an open field in our front half a mile wide, then a body of woods. I received orders to cross the river; Pender's division, under my command, commenced the movement. As I was about to move my division, a squad of cavalry debouched from the woods in our front and approached my troops.[41] Behind the epaulments mentioned, General Pettigrew and my staff, all mounted, saw them approach. We supposed it was the squad of cavalry that had passed us a few hours before. A United States cavalry flag was displayed. I told one of my staff to arrest the officer in charge of the squad and that I would prefer charges against him for displaying a United States flag. I thought he had had a fight with the Union cavalry and captured a flag, and was flaunting it in our faces, thus running the risk of having his men fired on. About this time the squad had approached within 175 yards of my position, and halted. I heard the officer give the command, "Draw sabers, charge!" They soon passed between the open space separating the epaulments, crying out, "Surrender, you d—— rebels, surrender!" A sergeant passed within a few feet of General Pettigrew and myself. In the melee which occurred, Pettigrew's horse reared and fell; as he was rising from the ground, the Federal sergeant shot him in the groin which proved fatal. The affair was over in less than five minutes; the entire squad was killed, wounded, or captured. My loss was General Pettigrew, and one Tennessee soldier.[42] We now moved towards the river and crossed the pontoon bridge. The following day we continued our march, reaching Orange Court House, where we wintered, 1863-4.

We remained quiet until October, 1863, when General Lee determined to move around General Meade's army, and threaten Washington. Hill's corps struck the Orange and Alexander Railroad at Bristoe Station, October 14, 1863; my division happened to be the leading division of the corps. A Federal corps was occupying this point when we reached Bristoe and was crossing the creek at that point.[43] Our approach hastened the crossing of this corps. There is a railroad cut at this point.[44] Hill, seeing the corps hastening to get out of the way, attributed their rapid retreat solely to his approach, but as it turned out they were hastening their movement to enable another corps, Warren's, to take their position.[45]

Of this Hill was ignorant, and he urged his troops, my division, to attack speedily, fearing, as he said, the retreating corps would escape across the stream without assault. I attacked with two brigades,[46] supplemented by the rest of my division; on reaching the railroad cut I found General Warren's troops occupying it and concealed by the cut. We received a terrific fire from the troops in the cut and were driven back with considerable loss. Generals Cooke and Kirkland, commanding brigades, were both wounded, and my horse was killed. We inflicted but little loss upon the enemy. I also lost some guns.[47]

Warren, the night of the 14th, continued his march towards Manassas Junction. The next day, October 15th, General Lee, General Hill and I rode over the field; Hill was explaining to General Lee the attack made by my division the day previous. Hill assumed all the responsibility of the attack. General Lee's only remark was, addressing Hill, "General, bury your dead." We then returned to Orange Court House, where we remained quiet until drawn out by General Meade crossing the Rapidan and taking up a position at Mine Run,[48] November 26th. General Lee was speedily in his front; we threw up temporary breastworks. General Meade ordered General Warren on December 2d to attack. General Warren made a careful reconnaissance and came to the conclusion, wisely, I think, not to attack our line, and so informed General Meade.[49] Had Warren attacked, his left and left center would have met my division. I was hoping he would attack; in order that I might square accounts with him for his treatment of me at Bristoe Station.

I always classed General Warren among the best of the general officers of the Army of the Potomac. He died from a broken heart, due to the treatment he received after winning the battle of Five Forks, April 1, 1865.[50] It was Warren who, on July 2d, when he arrived on the field of Gettysburg, at once recognized the military value of Little Round Top, and assumed the responsibility of detaching a passing brigade and ordering it to occupy this stronghold on Meade's left flank. Had the Confederates held Little Round Top the battle of the 3d would never have taken place. Meade could not have held his lines along the Cemetery Ridge, the Confederates occupying Little Round Top, as they would have done if left unoccupied. General Meade, receiving General Warren's report of the strength of our lines in his front, withdrew his army, recrossing the Rapidan and resuming his former position.

During the winter of 1863-4, I frequently visited General Lee in his headquarters; on one occasion he said to me, "General Heth, I understand some of my officers have criticised very severely my management at Gettysburg." I replied, "Yes, General, the Battle of Gettysburg has been criticised a great deal." "Well," he said, "all my officers know that I am always pleased for them to come and see me, and I will listen to any suggestions they may have to make, but they do not do so; and as stupid a man as I am can see after a battle is over the mistakes that have been made."

XX

The Federal and Confederate armies remained quiet until May 1864 when General Grant, then in command of the Federal army, commenced his march to capture Richmond. General Grant, knowing the strength of General Lee's army, supposed, when he crossed the Rapidan, that General Lee would retire

to the fortifications around Richmond, and would not dare to
face his large army, but General Lee had no idea of retiring
behind the fortifications of Richmond and standing a siege.
General Lee appears to have reasoned thus: "What will I gain
by retreating? I cannot expect any material gain in strength. This
is as good a time and as good a place to settle this issue as
I can expect to find." General Lee, I have always thought, was
the most belligerent man in his army.

When Grant crossed the Rapidan[1] on the 4th of May, General
Lee took the most direct roads to meet him. Ewell's II Corps
moving on the old turnpike leading to Fredericksburg, Hill's
III Corps on the Plank Road also leading to Fredericksburg,
Longstreet's I Corps moved down the Plank Road[2] but did not
reach the battlefield until after sunrise on the 6th. The leading
division of Hill's corps was Heth's. I struck the enemy at Mine
Run,[3] I think only a strong skirmish line, and drove this force
steadily before me until within four or five hundred yards of
the Brock Road which the enemy held in force. The Brock Road
at this point is perpendicular to the Plank Road. My skirmish
line was unable to drive the enemy's skirmishers any further;
they halted, and, the division coming up, line of battle was
formed.[4] All was quiet for an hour or more.

General Lee sent a staff officer to me, who said, "The
General is desirous that you occupy the Brock Road if you could
do so without bringing on a general engagement." I said, "Say
to the General that the enemy are holding the Brock Road with
a strong force; whether I can drive them from the Brock Road
or not can only be determined by my attacking with my entire
division, but I cannot tell if my attack will bring on a general
engagement or not. I am ready to try if he says attack." This
was between three and four o'clock as I remember. Before the
staff officer reached General Lee my line was assailed at 3:30
p.m. by a strong line of battle. My men were not behind
breastworks; the enemy came within ninety yards of my line.

My entire line now opened a destructive fire, and a very deadly
one it was. The enemy gave way, retiring to the Brock Road.
This attack was made by General Getty's division, VI Army
Corps.[5] When Getty attacked, Hancock's II Corps arrived and
rapidly formed line of battle in my front. The enemy now
attacked me again, and met with the same fate. This was
repeated seven times. General Getty of the Federal Army in
his reports, says, "They (meaning my division) held in the main
their ground and repulsed every attack."[6] Wilcox's division followed my division on May 5th. Ewell's Corps advancing on
the Old Turnpike, struck the enemy sometime before I became
engaged.[7] When Wilcox passed, General Lee was about a mile
from Brock Road and on the Plank Road. Ewell was actively
engaged. General Lee ordered Wilcox to go to Ewell's
assistance. Wilcox had to march a mile or more to reach
General Ewell. Wilcox had hardly put his division in motion
to execute this order when the enemy attacked me. General Lee,
seeing how heavily I was engaged, sent word to General Wilcox
to return to my assistance.

Wilcox rode ahead of his division and reported to me. I told
him I had successfully repulsed seven different attacks of the
enemy; that they had been, I believed, awfully punished, and
I thought the time had come now for us to take a hand in the
attack. As soon as Wilcox formed his line of battle we went
in. This proved to be a mistake on my part. I should have left
well enough alone. We found opposed to us not only Getty's
Division, but Hancock's II Army Corps; we succeeded in capturing a part of the enemy's breastworks, but were soon driven
out. Two divisions attacking five divisions, is hazardous and
apt to be unsuccessful. The enemy followed up their success
and we were driven back some half mile. Night put an end
to the battle of May 5th.

Wilcox's troops and my own were terribly mixed up. Our
men had been marching and fighting all day. Skirmishers were

thrown out; the men lay down and were soon asleep. I went to General Hill who was sick. Seated on a camp stool before his camp fire he said, shaking me by the hand, "Your division has done splendidly today; its magnificent fighting is the theme of the entire army." I replied, "Yes, the division has done splendid fighting, but we have other matters to attend to just now." I described to him the almost inextricable mixing up of Wilcox's troops and my own. "Let me take one side of the road and form line of battle, and Wilcox the other side and do the same; we are so mixed, and lying at every conceivable angle, that we cannot fire a shot without firing into each other. A skirmish line could drive both my division and Wilcox's, situated as we now are. We shall certainly be attacked early in the morning." Hill replied, "Longstreet will be up in a few hours. He will form in your front. I don't propose that your division shall do any fighting tomorrow, the men have been marching and fighting all day and are tired. I do not wish them disturbed."

A second and third time I saw Hill and begged him to order Wilcox to get his men out of the way. Wilcox saw Hill and seconded my efforts. The last time I saw Hill he got vexed and said, "D—— it, Heth, I don't want to hear any more about it; the men shall not be disturbed." The gravity of the situation was such that I determined to lay the matter before General Lee. I hunted for his tent one hour but could not find it. The only excuse I make for Hill is that he was sick.[8]

I walked the road all night; when I imagined I saw the first streak of daylight, I ordered my horse and with half speed rode down the Plank Road to see if Longstreet was coming. I rode two or three miles in the direction of Mine Run. No Longstreet. I hurried back. General Grant, I was informed afterwards, gave Meade orders to attack at daybreak. Meade informed General Grant that he should not be prepared to attack so early. The attack, fortunately for us, was deferred until sunrise.

A cannon was then fired, and the Union troops attacked.[9] I gave orders to my brigade commanders to retire along the Plank Road. It was impossible to fire a shot without firing into my own troops or those of General Wilcox. The regiments hurried to the rear, as did those of Wilcox.[10] In this melee a few men from both divisions were captured. Longstreet now appeared, and forming rapidly, checked the Federal advance. When his troops got in position, he charged and drove the enemy back, almost routing them. They only halted when they reached the Brock Road.

Had Wilcox and I been in line of battle, we could easily have repulsed the advance of the Federals, which would have given Longstreet time to have gotten on the left flank of Meade's attacking force, when Hill's corps could have advanced and, I believed then, and do now, that Grant would have been driven across the Rapidan. It was on this occasion that General Lee seized a regimental flag and was about to lead the regiment to the front, when his aide, Colonel Walter Taylor, took it from him. Men and officers protested against his exposing himself, and he was persuaded to go to the rear.

I think General Lee never forgave Wilcox or me for this awful blunder. When riding with me one day along my lines in front of Petersburg, I explained to him all that occurred between General Hill and myself on the night of the 5th of May. His reply was, "A division commander should always have his division prepared to receive an attack." I said, "That is certainly so, but he must also obey the positive orders of his superior." General Lee made no reply. He knew a splendid opportunity had been lost, one that never occurred again.

On the 7th of May General Grant commenced his movement towards Spottsylvania Court House, but General Lee reached there first. Both armies threw up breastworks, facing each other. My division lay in front of Spottsylvania Court House and held the extreme right of our army. On the 11th of May an angle of my breastworks was vigorously assailed by General Burnside. In front of the point where this attack was made the ground was level for about one hundred yards, then fell off abruptly; the attacking force, or some of them, came within thirty paces of my breastworks; at the same time my infantry poured a shower of lead into Burnside's troops. They were exposed to the raking fire of my artillery on my right, where I had some twenty pieces in position behind the epaulments. The artillery was well handled, using grape and cannister on the attacking force. If I remember correctly, Burnside made three assaults on this angle; each was repulsed with great loss. After this affair terminated and all was quiet, a young lieutenant got on the breastworks and was walking along when he was shot through the head by a sharpshooter. This was the only loss I met with. We counted 300 odd dead in front of our works, which being multiplied by five gives the usual number of wounded in an open field fight, as against seven in a battle in the woods. So we estimated Burnside's loss in this affair at 1800.

That evening General Lee came to the church in Spottsylvania Court House which I occupied as my headquarters. Quite a number of general officers were present, General A. P. Hill among the number. I remember General Grant was being severely criticised by them for throwing his men against our breastworks and having them slaughtered. After all had expressed an opinion General Lee said, "Gentlemen, I think that General Grant has managed his affairs remarkably well up to the present time." Turning to me he said, "My opinion is the enemy are preparing to retreat tonight to Fredericksburg. I wish you to have everything in readiness to pull out at a moment's notice, but *do not disturb your artillery,* until you commence moving. We must attack these people if they retreat."[11] The movement of the troops from Grant's left towards his right caused General Lee to suppose a retreat was contemplated when it was a movement preparatory to General Hancock's attack on

General Edward Johnson's lines the following morning, May 12, 1864, at what is known as the "Bloody Angle."[12]

Johnson often told me that the discomfiture he met with on the morning of May 12th was solely due to the fact that during his absence on his skirmish line all of the artillery defending his works, probably thirty guns, were removed, by whose orders he knew not. My belief is, the order General Lee gave me, to be in readiness to move, but not to move my artillery, when it reached Johnson was perverted into "Move your artillery." When Johnson returned from inspecting his skirmish line, he was convinced the enemy were preparing to attack his front. He found his artillery had disappeared. He at once sent word to General Ewell to return his artillery. When the artillery was sent back, Hancock had pierced Johnson's line and Johnson's artillery was captured before it could get in position. General Johnson and General Steuart[13] were captured. As these officers were being taken to the rear, Hancock rode up and shook hands with his old regimental friend and associate, Ned Johnson. He then offered his hand to Steuart. Steuart refused to take his hand, saying, under the circumstances he must decline to take his hand. Hancock replied, "Under no other circumstances would I have offered it."

When General Lee said in the church, "We must attack these people," Hill said, "General Lee, let them continue to attack our breastworks; we can stand that very well." I said, "General, you witnessed Burnside's attack of me this morning." "Yes," he said, "I did." I then told him my loss and what we had estimated the Federal loss to be. After some remarks, which I do not remember now, the General said, "This army cannot stand a siege; we must end this business on the battlefield, not in a fortified place." I thought at the time, visions of a siege, behind the fortifications of Richmond, were on his mind.[14]

On the 10th of May my division was ordered to take a circuit-ous route and drive the enemy from a position south of the Po and near the bridge crossing that river, not far from the Block House, on what is known as the Block House Road. I found the troops opposed to me to be Hancock's Corps; Hancock in his official report of this affair says that my division was driven back several times with great loss when attacking his troops. This is not my recollection of what occurred. My division was not driven back at any time that I am aware of during this fight, but steadily drove the enemy, until he succeeded in crossing to the north side of the Po on bridges he had erected.[15] Hancock says in his report, page 333, vol. XXXVI, series 1, *Rebellion Records:* "The enemy regarded this a considerable victory and General Heth published a congratulatory order to his troops, endorsed by General Hill and General Lee, praising them for their valor in driving us from our entrenched lines. Had not Barlowe's fine division (then in full strength) received imperative orders to withdraw, Heth's division would have had no cause for congratulations." It was by *General Lee's orders* I published the congratulatory orders to my division.

I then resumed my position in front of Spottsylvania Court House. On the 21st of May, General Grant commenced to move by his left flank. General Lee followed on roads running parallel to Grant's movements. On reaching the North Anna,[16] where both armies maneuvered for position, General Lee was between Grant and Richmond. On the 23d I had an engagement with General Warren but without any decisive results, save checking Warren's further advance.

The III Corps, May 25th, lay entrenched between the North Anna and Little River. On the 27th we commenced to move in the direction of Bethesda church, a few miles from Cold Harbor. Near Bethesda church I struck the IX and V Federal Army Corps. General Early was on my right. As the enemy were withdrawing from my front, preparatory to the grand attack he was to make on June 3d at Cold Harbor, General Early commanding

Ewell's Corps, (Ewell being sick) came to me and said that the enemy were retiring from our front, and that he proposed to attack, and asked me for a brigade to assist him. I told the General I was aware that the enemy was withdrawing from my front, and that I had already given orders to attack; that I would not give, or lend him one of my brigades, but would assist him with the entire division, which would be far better. We drove the enemy to the entrenchments he had thrown up near Bethesda church.

It was determined to attack their entrenchments; this was done. But as Rhodes, of Ewell's Corps, Early's division, failed to advance, my right flank became fearfully exposed and I gave orders to my brigade commanders to fall back. General Kirkland and one of my brigade commanders were wounded in this attack.[17]

On June 12th General Grant commenced his movements to capture Petersburg; General Lee followed, keeping between Grant and Richmond. My division crossed the James River on a pontoon below Chafin's Farm and proceeded to Petersburg.[18] I went into the trenches relieving some troops, my left resting on the spot where the famous Burnside mine was sprung. We remained in this position several weeks and were relieved and held in reserve; no fighting of any consequence occurred in which my division was engaged until 18th, 19th and 21st of August, 1864.

When General Grant determined to operate against Richmond from the south side of the James he ordered General Butler to send a force from his army and occupy Petersburg. Butler sent General W. F. Smith[19] to this duty. General Smith confronted the Confederate pickets at Petersburg before daylight on the 15th of June. The breastworks of that city were held by its citizens; none of the Army of Northern Virginia had at this time reached Petersburg.[20] General Smith, according to Grant's report, did not attack the Confederate lines until nearly sundown, when he carried the line northeast of Petersburg for some distance. After dark, Hancock with two divisions reached Smith. Hancock offered his troops to Smith. Nothing was done. The Federals could have marched into Petersburg with slight resistance. The following morning, the 15th, the Confederates were in force in front of the Federals and Petersburg was saved.

XXI

General Grant's tactics were to extend his lines to the left and occupy the railroads leading into Petersburg, over which General Lee received his supplies. On the 18th of August, 1864, General Grant cut the Weldon and Richmond railroad about two and one-half miles from Petersburg.[1] My division at that time was in reserve. General Hill ordered me to drive the Federals from the point they occupied near the railroad. I attacked the enemy with three brigades, drove them from two lines of breast-works, but could do no more. General Lee and General Hill rode up. The former, waving his hand to General Hill, said, "I think if you will send a force through those woods and strike them on their flank, you will find that flank in the air; at the same time that this force attacks, let General Heth attack as he did yesterday."

Orders to this effect were given. I told General Hill that I had noticed that when an attack of one force was made contingent upon the attack of another, things generally miscarried. So we calculated the distance this flanking force had to march, and as they were to commence their movements at a certain hour, they should certainly be in position by ten o'clock when

I would attack without waiting to hear their guns. At ten o'clock on the 19th, not hearing anything from the flanking party, I went in and drove the enemy from the two lines of breastworks I had carried the day previous.

After carrying the second line, I heard what I took to be skirmishing on my left. I do not think a thousand shots were fired. Soon the flanking force, instead of attacking, marched out of the woods with a large number; 1500 or 1800 prisoners. These prisoners were Federals who had been driven out of the breastworks by my division and in going to the rear had lost their way, and without organization had run into the flanking force. Had the officer in command of this force obeyed his orders and attacked, the entire Federal force on the Weldon road would have been captured. The commander of the flanking column saw that he could withdraw without fighting, having picked up in the woods some 1500 or 1800 fugitives.[2]

A general in the Federal army told me after the war ended that he never during the war was so much alarmed for the safety of his command as he was when the skirmishing commenced on his right; that, had the flanking force advanced, he would have been struck on the flank, and everything on the Weldon road would have been captured. On the 21st another attack was made on the enemy but failed to accomplish anything.[3] With the great and increasing strength of Grant's army, it was impossible for General Lee, with his small force, to prevent General Grant from cutting the Weldon railroad.

During the fight on the Weldon railroad there occurred an act of silly bravery on the part of a young girl worth mentioning. I was about placing some batteries in position near the Davis House on the Weldon road and went to the Davis House to see that the occupants were all away, as this house would be in the direct line of the enemy's fire when my batteries opened. I found in the house a young girl about eighteen. I told her to get out of the house. She seemed in no hurry to do so. In the meantime my batteries came up and I directed the officers where to place them. As soon as they were seen by the enemy, two or three Federal batteries opened. The Davis House was surrounded by a copse of young pine trees. A shell struck the house, the tops and young pines were falling fast, I begged her to hurry and get out of the range of the batteries, and finally got the girl out of the house. I never was before or after, subjected to such a terrible fire of artillery; the tops of the pines fell between us. I told her to run, and pointed out the direction she should take in order to get out of the line of fire. She stopped and with her arms akimbo said, "I will die before I will run." She stood still fully a minute shaking her fist at the Federal batteries and then deliberately walked in the direction I had indicated. She escaped unhurt.

As fast as General Grant could do so he kept extending his left, his objective point now being the Southside Railroad, the only road south of the James by which General Lee could receive supplies. It so happened that from this time to the day General Grant broke through the Confederate lines around Petersburg, my division was on the extreme right of our army. My orders were general, whenever General Grant extended his left, to attack him. I think, in compliance with this order, my division was engaged on an average every ten days from September 1864, to April 3, 1865, the day our lines were broken.

My headquarters during the summer and winter around Petersburg, were at what was known as the Pickeral House, four or five miles from Petersburg on the Boydton Plank Road about one hundred and fifty yards in rear of my breastworks. When we were retiring from the Bristoe affair, October 14, 1864, I camped for a day or two at the house of my uncle, Mr. Richard Cunningham, in Culpepper County; Lavinia, his aged cook, begged to accompany me. She was a great acquisition, a splendid old Virginia cook.

A friend of mine, Major Ficklin, was engaged in running

the blockade.[4] He loaded his steamer with cotton at Wilmington and carried it to Liverpool, returning with supplies most needed by the Confederate government, exchanging these again for cotton; he was very successful, one trip amounting to a fortune. I think he made six or eight successful trips to Liverpool and back. During the winter of 1864-5 Ficklin wrote me if I would send a wagon to Wilmington he would load it with good things. I did so. The wagon was loaded with canned goods, coffee, tea, sugar, hams, twenty gallons of brandy, and the same amount of whiskey, a dozen boxes of fine cigars, etc. By the same wagon he sent me a black horse which was the admiration of the army.

I had my wife and children with me during the winter of 1864-5. When at Orange Court House during the summer of 1863 I purchased a thoroughbred three-year-old Red Eye colt, and a beauty he was. My wife appropriated the Red Eye colt as her own. At reviews she always appeared on this horse. General Lee remonstrated with her for riding this horse, saying it was too spirited for her to ride. She would say to the General that she was not afraid of the horse, and felt she could manage him with ease. My wife, like many Virginia girls, had lived pretty much on horseback since she was ten years old, and was a splendid horsewoman, so I did not share the General's fear of her being injured.

As my division was, I believe, more frequently engaged than any on our lines, General Lee visited my line more frequently than he did others. There was hardly a week that he did not come to my headquarters. He would stop and have a chat with Mrs. Heth and play with my little daughter, filling his pockets with apples and claiming a kiss for each apple he gave her. When leaving he would request me to accompany him to the lines. On one of these rides we came to a point where I had thrown up an earthwork for artillery; the breastworks abutting on this earthwork were not completed, a gap of about six feet remaining to be finished. The General asked me if the gap would be finished that evening. I called my engineer officer and questioned him. He replied that it would be completed that evening. When my engineer officer reported I asked him if the gap had been closed. He said it had been. It appears that the engineer told the sergeant in charge of the working party to complete this work and they could then go to their regiments. He left, and so did the sergeant and his party. The following day General Lee came to my headquarters and as usual proposed a ride down the lines. When we reached the work there was still a gap. He said, "I understood you to say this gap had been closed." "Yes, General, my engineer officer reported to me last night that the work had been done." The General said, "I feel very uneasy about your wife riding that sorrel horse, he is a very spirited animal, and I think it would be well for you to ride him down these lines every day." I understood the reprimand, and felt it. On another occasion at my headquarters, he said, addressing my wife, "I don't think it safe for you to be here; General Grant may break through these lines some day and capture you and your little children, and it would grieve me to hear that General Grant had taken you for his cook."[5] It happened at that very point, our lines were broken and old Lavinia, my cook was captured; my wife had left for her home three days before.

During one of General Lee's visits he had my little daughter on his knee; he was devoted to children, especially little girls. The child said, "General, I want a lock of your hair." He replied, "Oh, no, you don't want any of this grey hair." She said, "No, I want some of yours." He said, "Get a pair of scissors and help yourself." This she did, and cut off a piece of hair as thick as my thumb, and then asked for a button from his vest. This was given her. "Now I am going to wrap these in a piece of paper and you must write your name on it." This he did. As the years have gone, these relics of the past, belonging to the good and great man became more and more precious and are cherished as most valued possessions.

One of my brigades was without a brigadier general. I requested General Lee to recommend Colonel William J. Pegram[6] for promotion and assign him to the brigade. The General answered, "He is too young—how old is Colonel Pegram?" "I do not know, but I suppose about twenty-five." The General replied, "I think a man of twenty-five is as good as he ever will be; what he acquires after that age is from experience; but I can't understand, when an officer is doing excellent service where he is, why he should want to change." "But, General, your officers have nothing to look forward to but promotion." The General said, "I would be delighted if Mr. Davis would find some one to command and relieve me. I would gladly command a regiment or a brigade."

Pegram was never made a brigadier general, but fell at Five Forks April 1, 1865. William J. Pegram was one of the few men who, I believe, was supremely happy when in battle. He was then in his element. I think I said once before that to Colonel Pegram I measurably owed my success at Reams's Station, August 25, 1864.[7] When I was going into battle, I always applied for Colonel Pegram's battalion of artillery to accompany me. His battalion fired the first shot that opened the battle of Gettysburg, July 1, 1863.

I went to General Lee's headquarters on one occasion on a matter of business and found him walking up and down his room; he asked me to be seated. Continuing his walk, he suddenly stepped in front of me and said, "General Heth, I am always pleased to see my officers and to listen to any suggestions they may have to make, but when they come and read me a manuscript of thirty pages containing nothing that I did not know before, I don't like it; my time is valuable." I said, "General, I have never read you thirty pages, or one page of manuscript." "No, you have not, but did you not meet General

Wise as you rode in?'' ''Yes, General, I met him at the gate.''
''Well, General Wise has been here for two hours, reading from
a manuscript to me, and it did not contain an idea I did not
know before. What shall I do with General Wise?'' I said,
''Send him to command one of the forts around Richmond.''
The General replied, ''Oh, no, that would never do, Mr. Davis's time is quite as valuable as my own.'' He then said, ''How
would it do to send him to fight it out with Chevalier Wicoff?
I believe he is somewhere in South America.'' On one occasion
when accompanying General Lee, riding down our lines, he
said, ''How can we carry on this war without additional men?''
I replied, ''The only solution of that problem that I know is
to put the negroes in the army.'' The General replied, ''I recommended that some time since, but to do so was not considered
advisable.''

During the latter part of March, Grant commenced his last
and successful flank movement to his left. He made a lodgement
on the Boydtown Plank Road near Burgess's Mill. On April
1, 1865, the battle of Five Forks was fought.[8] On the 2d of
April, General Wright ran over my weak lines; three of my
four brigades were taken out of the works on the 1st of April,
to meet the Federal force on the Boydtown Plank Road. The
works held by my division were now held by one small brigade.
There were not as many men behind the breastworks as there
were in the rifle pits in front of the works. General Wright had
a walkover. He swept down the vacated breastworks to Hatcher's Run.[9] Petersburg was evacuated by General Lee, April 3d,
and the Confederate army, without food, took up its march to
Appomattox Court House, where General Lee surrendered a
famished regiment of his once great army, April 9, 1865.

Several incidents worth mentioning occurred after the surrender of Appomattox Court House. On one of my marches in 1864
I saw on the roadside the running gear of an abandoned one-
horse vehicle. I directed one of my couriers to remain with

this relic and attach it to my headquarters wagon and bring it to camp. I had the wagon repaired, a body made for it, and covered with thick canvas. This was all done at my own expense. I considered this wagon as my private property. I wrote a note to General Seth Williams, General Grant's Adjutant General, and asked whether or not I would be permitted to take my effects home in this wagon. He replied that my note had been referred to the commanding general, who decided that I could not have the wagon. Not in a very good humor, I lay down in my ambulance to take a nap. I had not slept for three nights. I was about falling asleep when I heard the rattling of sabres outside and my name called. I arose and recognized Seth Williams and Rufus Ingalls, chief quartermaster of Grant's army. General Williams said, pointing to the small wagon, "Heth, is that the thing you have been writing about?" "Yes," I said, "and I hope it will be as useful to your army as it has been to me." He replied, "Old fellow, I had to answer your note as I did. The General thought it might establish a bad precedent. Have you any good ambulances in your division?" I said, "Yes." "Any good mules?" I said I had some splendid mules. Williams said, "Take the best ambulance, and hitch to it four of the best mules you have and go home in style." Turning to General Ingalls, he said, "That will be all right, Rufus, will it not?" General Ingalls replied, "Yes, take a half dozen if you wish." I was not slow in availing myself of this permission and I have always thought General Grant sent Seth Williams and Rufus Ingalls, both of whom were old friends, on this errand. I did not take six, but did take one, and four splendid mules, which, on arriving at my home, I turned over to my father-in-law, and it enabled him to make a crop that year.

XXII

The day of the surrender I went to General Grant's headquarters on some business. General Grant shook me by the hand most cordially and said, "Come into this room; I want to talk to you." We took seats. Grant asked, "Heth, do you remember when we were last together?" "In St. Louis, I believe in 1852." The General said, "Yes, and do you remember how near I came to breaking my neck and yours?" "Yes; it would have made little difference, as far as history is concerned if you had broken my neck, and now, as our troubles are at an end, I am glad that you got through safely; but, Grant, during the past three years I have wished a thousand times you had broken your neck when you ran into that cow." Grant laughed and said, "We went to Jefferson Barracks, did we not?" I replied, "We did." "Do you remember anything that occurred when we were at the barracks?" "No, nothing special." "Well," said Grant, "do you remember who were at the barracks on that occasion, I mean what officers were there?" "I remember some of then.. General Clarke, commanding the department; McDowell, adjutant general;[1] Hancock, adjutant of the Sixth Infantry; Bragg[2] with his battery; I don't remember now who the others were." "Yes," said Grant, "we called on all of them, did we not?" "Yes." "And you remember nothing special that occurred?" "I do not." "Well," said Grant, "I do: *not one of those fellows asked us to take a drink.*"

We chatted for half an hour about old times, kissing the beautiful girls in the army, about Mexico, our trip to Popocatepetl, but our war was not once referred to. Before leaving I said, "Your recollection of what occurred when we visited Jefferson Barracks in 1852 reminds me of the fact that we have not met for thirteen years, and that we have been chatting here for half an hour, and that you have not asked me once to take a drink. I have not had one for three months." He laughed and said, "I have nothing here to drink, but if you will send your orderly with mine, you will find something to drink at your quarters when you reach them." On my return I found two gallons of good whiskey in my ambulance.

On the 12th of April I reached my home on the James River, twenty miles above Richmond. The terms of our parole were somewhat indefinite. We were to go to our homes and remain there until regularly exchanged and not to be disturbed so long as we obeyed the laws in force in the States where we resided. Did this parole confine us *strictly to our homes*? I wished to visit St. Louis, Missouri. I wrote to my old friend and classmate Augustus H. Seward, U.S.A., stationed in Washington, and asked him to get me permission to visit St. Louis. He replied that it could not be granted. After some months had elapsed I found that those similarly situated as I was were going where they pleased and were not molested, so I went to St. Louis and stopped at the Southern Hotel.

I had not more than entered the room assigned me when there was a knock at the door and a soldier walked in saying that General Pope,[3] who was in command in St. Louis at the time, wished to see me. I packed my valise, followed my captor, and, depositing my valise at the office, accompanied the soldier to General Pope's office. I had known General Pope before the war. I wondered to what jail I would be consigned. On entering General Pope's office he arose, and smilingly approached and shook me by the hand, telling me how glad he was to see me, and that he wished to show me some correspondence which had taken place between General Halleck and himself. I was happy.

General Pope said, "You doubtless remember how unmercifully your papers pitched into me on account of an alleged dispatch of mine to General Halleck when I was in command near Corinth, saying I had driven the enemy twenty miles, captured

10,000 prisoners, artillery, etc?"[4] "Yes," I said, "I remember that very well, and that our papers gave you hail Columbia." Pope said, "That dispatch was a fabrication of Halleck's. I never sent such a dispatch to him. I did not propose to have any controversy with Halleck during the war, but determined to wait until it was ended and then to put myself right; so I wrote him this note."

The purport of Pope's note to Halleck was denying that he had ever sent him such a dispatch, and requesting Halleck to furnish him with a copy. Halleck replied that he had never sent a dispatch from him, Pope, to Washington that had not been received from him; that his papers were all packed away, and he should leave the following day for New York, en route to San Francisco. General Halleck remained some weeks in New York before leaving for San Francisco. Pope wrote a second note to Halleck, referring to the fact of his being six weeks in New York and again demanding a copy of the alleged dispatch. Pope denounced Halleck as the biggest liar in the army. I recollect that prior to the war John Pope enjoyed among his army associates the same reputation which he ascribed to General Halleck. I never heard how this controversy was settled.

When returning home I stopped in Baltimore for a few days at Barnum's Hotel. The day I arrived, a friend at the hotel asked me if I knew General Hancock. I told him I did. He said his office was only a few doors from the hotel where I would find him. I at once went to Hancock's office. He was in command of the troops in and around Baltimore. I never received a more cordial greeting. He asked me if I was afraid to come to his house and make it my home when in Baltimore. "Afraid! if I was not afraid of you on the 5th of May, 1864, nor at Reams Station August 25, 1864, why should I be now?" "Oh! I do not mean that, but what would your people say if you stopped with me?'' ''As to that I don't care a pinch of snuff what they say. I shall choose my friends without asking their permission; the war is over.''

My satchel was taken to his house, where I had a charming visit for two or three days. The first night I spent at Hancock's he asked how our monied accounts stood. I had no idea. I supposed I owed him something, and if I did, I could pay then. ''The boot is on the other leg,'' he said, ''I owe you a thousand dollars.'' ''It is very kind of you, and a delicate way of offering me a thousand dollars. I have money sufficient just now for my needs, and if I am ever forced to borrow money, I will apply to you. I have never borrowed money and never expect to; I will get something to do soon.''

''Excuse me, Heth, a moment, and I will prove to you that I owe you a thousand dollars.'' He returned very soon with an account book. In the early fifties, when stationed on the Arkansas River, I got a leave, intending to spend it in St. Louis. I had accumulated about a thousand dollars. Suddenly the Indians broke out at or near my post, and I was ordered to return immediately to my company. Hancock had said a great deal about buying lots in St. Louis and the opportunity of making money that offered. He had invested himself. I told Hancock before leaving that I wanted him to take the money and buy a lot for his baby, Russell. This he declined, but insisted upon purchasing a lot for me. After reaching my post he informed me of the purchase (a lot) in my name and asked me to send him pay accounts to complete the payment. I found a regular debit and credit account had been kept, and he handed me a note he made in my favor, endorsed by his father-in-law, Mr. Russell. Mr. Russell died some years before the war. Hancock had used as much of the money as was necessary to complete the payments on the lot; the balance he borrowed, the interest on which he used, or as much as was necessary, to pay taxes on my lot, crediting me with the balance. But for his kindness my lot would have been sold for taxes. During the past four years we had been trying our best to kill each other—another commentary upon civil war.

Soon after the war ended, I received a letter from my dear friend and classmate, General Burnside, requesting me to come to New York. I found him at the Fifth Avenue Hotel. Some time elapsed before I was shown to Burnside's room. On entering, he locked the door, threw his arms around me, and it was quite fifteen minutes before either of us uttered a word. Burnside said, "Heth, what are you going to do?" I replied, "I do not know, I intend to pitch into the first thing that offers, whereby I can make an honest living." He then said, "Your father at one time owned and worked coal mines near Richmond. How would you like to go into coal, buy or rent a piece of coal land, and work it?" I said that would suit me better than anything I could think of.

A tract of land on the James River was leased for twenty years, a royalty to be paid on the coal mined.[5] When this arrangement was completed, Burnside said to me, "Now I will go into this with you on one condition. I am Governor of Rhode Island; that occupies but little of my time; I am also president of the Providence Locomotive Works; that takes up some of my time, but every spare moment is taken up in building a railroad from Vincennes to Cairo, so I can't give my leisure to this coal enterprise. You must manage it. The only thing I promise to do is to *honor your drafts for what you may require to carry on the work.*" The coal enterprise was not a success; whether it was that the price of coal was too low, or we had to contend with too much water, or bad judgment, I can't say. Probably all entered into making it a failure. The price of coal at that time was barely sufficient to pay for mining. After a trial of two years the enterprise was abandoned.

Burnside then procured for me the appointment of special agent in the Treasury Department, and I was sent to Brownsville, Texas, near the mouth of the Rio Grande. I found at Fort Brown the 20th Infantry. I had letters to some of the officers stationed at Fort Brown, and my old friend General Sykes was in command,[6] a splendid man, a fine officer, and much beloved by his regiment and army associates. The country north of Brownsville was a hunter's paradise. I am almost afraid to mention a bag of game General Sykes and I made on one occasion, and would not, but there are so many of the 20th now living who know the facts that I will not hesitate to state the results of a day's shooting.

A party was made up for a week's hunt—General Sykes, Captains John C. Bates and Bradley, Lieutenants Lord, Hammer, Rodman and Huston[7] and possibly others, and the writer. These hunts were conducted very differently from those to which I had been accustomed when in the U. S. Army. We had an escort of eight or ten cavalrymen, two wagons, an ambulance and a buckboard, two hospital tents, wall tents, a cooking stove—in a word, everything necessary for a luxurious time. We went about twenty miles north of Brownsville, selected a beautiful camping ground; before daybreak the younger gentlemen of the party were off for deer, which were found in great numbers in the chapparal.

General Sykes and I took it leisurely, got our breakfast, and in thirty or forty acres around our camp could have shot partridges all day. When tired of shooting partridges, we would go into the marshes adjacent to the lakes, which abutted, and shoot jack snipe. The lakes were filled with ducks and every variety of wild geese I had ever seen, and some that I had never seen. We shot geese, brant and ducks until we were tired, then got into the buckboard and drove through a body of woods.

When driving along a wood road a band of peccary crossed

in front of us. We slipped into our guns, buckshot cartridges, and knocked over a couple of peccary, then loaded for turkeys, got out of our wagon and had not gone twenty steps when a deer jumped up, at which we both fired and did not stop him. We bagged several turkeys.

On returning to camp the dogs came to a dead point. Sykes said, "Suppose we empty our guns at these partridges; you remain here, and I will go on the other side of the small clump of chapparal, and if the birds fly in my direction, I will get a shot and if in yours you will have a crack at them." Sykes with the dogs went on the farther side of the chapparal; the dogs trembling with excitement went into the chapparal and up jumped a wild cat. It ran directly towards me. When within a few yards from me I fired, and it fell dead. Here was a bag of game which I challenge to be beaten in one day's hunt—partridges, jack snipes, geese, brant, ducks, peccary, turkeys, a wildcat, and a shot at a deer. Should this be doubted by any one, I refer the doubting Thomas to that model gentleman and soldier, Colonel John V. Bates, of the Second Infantry, then a captain in the 20th Infantry, whom I hope to see soon promoted to a brigadier general in the U. S. Army;[8] also to Major William H. Hammer, paymaster, U. S. Army who is the crack deer hunter in the army, a splendid man in every respect.

The only drawback to this hunters' paradise is the climate; the game killed must be consumed very soon, or it spoils from the excessive heat. On my second hunt I took out part of a sack of salt and salted down the deer hams, thus preserving them.

My special duty at Brownsville was to watch for smugglers. I became well acquainted with the ladies whose husbands were stationed at Fort Brown. Frequently I was asked by some of them if I would like to go to Matamoras, a Mexican town opposite Brownsville. I usually consented. They did their

shopping in Matamoras. When crossing the ferry over the Rio
Grande they would ask me to help them with their bundles.
I found out before leaving Brownsville that these dear creatures
were using me, an officer of the Government, sent to
Brownsville to prevent smuggling, as the medium by which they
could smuggle small packages across the river. I do not suppose
the duty on all the packages I ever took across the river would
have amounted to twenty-five cents, but they had their fun all
the same. I came to the conclusion that women were natural
born smugglers; for the sake of smuggling they would go over
the river to Matamoras and pay fifty cents for an article that
they could purchase on our side of the river, in Brownsville,
for forty. My stay at Fort Brown was rendered very pleasant
by the kindness received from the officers of the 20th Infantry,
among whom were my dear friends, Lieutenants (now Captains)
Rodman, Huston and Maize,[9] Lieutenant Lord and others.

The Secretary of the Treasury, Mr. Sherman,[10] was desirous
of the nomination for President and in order to strengthen his
chances could tolerate no Democrat in office; so I lost my place.
I was then appointed to do some work in the State of South
Carolina, on the Waccamaw River; my station was Georgetown,
S. C., where I spent three very happy years.[11] When Mr. Cleveland became president, Secretary Lamar appointed me special
Indian Agent in the Interior Department.[12] My duty was to
inspect Indian agencies and Indian schools. This duty caused
me to visit all the Indian agencies in the west. When Mr. Harrison was elected President, I, in common with other Democrats,
lost my place as a matter of course.[13] At the request of the
Superintendent of the Census I was asked to take the census
of the Indians in Washington and Oregon.[14]

I happened to be in New York in 1880, soon after Hancock
was nominated by the Democratic Party for President. I spent
several days with him at Governor's Island. The principal topic

of conversation related to our Civil War, but knowing how sensitive he was about the battle of Reams Station, August 25, 1864, we never touched on that. In the history of II Corps, Hancock's Corps, which was in the engagement at Reams Station, I find:

It is not surprising that General Hancock was deeply stirred by the situation, for it was the first time he had felt the bitterness of defeat during the war. He had seen his troops fail in their attempt to carry the entrenched positions of the enemy, but he had never before had the mortification of seeing them driven, and his lines and guns taken, as on this occasion. Never before had he seen his men fail to respond to the utmost when he had called upon them personally for a supreme effort, nor had he ever before ridden towards the enemy, followed by a beggarly array of a few hundred stragglers who had been gathered together and again pushed toward the enemy. He could no longer conceal from himself that his once mighty corps retained but the shadow of its former strength and vigor. Riding up to one of his staff in Werner's battery, covered with dust and begrimed with powder and smoke, he placed his hand upon his Staff officer's shoulder, and said, "Colonel, I do not care to die, but I pray to God that I may never leave this field."

Again I have read that if Hancock's heart could have been examined there would have been written on it "REAMS," as plainly as the deep scars received at Gettysburg and other fields were visible."[15]

We cannot always expect to be successful in war. Hancock was sensitive and had much laudable ambition: General Meade, commanding the Army of the Potomac, wrote to Hancock the day of the battle, August 25, 1864:

Dear General:

No one sympathizes with you more than I do in the misfortune of this evening. ——— I am satisfied that you and your command have done all in your power, and though you have met with a reverse, the honor and escutcheon of the old Second is as bright as ever. —— Don't let this matter worry you, because you have given me every satisfaction.

Truly yours,
George G. Meade,
Major General.[16]

Major General Hancock,
Commanding Second Corps.

When taking leave of Hancock I said to him, "Of course you will be elected President, and I wish you to make a promise." He interrupted me and said, "Heth, I have made it a rule, by which I shall be governed, to make no promises. There was a Major General in my Corps, one of the best in the army, who wants me to appoint him ambassador. I will not do it, for I do not think he would fill creditably the position he asks, and I am determined to appoint no man to office that I do not believe qualified to fill it. I have told you that I intended to look out for you and I shall do so."

I said, "I am not after an appointment; the promise I wish you to make me is something personal to yourself. When you become President of the United States, you will have a great deal of entertaining to do. You will have to entertain crowned heads possibly, or those that are to wear crowns, the Justices of the Supreme Court, Senators and distinguished people. I want you to promise me at these functions *not to mash your potatoes.*" "To the devil with you and your potatoes," was his reply.

XXIII

After the war when mining coal in Virginia on the James River, my family suffered much from chills and fevers; to eradicate the malaria I sent them to the Rockbridge Baths and Springs.[1] General Lee and some of his family arrived at the Springs the day my wife and children reached there, and at General Lee's request Mrs. Heth was assigned to his table in the dining room. General Lee was the embodiment of order and punctuality. When the bell rang for meals the General was one of the first to enter the dining room; his daughter, Miss Agnes,[2] was not infrequently late. One morning at breakfast, Miss Agnes was late. The General said to her, "Miss Agnes, there is a family in this part of the country, Harman by name, and they take their breakfast by candle light every morning. How would you like to marry one of the Harman boys? Then I think you would be ready for your meals." Miss Agnes blushed and blushed, but said nothing.

Mrs. Heth was late for breakfast one morning. She was ashamed to meet General Lee, so concluded to wait and take breakfast at the second table with the children and nurses. This also occurred at dinner that day, and she adopted the same tactics rather than face the general. As she opened her cottage door going to dinner, whom should she meet at her door but General Lee, who said, "I did not see you at breakfast this morning, nor at dinner. I was afraid you or some of your dear children were sick, and I came to enquire after you." Mrs. Heth said, "General, to tell you the truth, I was late for breakfast, and again for dinner, and I was ashamed to meet you." The General replied, "Madam, my habits of order and punctuality were learned from my mother"—a pertinent and just reminder to a young mother; Mrs. Heth says she remembered it and has ever tried to profit by it.

In 1877 I was in business in Richmond, Virginia.[3] I received a letter from my old friend General Burnside, who was then one of the senators from Rhode Island, asking me to make him a visit in Washington. His wife had died some months previous, and he thought that a visit from me would do him good. I went to Washington and remained with him some two or three weeks; mentally he was in a bad way. He told me that in walking from the avenue to the capitol, which he did every day for exercise, frequently his wife was as much by his side as she ever was when living; he added, "You know I am no spiritualist. I have asked my friends on the committees to throw as much work upon me as possible." He would work until two o'clock at night upon committee business and then, walking in a restless way about the room, he would see a piece of silver, china, or something that reminded him of his wife, when he would break down completely and throw himself on the lounge where I was reclining, throw his arms around my neck, and cry like a child.

I tried in every way I knew to console him. One night after one of these paroxysms, he jumped up and said, "Heth, I tell you what we want." "What is it?" He replied, "A dinner party." "Why did we not think of that before." "How do you get on with Grant, Sherman, and the old fellows you knew before the war?" I said, "Just as well as if there had been no war." "Well," he said, "We will have them all here to dine." In a few days the function came off. General Grant was not there; he was ill; General Sherman, Parke,[4] Van Vliet, Warren and all the old ones in Washington we knew were present, and several senators. As I remember some fourteen or fifteen made up the party. We sat down to dinner at seven and got through about *three o'clock*. The Florida War, the Mexican War, and finally our Civil War formed the topics talked over.

I was seated next to General Sherman; some incident connected with our war was discussed, when Sherman turned to me and good naturedly said, "Heth, but you damned rebels did so and so on that occasion." I said, "Stop, Sherman, and think, if there are two men in the world that should go on their knees and thank the Almighty for raising up the rebels, those two men are Grant and yourself; but for the rebels you would now be teaching school in the swamps of Louisiana[5] and Grant would be tanning bad leather at Galena." Sherman placed his hand on my shoulder and said, "That is so, old fellow."

A short time after the Federal dinner party, Burnside said, "Heth we must now have a Confederate dinner party, and you make out a list of your Confederate friends and I will invite them." So, Ran Tucker,[6] Generals Ransom,[7] Gordon,[8] Bev Robertson,[9] Field,[10] and many others composed the party. We had a delightful time, the dinner lasting about as long as the Federal dinner and quite as much champagne and punch were consumed.

During the summer of 1874 General John B. Hood and I were requested to go to Canada by the insurance company we were working for, and report upon the advisability of establishing our company in the Canadian Dominion. We stopped for a week at the Queen's Hotel near the mouth of the Niagara river. We found Generals Joe Hooker (retired), and Dick Taylor at the Queen's; I knew General Taylor before the war and had read in our papers much about his reception by the Prince of Wales during his recent visit to England, and of his visits to Sandringham, a guest of the future King of England.[11] General Taylor was one of the most accomplished men I ever met; he had been a great reader, and remembered what he read, thoroughly posted in politics, science, art, finance, and the current literature of the day, and was the most charming raconteur I ever encountered.

I was anxious to hear him give an account of his visits (two a week each) at Sandringham. One evening we were seated in front of the Queen's Hotel enjoying our cigars and I asked him to give me an account of his visits to Sandringham. I will give, as nearly as I can recollect, a description of his visit to the Prince of Wales.

He commenced by saying, "When you are admitted into the house of an English nobleman you are treated precisely as you would be in the house of a Virginia, South Carolina or Louisiana gentleman. When I was asked by the Prince of Wales to make him a visit of a week at Sandringham, I went with my servant to the depot nearest Sandringham, where one of the Prince's carriages met me. I was driven to the Palace. When the carriage stopped, the Prince came out and gave me a cordial welcome and we entered the palace. He took me to a room and presented me to his wife, then said, "General, probably you would like to walk to your room;" he conducted me himself.

"General, as you are a soldier I thought it would interest you to see these prints which I have had hung up; they were sent to me by my brother-in-law, the Crown Prince of Prussia,[12] and represent the battles of the Prusso-Austrian War; there is a libretto on the table which gives a short account of the battles fought. Don't make any change in your dress, we dine at seven o'clock; when you are ready, come down and the princess will give you some luncheon." The luncheon consisted of tea, chops, sherry, etc.

After lunch the princess said, "Would you like to walk around the rooms and see the statuary and paintings?" I accompanied Her Royal Highness. I noticed in every room a taper burning. She said, "I see you are wondering why tapers are burning in each room; the prince is a great smoker and I wish him to have a light for his cigar when he desires to smoke."

The only formality I perceived was when going to dinner. The guests, and there were usually some half dozen, assembled in a large room adjoining the dining room. Five minutes before dinner the prince and princess would enter this room, and the guests unknown to the princess would be presented to her. The folding doors would be thrown open and dinner announced. The prince, conducting the princess, would lead the way, and the guests followed. When seated, the prince opened the conversation, and then matters were conducted as at any gentleman's table. The prince informed me that since he has taken charge of Sandringham, the revenue from the estate has increased some five to ten thousand pounds. He showed me a set of books which he kept himself, and they were admirably kept. The questions he put to the workman on the road and elsewhere showed practical ability. I came to the conclusion that he was a good business man. During my second and last visit to Sandringham, as I was leaving, I said to the princess that I supposed that I should never meet her again. She said, "It will be your own fault if you do not; I shall be in London during the winter and will be glad to have you call and see me."

There is a club in London of which the Prince of Wales is ex officio president. To be admitted as a member of this club a person's name must be up for twenty years; a father puts up the name of his son when a few years old, and if there is no objection raised against him at the proper time, he is balloted for and admitted. The Prince of Wales, as president, has the authority to nominate two each year as members. The year Dick Taylor was in London the prince nominated Lord Wolseley[13] and General Taylor. General Taylor was famed for his magnificent game of whist. On one occasion the Prince of Wales was playing whist at the club and lost the game by a bad play. Dick Taylor was looking on and noticed the mistake the prince had made; nothing was said by the parties in the game, but the

prince saw they thought he had played badly. The prince turned
to General Taylor and said, "General Taylor, do you not think
I played correctly?" Dick said, "I think, Your Royal Highness,
it was the d——d meanest play I ever witnessed." The prince
laughed as did the others.

When the prince is invited to dine and accepts the invitation,
a list of the guests he is to meet is sent him, and he is expected
to strike from it any name he chooses. To these functions Dick
Taylor was always invited. On one occasion he accompanied
the Prince in his brougham to some place in London. The
brougham was dismissed; pretty late at night Dick accompanied
the prince on foot, to the entrance of his palace; when en route
they were persecuted by two girls; they tried to avoid them but
the girls were persistent; on reaching the entrance to the palace
the sentinels gave the usual salute; seeing this, one of the girls
turned to the other and said, "My God, Sal. it is the Prince."
They caught hold of their skirts and scampered for dear life.

Dick Taylor said soon after the arrival of the princess in London, he called to see her and had a charming visit. In due course
of time he called again. When playing whist at the club one
evening, after his second call upon the princess, he was asked
by a gentleman to let him have a few minutes conversation with
him when he had finished his game. They went into an adjoining room, when the gentleman said, "You are aware I am the
Lord Chamberlain to Her Royal Highness and the Princess of
Wales, and I assure you, General, there is no man in England
that has a higher admiration for you than I have, but it becomes
my duty to say to you that it is not customary for gentlemen
to call on Her Royal Highness as you have done." Dick Taylor
said, "Of course, I had to shield the lady; I could not say that
my visits were made on her invitation; so I apologized and
excused myself, owing to my Republican ignorance of what was
due to Royalty." Dick, in continuing this part of his narrative

said, "I did not intend this should end without mentioning the matter to the Prince of Wales, so the first opportunity that presented itself, I said to the prince I was sorry to have made this blunder, but that he must attribute it to my ignorance." He replied, "Oh, you American gentlemen are so fascinating that we have to guard against you."

From the Queen's Hotel Hood and I went to Toronto. We were invited by Mr. Coburn, President of the Upper Toronto College, to dine with him.[14] When dinner was half over a gentleman walked in, who Mr. Coburn introduced as Mr. Smith. The topic of conversation, when Mr. Smith took his seat, was our Civil War. Soon Mr. Smith joined in the conversation; no one was anxious to talk after he began; we were all attentive listeners. Mr. Smith was as well posted on our battles as either General Hood or myself; he had evidently made a careful study of our Civil War, and was accurate as to dates and all details. Who could this Mr. Smith be? He turned out to be Goldwin Smith,[15] the former professor of history at Oxford, England, and then holding some office under the Canadian Government, a man of great research and erudition. Mr. Smith said, "I wish to relate to you a piece of unwritten history connected with your Civil War, which, probably you have not heard. You are aware of the fact that England and France agreed that when the time came to recognize the Southern Confederacy, their action should be simultaneous. Napoleon III was tired of this arrangement, and he determined to act alone; orders were about being issued for his fleet to assemble in the Gulf of Mexico when he would recognize the Confederacy and raise the blockade;[16] when this was on the point of consummation General Lee surrendered.

General Lee, as I have before said, not excepting Jackson, was the most aggressive man in his army. No one ever went to General Lee and suggested an aggressive movement who was not listened to attentively, and if convinced that there was a remote chance of striking the enemy a blow, was not permitted to make the attempt. On one occasion I went to the General and requested permission to make an attack on the enemy's line about a mile from where they rested on Hatcher's run. He consented and said, "I will send Gordon to assist you."

General Gordon and I were riding down the Boydtown Plank Road to a point where a wood road turned off which we had to follow in order to reach the point where the attack was to be made. In the angle, between the Boydtown Plank Road and the wood road was an abandoned school house; I halted here awaiting the arrival of the head of the column. Gordon's staff and couriers and my own were, of course, with us. General Gordon said to me, "We are about to go into battle and if there is no objection, I propose we go into this school house and have prayers." Gordon ordered his staff and couriers into this house, as I did my own. I looked down the road and saw one of my aides, my brother, talking to a friend; I called to him and said, "Go into that house." He put his hand up to his mouth and replied so that all could hear him, *"Thank you, Brother Henry, I have just had one."*

I remember in this battle, Pegram's battalion of artillery coming into battery, Pegram on his horse among his guns as unmoveable as a statue, and giving his orders as though he was on parade and no shot and shell were whistling around his guns; and I recall also the appearance of that "Little Game Cock," Gordon McCabe,[17] swinging his cap around his head cheering his men, and like his chief, happiest when in battle.

As the years roll by the grand central figure of our war becomes more and more conspicuous and future generations will place him as a general in the fore rank, beside Alexander, Hannibal, Caesar, Wellington and Napoleon. Robert E. Lee is so far ahead of our other soldiers that our war produced that it appears a travesty to institute a comparison; yet our Civil War developed many splendid soldiers. "When God made Lee, he rested himself."

XXIV

I have been requested to give my impression of the character of the Indians with whom I was so long associated and to say more about their customs and habits. It is needless to say that the wild nomads of the plains of America have greatly changed since the disappearance of the buffalo and their compulsory residence on Indian reservations, it will be a mere question of time when they will disappear; that baneful and sure destroyer of human life contracted from the white man is in their blood; this, accelerated by fire water, will hasten their disappearance. I suppose that any facts relating to these people, who, less than four hundred years ago, were the undisputed owners of the continent of North America, will be read with interest by the archeologists and indeed by many others who are interested in the betterment of these people.

The Indian tribes of the plains differ greatly; the Sioux and the Cheyennes are virtuous, they are fine looking, brave and manly. The Arapahoes, Pawnees and Kiowas were immoral and badly diseased.[1]

My experience among the Indians convinced me that if you treat Indians fairly, are firm with them, never deceive them, never make a promise to them that you cannot fulfill, they will be your friends; once break your word with an Indian, and he will never trust you again; you have made an enemy for life. I have often heard it said that no treaty made with Indians by our government had ever been carried out; this is an exaggeration. I will give, to me, the greatest injustice perpetrated on Indian tribes in which, unwittingly, the treaty-making power of our government became badly involved.

Before Alaska was purchased, possibly now, the most valuable fishery in the United States was the Columbia River in Oregon. Several bands of Indians occupied the country adjacent to the Columbia River, controlling the fishing rights of this stream. For centuries these Indians had obtained their food supply by taking salmon from this river. The salmon of the Columbia river as food was to these Indians what the buffalo were to the nomads of the great plains of America, or bread is to the white man. In 1855 the white man appears on the scene; he sees that taking salmon in the Columbia River may be made a most valuable franchise. The first step is to remove the Indians on the Columbia to some other point; a treaty is made with these Indians, concluded June 25th, 1855, and ratified April 18th, 1859, by which they agree to cede to the United States all their right and title to the country claimed by them bordering upon the Columbia River and move to a tract of land seventy miles south, known now as the Warm Springs Reservation; but the Indians required the following clause to be inserted in the treaty:

Provided also That the exclusive right of taking fish in the streams running through and bordering said reservation, is hereby secured to said Indians, and at all other usual and accustomed stations in common with citizens of the United States, and of erecting suitable houses for curing the same;

also the privilege of hunting, gathering roots and berries and pasturing their stock on unclaimed land in common with citizens is secured to them. . . .[2]

This continued for ten years; the whites found that taking salmon from the Columbia river was a rich bonanza; means must be taken to prevent the poor Indians from participating in this bonanza. In 1865 we find that I. W. Perit Huntington, Superintendent of Indian Affairs in Oregon, acting Commissioner, on behalf of the United States, made a supplemental treaty with these Indians. Under Mr. Cleveland's first Administration, as a special agent of the Indian Bureau, I had charge of the Warm Springs Reservation for several months, and I became well acquainted with the Indians on this reservation. It appeared that I. W. Perit Huntington promised the whites interested in salmon fishing on the Columbia River (there can be little doubt for a consideration) that he would arrange it so that in the future the Warm Spring Indians would be prohibited from interfering with them by taking salmon from that river.

At that time the Snake Indians of Oregon were at war with the whites. Huntington visited the Warm Springs Reservation, called the Indians together in council and stated to them that the Snake Indians were on the war path and that the whites who were hunting for the Snakes would be unable to distinguish them from Snake Indians, and they risked being shot as Snakes; this could be avoided by their consenting and signing a paper to the effect that they would not leave their reservation without a written pass from their agent. This pass, in the event of their meeting whites when not on their reservation, they would wave to the whites, who would thus know that they were friendly; to this the Warm Springs Indians readily agreed. Huntington now obtained the signatures of the Indians on a separate sheet to this agreement duly witnessed by the interpreters and three other witnesses.

A forged treaty containing the following claim was now prepared and the signatures of the Indian witnesses appended thereto; the clause in question read as follows:

Article 1[3]

It having become evident from experience that the provision of Article 1, of the treaty of the twenty-fifth of June, A.D. eighteen hundred and fifty-five, which permits said confederated tribes to fish, hunt gather berries and roots, pasture stock and erect houses on lands outside of reservations and which have been ceded to the United States, is often abused by the Indians to the extent of continuously residing away from the reservation and is detrimental to the interest of both Indians and whites; therefore it is hereby stipulated and agreed, that all the rights enumerated in the third proviso of the first section of the before-mentioned treaty of the twenty-fifth of June, eighteen hundred and fifty-five, ——that is to say, the right to take fish, erect houses, hunt game, gather roots and berries and pasture animals upon lands without the reservation set apart by the treaty aforesaid——are hereby relinquished by the confederated Indian tribes and bands of Middle Oregon parties to the treaty.

The following year the Indians went as usual to catch salmon, and were informed by the whites that by a treaty they had surrendered all their rights to fish in the Columbia River. The Indians were astounded. They insisted that nothing had been said to them about relinquishing their treaty rights to fish in the Columbia; the chief interpreters and whites made affidavits to this effect. What was to be done? The forged treaty had been ratified March 2, 1867, and proclaimed March 28, 1867. All land adjacent to the Columbia River controlling the fishing

privileges had been secured by the whites through the Land
Office and paid for. The Indian Bureau was informed of this
fraud and made an effort to repair the damage done the Indians,
but without result. The reason that nothing was accomplished,
is to me apparent; the whites who purchased the fishing
privileges on the Columbia River are voters, the Indian has no
vote. The Commissioner of Indian Affairs in his report sent to
Congress, quotes from the reports of Indian Agent Gessner[4] as
follows:

> When the Piutes were murdering the defenseless settlers
> and keeping the soldiers at bay the Government called upon
> the Warm Springs Indians for help, and it came. When
> the Modocs held the lava beds, and there were graves of
> over one hundred and ninety soldiers slain in the futile
> attempt to dislodge them from their stronghold, the
> Government turned imploringly to the people here for help,
> promising them, if killed in battle, or wounded, they would
> be pensioned, (which agreement was never complied with).
> Help came quickly and the result is known everywhere,
> and yet when the people here or their agent asked for what
> they were promised and what they should have, the
> Government is silent as the grave.

A Warm Springs Indian in remonstrating with his agent
against the fraud practiced on them said, "If I had a hired man
and he should go out and steal something from you, I would
not accept it, and that this was a parallel case and that the
Government should not receive property stolen by a hired man
like Huntington."

I was conversing with an old officer of the army, now on
the retired list, he said, "I am glad you propose to give an
account of your experiences and what you learned about the
habits and customs of the Indians as you found them sixty years

ago. Who is there now living who had your experience? There is no one, and who in the army sixty years ago lived as long among the nomadic or buffalo Indians as you did? No one as far as I know.''

On the reservation, the Indians are presumed in time to become self-sustaining by tilling the soil. Their habits and customs are changing fast; the use of the bow and arrow, used by him in war and for obtaining food, has, or will, become obsolete; he is now armed with the repeating and precision rifle.

Marriage among them when nomads is worth handing down. A young Indian buck (Man) desiring to take a young squaw for his wife commenced by depositing at the door of her lodge, or tepee, game he had killed, and probably having a stolen talk with her when occasion offered. No marriage could take place until a horse or horses, were given and accepted. Finding out how many horses the father of the girl required for his account, the horses would be picketed in front of the girl's tepee and if driven away the next morning with the horses belonging to the father, the young buck was the accepted suitor of the daughter, who was then dressed in her bridal dress, consisting of a skirt of buck skin, or elk skin, elaborately trimmed with elk's teeth and beads, a pair of red or blue leggings and a new pair of moccasons upon which beads or porcupine embroidery was much in evidence, and she was ready as a bride for the inevitable supper, with a fat puppy or dog as the *piece de resistance*. A lodge was provided, made of dressed buffalo skins, buffalo robes for bedding; a couple of blankets, a camp kettle and a large iron fork, pretty much composed their outfit. She was also given as many horses as the generosity of the father could stand to part with; an axe, kitchen knives and the tools used in preparing the buffalo robe for commerce, were a part of her inheritance. The Indian women doing all the work, became, as I have before said, very strong; parturition with them apparently gives them no trouble, no concern.

I was riding with the Indians one day when they were moving to another camp ground to obtain better pasture for their animals; I noticed a squaw, the wife of an Indian I knew, ride off, leaving the party. I asked her husband where she was going; He replied, "Not far, she will be in camp by the time we reach there." Very soon after reaching the camp ground the squaw appeared, dismounted from her pony, and handed to her husband to hold a new-born baby, wrapped in a blanket. She went to work as usual, putting up the lodge, making down the beds, bringing the water, etc., as though nothing unusual had occurred. As soon as the bed was made, the buck laid the blanket down in the grass, went to his lodge, lit his pipe, and smoked.

Disposing of the dead among the Indians differs in different tribes. Some inter the body in the ground as the white man does. Others wrap the body securely in clothes, blankets, or buffalo robes, erect a scaffold on four posts or poles securely planted in the ground, and about six or seven feet high, upon which the body is placed. Others place the body in trees, where a scaffold is erected for its reception.

On one occasion as I was going into camp on the bank of the Arkansas River, a Cheyenne Indian boy about twelve years old whom I knew well, came to our camp. A large dead cottonwood tree was near my tent; in this tree was a scaffold on which were, I presume, the remains of a dead Indian; my servant was collecting buffalo chips with which to cook our supper; wishing to see what the Indian boy would say, I told him if he would climb the tree and cut the cords which secured the scaffold, the sticks of which would give us all the fuel we required, I would give him a cup of sugar. He answered, "No, no," that the devil would get him if he did that. The Indian sign which he made for devil was putting his fingers in his mouth and eyes, and stretching them open. "Big mouth and big eyes would get him," he said.

When in charge of the Warm Springs Reservation, an Indian accompanied by a squaw came to my office and requested me to marry him. An Indian Agent is now, not infrequently, called upon to perform the marriage ceremony. The Indian had his fishing rod in his hand. I used the Episcopal form in the ceremony, or as much of it as I could remember, having no prayer-book with me; a certificate of marriage was given the squaw, and the marriage duly recorded in a book kept in the office for that purpose. I told the interpreter to tell the Indian to salute (kiss) his bride; the squaw ran and hid behind a door, and nothing could persuade her to leave her hiding place. The Indian left and the squaw followed him. On leaving the office the Indian went in an exactly opposite direction from the squaw. I made the interpreter call him back. I abused him soundly, told him that white men always accompanied their brides home, and the idea of his going fishing and not accompanying his bride home was something I could not tolerate; that unless he went home with his wife I would unmarry him then and there, and give the girl to another Indian who was in love with her.

He said that in coming up the creek he saw a fine big salmon in shallow water, and that as soon as he caught the fish he intended to go where his wife was. I told him to go and catch the salmon, to bring it to the office and let me see it, and then he could take it to his wife. In about twenty minutes he returned with a fine salmon, weighing twelve or fourteen pounds. I gave him about as much beef, some sugar and coffee, and sent him on his wedding tour rejoicing.

In all my intercourse with Indians I never saw an Indian kiss his wife, or a wife kiss her husband. I do recollect having seen an Indian mother or father kiss a child.

When I visited the Cheyenne and Arapahoe Agency as Special Agent under Mr. Cleveland's first administration on an inspecting tour, I inquired after some of my old Cheyenne friends that I had known on the Arkansas River forty years before when they were as happy as a people could be and as independent, rarely out of sight of buffalo. I found all dead; some died a natural death, most however, had been killed in battle, fighting their Indian enemies, or their more implacable enemy, the white man. I have mentioned before that "Old Bark,"[5] the chief of the Cheyenne, had two very pretty grand daughters, about twelve years old in 1850. I inquired whether Eoneva and Nahanney, the names of the two girls, were living. I was told they were, and married; that Eonova had grown children. Nahanney was not living on the reservation, but Eoneva was. I sent for Eoneva and her husband; they came to the Agency. I enquired of Eoneva about her relations, my friends, with whom I had so often hunted buffalo. They were all gone; most of them fell fighting the white man; we talked long about the happy times we had on the Flint Water, the Indian name for Arkansas River. As we conversed, of course using the sign language, I saw the tears flow down Eoneva's cheeks; evidently her thoughts were on those happy childhood days on the Arkansas River when every wish an Indian had could be gratified; all was changed now, buffalo all gone, and confined by the white man to what, in comparison to their former hunting grounds, is a prison.

With tears in her eyes, she approached me, put her hands behind my head and kissed my forehead; her husband, "Young Whirlwind,"[6] whose father I had known, approached me and said, "Yo-ba-me-ats, Eoneva and I give you this lion skin; keep it, the road that you travel our children shall follow; in forty years you have never told an Indian a lie." This I consider, coming from an Indian, who had no reason for saying what he did not believe, was the most beautiful and highly prized compliment I ever received. So unusual was this from an Indian, that an intimate friend has suggested that it be engraved on my tomb stone.

It must be borne in mind that the Indians, as I knew them,

had never been instructed as we have been in the Commandments, given by God to Moses on Mount Sinai. We have all noticed that many young children will, at times, take what they wish, and when asked if they have done so will tell an untruth; this is the child's natural defense. Now the Indian is only a full grown child, but while you may not trust to an Indian's honesty, you can trust *his honor*. Leave an Indian in charge, as an Indian trader sometimes does of his store, and every penny taken in will be accounted for, and nothing will be missing, but after being relieved from his trust, *look out*.

When the publication of the Rebellion Records[7] was commenced, the impression quite generally entertained in the South was that the purpose of this work was to be a one-sided affair to glorify the prowess of the Northern Army and belittle that of the South.

Those who have examined the work, now nearly completed,[8] have come to a very different conclusion. No fairer compendium of a war has ever been collated. The work contains every report, letter, order or dispatch made by officers in command or participating in the battles, engagements, etc., known to be authentic and bearing on the subject treated; these are given without comment.

Under an act of Congress directing that the lines of the two armies participating in the Battle of Antietam, or Sharpsburg, should be marked, the Secretary of War, the Honorable Redfield Proctor, appointed a board consisting of one officer representing the Northern Army and one representing the Southern Army to do this work. I was unknown to the Secretary. At the suggestion of friends, Secretary Proctor appointed me on this board.[9] I had occasion to examine the Rebellion Records containing the reports, etc., bearing upon this, the bloodiest one day's battle of the war, September 17, 1862.

Nothing could have been compiled fairer than the facts collected in this volume, and so it is in all; a single idea seems to have been the guide of the gentlemen comprising the board of publication, authenticity. The future historian of the Civil War, or of any campaign of the war, will find all the data bearing on the same faithfully recorded. I am satisfied no such collection of *official data*, treating of any war, ancient or modern, has ever before been so truthfully and conscientiously compiled. The North and South owe a debt of gratitude to Colonel R. N. Scott,[10] in charge of this work and his able assistants.

Colonel Scott died after devoting ten years to this work. Colonel H. M. Lazelle succeeded him and remained at the head of the board until relieved and ordered to West Point.[11]

Under an act approved March 2, 1889, directing, "that hereafter the preparation and publication of said records shall be conducted under the Secretary of War, by a board of three persons, one of whom shall be an officer of the army and two civilian experts to be appointed by the Secretary of War," the following board was appointed:—George B. Davis, major and judge-advocate general; Leslie J. Perry, civilian expert; Joseph W. Kirkley, civilian expert.

Major Davis, after serving years, was relieved and ordered to West Point, and Major George W. Davis, 11th Infantry, succeeded him.[12]

The Secretaries of War have been wonderfully fortunate in their selections of both officers and civilian experts composing the board of publications; they have been, and are still, fair, intelligent and levelheaded gentlemen. Mr. J. W. Kirkley, civilian expert, connected with the work since its incipiency, is, I think, regarded as the genius and animating spirit of this great work.[13]

There was comparatively little trouble in procuring documents pertaining to the Union side, but not so with those of the Confederate. Many Confederate reports and papers were lost and destroyed when the war ended; large expenditure of money by the Government secured valuable authentic documents.

Credit is due to General Marcus J. Wright and Colonel Edwin J. Harvie, Confederate officers employed by the Secretary of War, for valuable Confederate records secured by them.[14]

In closing these reminiscences my thoughts turn to many old army friends with whom I have had the most pleasant intercourse and from whom I have received acts of kindness and consideration since my wanderings brought me to Washington.

When on the Sioux expedition in 1855, many will remember a negro melody then much in vogue, "The other side of Jordan." The officers of our column amused themselves on the march, composing doggerel to this air, bringing in the names of officers on the expedition. I recall now but one of these *poetic effusions*.

> "And there is old Van Vliet, that quartermaster sweet,
> The buffalo bull did charge on.
> The bull came to bay, and his horse ran away,
> And tossed him on the other side of Jordan.
> Then pull off your coat and roll up your sleeve,
> For Jordan is a hard road to travel I believe."

To General Van Vliet, "that quartermaster sweet," General D. H. Rucker (dear, good, honest old Rucker,) Generals H. G. Wright, D. W. Flagler, John G. Parke, Absolam Baird,[15] R. C. Drum,[16] John C. Kelton, Robert Williams, G. D. Ruggles, Robert MacFeely, M. R. Morgan, Alexander Perry, and others, I return my thanks for acts of kindness. My warm friends and classmates, O. B. Willcox and John S. Mason,[17] whose society I so much enjoy, also my classmates and dear friends, Generals John Gibbon and W. W. Burns,[18] both now "over the river," I remember with affection. I can never forget the Sunday evenings General Gibbon and I spent at Miss Sarah

Coleman's hospitable mansion, where our youthful days and escapades at dear old West Point, were gone over and enjoyed by Miss Sarah[19] as much as she did fifty years past.

I was ever welcome at the hospitable mansion of my quondam messmate and always friend, Colonel E. McK. Hudson.[20] The cadet hash at his house was made by "Old Bev." Robertson and myself, when General Sheridan, who had just dined with some foreign minister, *and had no appetite for hash,* came in and ate a pound or two, the old time taste coming back to him, as it did to us all. The potatoes and bread, to carry out the delusion, were supposed to have been stolen from "old Rucker's," next door.

The delusion of West Point cadet life was only broken by Hudson bringing in a big bowl of the delicious punch he knew so well how to brew and insisting upon opening a half dozen bottles of champagne which, though not en regle at a cadet hash, we enjoyed. The amount of hash consumed by Bev. Robertson and myself would have killed any one not provided with the West Point stomach and the digestion inherited from cadet life.

I should be remiss not to mention the many acts of kindness received from my friend and former sergeant of my Company, E., 10th Infantry, by all odds the best first sergeant I ever knew, now Captain Thomas C. Trumbull, Superintendent of the blank room of the Quartermaster's Department.

XXV

The year spent in Raleigh, N. C. was a most happy one.[1] We left there many kind and devoted friends, the Battles, the

Hoggs, the Blunts, that splendid soldier General Hoke, General W. R. Cox, now Secretary of the United States Senate, the Heywoods, Mr. Barringer, Doctor Simons, principal of the Young Ladies' Seminary, Doctor Mason,[2] the good pious eccentric pastor of the Episcopal Church of whom many amusing stories were circulated. The Doctor was devoted to gardening; it was said he once planted his spectacles, filling his pockets with potatoes. On another occasion, when walking on the sidewalk he ran into a lamp-post, wheeled around and exclaimed, "Young man, have you no respect for age?" It was told that one Sunday he brought the wash bowl from the vestry room and placed it on the desk of the pulpit, leaving his sermon where the basin should have been. Whether these stories told on this good old man were true or not, I can't say, but they were circulated far and wide. Dr. Mason died while we were in Raleigh, beloved and regretted by all.

The sight of a North Carolinian, and the touch of his hand, opens a warm valve in my heart. No brigades in any army surpassed in gallantry those of John R. Cooke and William McRae.[3] The casualties and the killed and wounded among the North Carolina troops show a greater percentage of loss than those from any other state. The little reputation I gained during the war was measurably the reflection of gallant deeds which history will credit to my brave Mississippians, Tennesseeans, Virginians, and "Tar Heels."

Who among the North Carolinians of the Army of Northerm Virginia does not remember old Aunt Abby House,[4] living on a small farm which she cultivated herself? She devoted her time and her means to supplying "her boys" as she called them, in General Lee's army, with clothing and edibles. Aunt Abby, far past three score and ten, was a frequent visitor to the army when we lay around Petersburg in the winter of 1864-5. She would sometimes request a few days' furlough for one of her boys. The story was told that when interceding with General

Lee for a leave for one of her boys, the General placed his hand on this old woman's shoulder; assuming the most kitten-like attitude she said, "Take your hand off, Bob Lee, I permit no familiarities." Aunt Abby carried her point, and never failed in like mission. She promised that her boys should be returned on the day agreed upon, and she never failed to bring them back. The Legislature of North Carolina should appropriate a small sum to mark the spot where brave and kind-hearted Aunt Abby rests. What do you say to starting this monument, Generals Cox and Hoke?

On the outskirts of Raleigh was the beautiful old homestead of the Hon. Mr. Saunders,[5] formerly our minister to Spain. Our gallant and hospitable General Bradley T. Johnson[6] married his daughter. I am informed that Bradley is now residing in Amelia County, Virginia, one of the poorest in the state, save the adjoining county, Chesterfield, in which I was born, unable to raise tobacco, wheat or corn. I understand General Bradley has turned his attention to raising land terrapins and bullfrogs; may he make a success of this new venture. How would it answer, Bradley, to cross the land terrapin with the diamond-back? If a success, your fortune is made. I inquired the price of one diamond-back I saw yesterday in a shop window and was asked ten dollars. My mouth watered to possess this beautiful specimen of the genus chelonia, but I need not say that I did not invest.

Colonel James L. Corley,[7] chief quartermaster of the Army of Northern Virginia, came to Raleigh about the time I did; we each had our families with us. I proposed to Corley (we had been lieutenants in the same regiment, the Sixth U. S. Infantry,) that we should rent a house, live and mess together. He consented, provided Mrs. Heth would assume the general management. We lived happily together one year, when I went to Richmond and he to Norfolk. We became devotedly attached to the Corleys. On parting, Colonel Corley said to Mrs. Heth,

"If yours has been the strongest government I ever lived under, it is certainly the best and happiest."

Dear old Richmond! it is the first city I remember. Here much of my youth was spent; here my father and brother resided a part of each winter; here I learned to swim in the falls of the "noble Jeems," and here I fought my first battles with the butcher cats, a war that has existed for a hundred years, and I believe is still carried on, proving to me that man is by nature a belligerant animal. I was most affectionately and kindly received by relatives and friends.

When President Hayes removed the troops from the Southern States, where by their presence the much-despised carpet-baggers were kept in power, the people of Richmond were joyous beyond expression. A committee of three, Colonel Thomas Carter, Mr. Gray and the writer were sent to Washington to request the President and his cabinet to visit Richmond and be the guests of the city.[8]

When the statue of Stonewall Jackson was unveiled,[9] I was named as the acting marshal of the occasion. When the statue of Lieutenant General A. P. Hill[10] was unveiled, I was in supreme command. When Mr. Davis's remains were interred at Hollywood I commanded the visiting troops.[11] I was ever treated as one of her favored sons. My friend Governor James L. Kemper[12] was anxious that I should be a candidate for Governor, but I had no taste for political honors.

The kindness I received from my dear friend General Joseph R. Anderson, to whom the City of Richmond owes so much, and who left a son, Colonel Archer Anderson,[13] a splendid soldier and man of great business capacity, worthy of and capable of carrying on the work performed by his noble father, Mr.

"Norwood"

John Montague, that ever ready and witty gentleman, was, and is, my friend, [as also are] Colonel William Palmer and Uncle George, to whom I am under obligations for favors received. Many happy hours I have passed with Judge Minor, Phil. Haxall, Willie Trigg, the Dunlaps, Cabells, Leigh Paige, the Wises, Dr. McGuire,[14] that skillful surgeon, Dorsey Cullin, Frank Chamberlain, Boulware, my old friend Dr. James McCaw, Charles U. Williams, R. T. Daniel, Dr. Barksdale and his brother George, Mr. Thomas Branch, Oscar Cranz, Mr. Ott, James Dooly and his good wife, the Peytons, Wellfords, and a host of others. There resides in Richmond one I learned to love and admire, who was associated with me in business, Colonel John B. Cary,[15] a man of the greatest rectitude of character and capable of filling any position with credit to himself, his state, or his country, to which he might be called. Long may he live and prosper. Dr. Minnigerode,[16] our beloved pastor, the saintly Dr. Peterkin,[17] Dr. James B. Hoge,[18] are examples worthy of the Savior whose precepts and example they followed and taught others to imitate.

There lived with us in Richmond for years James Davis and his wife. James Davis[19] was a young man of rare ability as a lawyer, and so esteemed by the entire legal faculty of Richmond. There was born to them while living with us a child who on the death of her mother we cared for as our own, and learned to love as such. This little girl, named for my wife, has developed into a splendid character, a worthy member of the Davis family, which for several generations has reflected credit upon Virginia's famous University, founded by that great statesman, her ancestor Thomas Jefferson. It is she to whom I allude in these unworthy pages, "ours by adoption and sincere affection."

I would be remiss not to mention that grand soldier, General John R. Cooke, who commanded a North Carolina regiment in the hardest-fought battle of the war, Sharpsburg or Antietam. Being told by a general officer that the position he was holding must be held at all hazards, he replied, "General, I have not a cartridge left, but so long as one man lives that flag shall wave over here;" and there he remained, and without a cartridge made one or more charges on the enemy. The record made by Cooke's and McRae's brigades is one of unbroken glory and will be pointed to and admired by the great American nation in all future times.

Soon after reaching Richmond I became a member of the Richmond Club, where I spent many pleasant evenings. Boston, played for a moderate stake, was the principal amusement. My friend Buck Royal was generally the winner. After enduring the sighing and whistling of my friends Buck Royal and poor Sallie Watkins[20] for three years, some of the older members of the club determined to start a new club. General Dabney H. Maury (the gallant Virginia soldier who has given us the most charming and delightful book of the century), and others with whom I united started the Westmoreland Club,[21] which developed into one of the finest clubs in the South. I was honored as its first president. The Westmoreland Club was so quiet and orderly that at times I was fain to wish for Buck Royal's whistle to break the silence. When I am taken to Hollywood—and it will not, in the course of nature, be long, I wish you, dear Buck, to whistle taps over my grave.

I desire in closing these reminiscences to return my thanks and express the obligations I am under to my dear friend, that good soldier during the war, and now skillful physician, Doctor George Boyd Harrison,[22] who by attentive and splendid management saved my life many times when attacked by pneumonia. I also thank our dear friend and pastor, a grand soldier, now a distinguished divine, The Rev. Doctor Randolph K. McKim[23] of Epiphany Church, Washington, D. C., for which church my wife has labored assiduously until her health gave way, and in whose fold I have been numbered, for it would be to me everlasting torture to be separated from her I adore.

Heth's Grave, Hollywood Cemetery, Richmond

Notes

Chapter I

1. John Heth, Henry's father, was the owner of Blackheath. It was located on the edge of Midlothian about ten miles west of Richmond. Ida J. Lee, "The Heth Family," *The Virginia Magazine of History and Biography*, XLII, No. 3 (July 1934), 280.

2. John Heth resigned from the navy in 1822. He married Margaret L. Pickett, daughter of George E. Pickett of Richmond. Ibid. George Pickett was the grandfather of Major General George E. Pickett, Confederate State Army, thus, Henry Heth and George Pickett were first cousins. Robert A. Brock, "Orderly Book of Major William Heth of the Third Virginia Regiment, May 15-July 1, 1777," *Collections of the Virginia Historical Society* (new Ser.), XI (1892), 320-21.

3. In 1837 John Heth incorporated the Blackheath mines and adjacent properties to form the Blackheath and Huguenot Coal and Iron Company. His partners in this enterprise were: Dr. John Brockenbrough, President of the Virginia Bank, and William H. MacFarland, President of The Farmers' Bank, Richmond. Ibid., 320.

4. The two Peugnet brothers, former Napoleonic officers, operated this semi-military school. They specialized in preparing can-

didates for entrance to the U.S. Military Academy. Hamilton Basso, *Beauregard the Great Creole* (New York: Charles Scribner's Sons, 1933), 16-17.

5. Sackett, a member of the Class of 1845, served in the U.S. Cavalry until the Civil War. During the war he was a staff officer under McClellan and later, Burnside. George W. Cullum, *Biographical Register of the Officers and Graduates of the U.S. Military Academy at West Point* (Boston: Houghton Mifflin and Company, 1891), II, 234-35.

6. Joseph N. G. Whistler was a member of the Class of 1846. He served as an infantry officer in the Mexican War, the Civil War and subsequently on the frontier. Ibid., 297.

7. Choteau cannot be identified.

8. The Pratts and Nidletts cannot be identified.

9. After graduation Prime, an engineer officer, served in New York, California and Alabama prior to the Civil War. During the war he served as chief engineer in the Departments of Kentucky, Cumberland and Ohio; subsequently, he served as chief engineer under Grant during the Mississippi Campaign. Cullum, *Register*, II, 401.

10. "Rooney" Lee was a Harvard man. He served in the 6th U.S. Infantry prior to the Civil War. During the war he was a cavalryman under J. E. B. Stuart. Mark Mayo Boatner III, *The Civil War Dictionary* (New York: David McKay Co., 1959), 477.

11. John Heth died 30 April 1842. Brock, "Orderly Book," *Collections, Virginia Historical Society*, XI, 320.

12. Norwood was on the south side of the James, 17 miles west of Richmond. The 2065-acre estate had been the property of Henry Heth, grandfather of the memoir writer. At the time of John Heth's death Norwood belonged to Miles Carey Selden, husband of Harriett Heth, John's sister. Douglas Vanderhoof (ed.) *The Book of Nancy Selden Vanderhoof* (Richmond: privately published 1934), 82.

13. Heth accepted the appointment, 15 March 1842. Letter, Henry Heth to James M. Porter, Secretary of War, 15 March 1842, Adjutant General's Office, Letters Received Book, 1842, National Archives.

Chapter II

1. Heth qualified for admission of 27 June 1843 and was

admitted on 1 July. Post Orders, No. 2, Headquarters U.S. Military Academy, 27 June 1843, U.S. Military Archives, West Point, New York.

2. Pickett graduated last in the Class of 1846. Cullum, *Register,* II, 304.

3. Heth graduated last in the Class of 1847. Official Register, United States Military Academy, 1844-47, U.S. Military Academy Archives.

4. This tavern was in Buttermilk (now Highland) Falls on the Hudson just below West Point. Benny Havens closed his business in 1859. Sidney Forman, *West Point: A History of the United States Military Academy* (New York: Columbia University Press, 1950), 90n.

5. Heth is in error. Legendre wrote *Elements of Geometry,* a standard text for the Fourth (first year) Class throughout the nineteenth century. Lacroix's *Traite de Calcul differential et de Calcul integral* was the Third (second year) Class text. Ibid., 52-55.

6. At the end of his Fourth Class year in June 1844 Heth stood 38th in a class of 53 cadets. *Official Register,* 1844-47, U.S. Military Academy Archives.

7. At the end of his Third Class year Heth stood 39th in a class of 44. Ibid.

8. Buckner, a Confederate, and Hancock, a Union officer, were members of the Class of 1844. Cullum, *Register,* II, 198, 201.

9. Whiting, a Confederate; W. F. Smith, a Union officer; Fitz John Porter, a Union Officer; E. K. Smith, a Confederate; Sackett, a Union officer; and Bee, a Confederate, were members of the Class of 1845. Ibid., 208-236.

10. McClellan, Reno, Couch, Sturgis, Stoneman, and Jones were Union Officers. Maury, Wilcox, and Pickett were Confederates. All were members of the Class of 1846. George F. Evans, also a member of this class, died 29 March 1859. Possibly Heth has confused him with N. George Evans, a Confederate, who was a member of the Class of 1848. Ibid., 250-284, 365.

11. All except A. P. Hill remained with the Union. Other generals from this class were Horatio G. Gibson and Tredwell Moore, both Brigadier Generals, U.S. Volunteers. Ibid., 308-339.

12. At the end of his Second Class year in June 1846 Heth stood 36th out of a class of 40 cadets. *Official Register,* 1844-47. U.S. Military Academy Archives.

13. Fort Clinton, originally Fort Arnold, was located on the edge of the "The Plain," the cadet drill field and summer camp area. Forman, *West Point*, 12.

14. Augustus H. Seward graduated four files above Heth. He served in the 8th and 5th Infantry Regiments prior to the Civil War. During the war and subsequently he served as a paymaster. Cullum, *Register*, II, 340-41.

15. Kemble, a New York Congressman, wrote two letters of recommendation for Heth: Gouverneur Kemble to Colonel Joseph G. Totten, Chief of Engineers, 30 January 1843, and Gouverneur Kemble to James M. Porter, Secretary of War, 16 March 1843, Adjutant General's Office files, Records Group 94, National Archives.

16. Francis G. Brown of Ohio did not graduate. *Register of Graduates*, 1963, 238.

17. These were Maria and Virginia. Charles W. Elliott, *Winfield Scott The Soldier And The Man* (New York: Macmillan & Co., 1937), 216.

18. Cullum does not list Walter Scott as a graduate.

19. Maria B. Mayo Scott was the daughter of Colonel John Mayo of Bellville near Richmond. Elliott, *Winfield Scott*, 212.

20. McAllister graduated fourth in the Class of 1847. He was an ordnance officer throughout his career. Cullum, *Register*, II, 307-8.

21. Burns graduated 28th in the class. During the Civil War he was a Major General of Volunteers, serving in the Army of the Potomac. Afterward he was Assistant Commissary General of Subsistence. Ibid., 337.

22. Valentine entered in 1844 but failed to graduate. *Register of Graduates*, 1963, 236.

23. Baize is a coarse woolen cloth.

24. Roe's or West Point Hotel was located on the edge of the military reservation. Lloyd Lewis, *Captain Sam Grant* (Boston: Little, Brown & Company, 1950), 61.

25. For being absent from the hospital between "Retreat" and 11 P.M. on 23 August 1846 Heth was confined to quarters for two weeks and required to perform eight extra guard tours. Special Orders 124, Headquarters U.S. Military Academy, 31 August 1846. Post Orders No. 3, U.S. Military Academy Archives.

26. Frederick A. Smith, Captain, Corps of Engineers, was an instructor in Practical Military Engineering. Diploma, U.S. Military

Academy, Henry Heth, 23 June 1847, Heth Papers, 5071, University of Virginia Library.

27. Henry Brewerton, Captain Corps of Engineers, was Superintendent. Ibid.

Chapter III

1. George W. Cullum, then a Captain, Corps of Engineers, was an instructor of Practical Military Engineering from 1848 to 1851. He is the author of the *Biographical Register of the Officers and Graduates of the United States Military Academy*. Cullum, *Register,* I, 535.

2. 1st and 2nd Cavalry, 9th and 10th Infantry. *Official Army Register,* 1856, 14, 15, 28-30.

3. McIntosh was a member of the Class of 1849. He was appointed Second Lieutenant, 8th Infantry, 15 May 1851 and First Lieutenant, 1st Cavalry, 16 January 1857. Although he graduated last in his class, the promotion to captain placed him ahead of all of his classmates except Joseph L. Tidball and Richard W. Johnson, both of whom were promoted to captain in 1855. Cullum, *Register* II, 390-91, 399-400.

4. Colonel James S. McIntosh. Ibid., I, 400.

5. The sister could be either Lavinia Randolph Heth, born 31 March 1827, or Elizabeth Chevallie Heth, born 28 October 1829. Ida J. Lee, "The Heth Family," *Virginia Magazine of History and Biography,* XLII (July 1934), 279.

6. Probably she was the wife of George Cadwalader, a Philadelphia lawyer who served as a general in the Mexican War and in the Civil War. Mary, his wife, was the daughter of Clement Biddle of Philadelphia. *The National Cyclopaedia of American Biography,* XII (New York: James T. White and Co., 1904), 269.

7. See note 32, Introduction.

8. A verse from this song is quoted in *Cadet Life at West Point* George S. Strong, (Boston: T. O. H. P. Burnham, 1862), 14.

9. Daniel M. Beltzhoover was a member of the Class of 1847. He was a Confederate general during the Civil War. Afterwards he taught school in Mobile, Alabama. Cullum, *Register,* II, 313-14.

10. Bradford R. Alden, Captain, 4th Infantry, was Commandant

of Cadets and Instructor of Infantry Tactics from 14 December 1845 to 1 November 1852. Because of wounds received against the Rogue River Indians in 1853 he was unable to participate in the Civil War. Cullum, *Register,* I, 488-489.

11. James Bankhead of Virginia. He was not a West Pointer. *Official Army Register,* 1847, 15.

12. Possibly they were the daughters of James Coleman, a wealthy ironmonger and owner of Elizabeth Furnace, Lancaster, Pa. *National Cyclopaedia,* XII, 421.

13. Dabney H. Maury, *Recollections of a Virginian In the Mexican, Indian, and Civil War* (New York: Charles Scribner's Sons, 1894), 22.

14. At graduation Maury ranked 37th in a class of 59. Cullum, *Register,* II, 284.

15. Samuel Ward, the elder brother of Julia Ward Howe, left the banking firm in 1839. His first wife, Emily Astor, died in childbirth. He married Medora Grymes in 1844, but they separated. Ward lost his fortune in 1849. *Dictionary of American Biography* (New York: Charles Scribner's Sons, 1936), XIX, 439.

16. Sweet Springs is in Monroe County, West Virginia, south of White Sulphur Springs. *Rand McNally Commercial Atlas,* 91st ed. (New York: Rand McNally Co., 1960), 465.

Chapter IV

1. C. G. Hunter, Lieutenant, U.S. Navy, commanded the U.S.S. Scourge, a steam-propelled gun boat, during the blockade of the town of Alvarado. Against Perry's orders Hunter opened fire on the town. In so doing Hunter brought about the surrender of Alvarado to American forces, but he was court martialed and cashiered for disobedience. Hunter's punishment outraged public opinion in the United States. Justin H. Smith, *The War With Mexico,* II (New York: The Macmillan Co., 1919), 345.

2. Maury, *Recollections,* 22.

3. They were all instructors at West Point, "Claudy" being Claudius Berard, Instructor in French from 1815 to 1848. Forman, *West Point,* 52.

Chapter V

1. Both officers were members of the Class of 1836. Roland A. Luther had been wounded at Palo Alto in May 1846 and reassigned to recruiting duty at Fort Hamilton. John F. Roland had been brevetted for gallantry at Palo Alto, Resaca De La Palma, and Monterey. He also had been reassigned to Fort Hamilton. Cullum, *Register,* I, 642-44.

2. The exact date of Heth's arrival cannot be fixed. He was still at Fort Hamilton in early October 1847 but evidently had arrived in Vera Cruz prior to February 1848. Letter, Henry Heth to the Adjutant General, 7 October 1847, subject: Acceptance of Commission. Adjutant General Letters Received Book, 1847, Item 23, National Archives; and letter, Henry Heth to the Adjutant General, 24 January 1848, subject: Request for Transfer. Adjutant General's Office Files, Record Group 94, National Archives.

3. Wilson had commanded the 4th Brigade, 1st Division, under Twiggs at Monterey. Later, he succeeded Worth as Governor of Vera Cruz. Smith, *War With Mexico,* I, 492; II, 221, 457.

4. Robert S. Granger was a member of the Class of 1838. He was promoted to Captain, 1st Infantry in September 1847. During the Civil War he served in Middle Tennessee and Alabama and later commanded the 11th Infantry on occupation duty in Richmond. Cullum, *Register,* I, 719-20.

5. Frederick J. Denman was a member of the Class of 1842. He served with the 1st Infantry until his death in March 1853. Cullum, *Register,* II, 134-135.

6. Electus Backus, Class of 1824, was brevetted to major on 23 September 1846 for gallantry at Monterey. He commanded the castle of San Juan de Ulloa in 1847. Backus was in Garland's brigade at Monterey and later wrote a highly critical account, maintaining that the 3rd and 4th Infantry "were entirely inadequate to do the job required." Cullum, *Register,* I, 335-36; and Smith, *War With Mexico,* I, 502.

7. Probably this was Hugh Brady who had been commissioned Ensign of Infantry in March 1792 and rose through the ranks to Major General in 1848. Brady fought at Chippewa and Lundy's Lane. Later he was a member of a board of inquiry which investigated Scott's failures in the Seminole Campaigns of 1836. Francis P. Heitman, *His-*

torical Register And Dictionary of the United States Army (Washington: Government Printing Office, 1903), I, 239; and Elliott, *Winfield Scott,* 185, 326-27.

8. Heth refers to extra mounts the quartermaster kept on hand as replacements for other horses which became disabled.

9. Cholula is about eight miles northwest of the town of Puebla in the State of Puebla. The pyramid, erected to the god Quetzalcoatl, still stands. It is 177 feet high and covers an area of 45 acres. *Encyclopaedia Britannica* (Chicago: William Benton, 1958), V, 619.

10. Joseph Selden was appointed Second Lieutenant, 8th Infantry in July 1838. He won brevets for gallantry at Contraras, Churubusco, and Chapultepec. A Confederate during the Civil War, Selden was assigned to the Office of the Adjutant and Inspector General. He was probably a cousin of Heth's wife, Hariett Selden. Heitman, *Historical* Register, I, 873; and Lyon G. Tyler, "Genealogy," *William and Mary Quarterly Historical Magazine,* VI (April 1898), 237.

Chapter VI

1. The commission was issued on 7 February 1848, with date of rank of 22 September 1847. Commission as Second Lieutenant, 6th Infantry, Secretary of War to Henry Heth, 7 February 1848, Heth Papers, 5071, University of Virginia.

2. Newman S. Clarke, a Vermonter, was commissioned Ensign, 11th Infantry in March 1812. He was brevetted for gallantry at Niagara in 1814 and again at Vera Cruz in 1847. Subsequently, he was on frontier duty until his death in 1861. Heitman, *Historical Register,* I, 307.

3. William H. T. Walker was a member of the Class of 1837. He was brevetted for gallantry in the Seminole Campaign of 1837-38. Later, Walker served as a Major General Confederate States Army. Cullum, *Register,* I, 694-95; and Ellsworth Eliot, Jr., *West Point in the Confederacy* (New York: The Sevart Corp., 1941), 451-452.

4. Armistead was a member of the Class of 1847, but he failed to graduate. Allegedly, he was dismissed for breaking a plate over Jubal Early's head. Armistead won two brevets for gallantry while serving with the 2nd Infantry in Mexico. He fell while leading one of Pickett's brigades. The monument marks the "High Tide of the

Confederacy.'' Boatner, *Civil War Dictionary,* 26.; and LaSalle Corball Pickett, *Pickett and His Men* (Philadelphia: J. B. Lippincott Co., 1913), 125-26.

5. Edward Johnson was a member of the Class of 1838. He served in the 6th Infantry until the Civil War. Johnson entered the Confederate Army as a colonel and had reached the grade of major general by 1863. He commanded the ''Stonewall Brigade'' at Gettysburg, participated in the Wilderness Campaign, and was captured by Hancock at Spottsylvania. Eliot, *West Point in the Confederacy,* 363.

6. Buckner was a member of the Class of 1844. He served in the 6th Infantry until 1851, then in the Commissary Department until his resignation in March 1855. During the Civil War he surrendered Fort Donelson, and later fought at Perrysville, Chickamauga and Atlanta. In 1887 Buckner was elected Governor of Kentucky. Ibid., 308-9.

7. ''Ridge fell, and no man died that night with more glory—yet many died, and there was much glory.'' Sir William F. P. Napier, *History of the War in the Peninsula And in the South of France From A. D. 1807 to A. D. 1814* (New York: Redfield, 1856), 371.

8. At this time Burnside was assigned to the 2nd Artillery. Cullum, *Register,* II, 318.

9. Cuernavaca is about 55 miles south of Mexico City. John Bartholomew (ed.), *The Times Atlas of the World* (London: The Times Publishing Co., Ltd., 1957) V, Plate 113.

Chapter VII

1. Probably this was ''Usted me has amante.'' (Let me be your sweetheart.)

2. Lovell, a member of the Class of 1842, received a brevet for gallantry at Chapultepec. Later, he was a Confederate major general and was Farragut's luckless opponent at New Orleans. After the Civil War Lovell was a civil engineer in New York. Cullum, *Register,* II, 122.

3. Porter, a member of the Class of 1845, was brevetted at Molino Del Rey and Chapultepec. During the Civil War he was a major general of U.S. Volunteers. He received a brevet for gallantry at Chickamuga. In August 1862 Porter was cashiered for failing to

obey Pope's orders at Second Bull Run, but he was reinstated in 1886. Cullum, *Register*, II, 220.

4. Willcox stood eighth in the Class of 1847. After the Mexican War he served at various military posts until he resigned in 1857. During the Civil War he became a Major General U.S. Volunteers, seeing action in east Tennessee, the Richmond Campaign, the Wilderness, and Petersburg. Cullum, *Register*, II, 310.

5. Tacubaya is a district in the southwestern part of Mexico City. *Times Atlas*, V, Plate 113.

6. Andrew Porter was a member of the Class of 1840 but failed to graduate. He received brevets at Contreras, Churubusco, and Chapultepec. During the Civil War Porter was a Brigadier General, U.S. Volunteers. Heitman, *Historical Register*, I, 798.

7. Richard H. Anderson was a member of the Class of 1842. He served in the 1st, and later, the 2nd Dragoons until his resignation in March 1861. During the Civil War Anderson served in the Army of Northern Virginia, becoming a lieutenant general in the last year of the war. Eliot, *West Point in the Confederacy*, 291.

8. Charles P. Stone was a member of the Class of 1845. He received brevets in the Mexican War at Molino Del Rey and Chapultepec. During the Civil War he served as Inspector General of D. C. Volunteers. Cullum, *Register*, II, 214.

9. Richard H. Long, a member of the Class of 1847, died in January 1849 while serving on the frontier. Ibid., 322.

10. Montgomery P. Harrison, another member of the Class of 1847, was killed in action near the Colorado River in Texas, 7 October 1849. Ibid., 339.

11. This is incorrect. Either Diego de Ordez, one of Cortez's men, or Francisco Montano who scaled the mountain in 1522 was the first. *Encyclopaedia Britannica*, XVIII, 230.

12. Popocatepetl is 17,883 feet high. Orizaba is 813 feet higher. Ibid.

13. Frederick William Church "Great Fall at Niagara," "Andes of Equador," "Heart of the Andes," and others. *Encyclopaedia Britannica*, V, 669.

14. Grant, who was regimental quartermaster, 6th Infantry, gives a similar account of the expedition to Popocatepetl and the visit to the caves in the spring of 1848. Ulysses S. Grant, *Personal Memoirs* (New York, Charles Webster and Co., 1885), I, 180-90.

15. As a Second Lieutenant, 6th Infantry, Hancock participated

in the fighting at Contreras, the hacienda of San Antonio, and Churubusco. He won brevets for these actions. Alfred Hoyt Bill, *Rehearsal for Conflict: The War With Mexico 1846-1848* (New York: Alfred A. Knopf, 1947), 271-78; and Cullum, *Register*, II, 201-5.

16. Pickett, a Second Lieutenant, 8th Infantry, won brevets at Contreras and Churubusco on 20 August 1847. He was brevetted Captain for gallantry at Chapultepec 13 September 1847. Cullum, *Register*, II, 304.

17. An escopeta is a small shotgun.

18. James Longstreet was hit while carrying the colors in the assault on Chapultepec. Pickett retrieved them. The "Stars and Stripes" were hoisted at 9:30 A.M. Bill, *Rehearsal for Conflict*, 269.

19. They were men of the San Patricio Battalion, a unit made up of Irish adventurers and American deserters. They surrendered to the 3rd Infantry at Churubusco. Ibid., 279-81.

20. William Selby Harney, a native of Nashville, entered the army as a Second Lieutenant, 1st Infantry in February 1818. He served against the Seminoles, receiving a brevet to Lieutenant Colonel. During the Mexican War Scott relieved Harney of command of the cavalry and appointed Sumner, Harney's subordinate. Harney relinquished command initially but later resumed it in violation of Scott's orders. He was court-martialed and required to apologize to Scott. Polk and Marcy, however, upheld Harney and reprimanded Scott. Subsequently, Harney served on the frontier, participating in several Indian campaigns. During the early part of the Civil War Harney was relieved from duty for having made an agreement with Price, the Confederate General, that neither would molest state troops in their area. Dumas Malone, ed., *Dictionary of American Biography* (New York: Charles Scribner's Sons, 1932), VII, 280.

21. Ratifications were exchanged on 31 May 1848. By 31 July the last American troops had evacuated Mexico. Bill, *Rehearsal for Conflict*, 322, 324.

22. Ralph W. Kirkham won Brevets for gallantry at Contreras, Churubusco, and Chapultepec. After the Mexican War he served in Missouri, California, and Washington. During the Civil War, Kirkham was Quartermaster, Department of the Pacific. Cullum, *Register*, II, 139-40.

23. Leonidas Wetmore joined the 6th Infantry in December 1839. He was breveted at Molino Del Rey in November 1847. Wetmore died in November 1849. Heitman, *Historical Register*, I, 1021.

Chapter VIII

1. Gustavus Loomis graduated from West Point in 1811. He had been Lieutenant Colonel, 6th Infantry since September 1840. After the Mexican War Loomis served on the frontier, assuming command of the 6th Infantry as a colonel in March 1851. During the Civil War he was a recruiting officer in Connecticut and Rhode Island. Cullum, *Register*, I, 97-8.

2. Daniel Emanuel Twiggs, a Georgian, had fought in the War of 1812. During the Mexican War he won a brevet at Monterey and was also awarded a sword by Congress. In the early days of the Mexican War Twiggs and Worth feuded over the succession to Taylor's command, Scott finally deciding in favor of Twiggs. Afterwards Twiggs commanded the Department of Texas. At the outset of the Civil War he surrendered the troops in his department and was cashiered. Twiggs then joined the Confederate Army as a major general. He was the oldest of the former U.S. Army officers in the Confederate service. He died in July 1862. Ezra J. Warner, *Generals in Grey* (Baton Rouge, Louisiana State University Press, 1959), 312; and Bill, *Rehearsal for Conflict*, 85, 86.

3. Albemarle Cady, Class of 1829, won a brevet at Molino del Rey. He remained with the 6th Infantry until 1861. During the Civil War he served in Oregon and California until he retired in 1864. Cullum, *Register*, I, 437-38.

4. John B. S. Todd, Class of 1837, served with the 6th Infantry until he resigned in September 1856. He reentered the service as Brigadier General, U.S. Volunteers in September 1861. Initially, Todd served in the North Missouri District, and later commanded the 6th Division, Army of the Tennessee. Cullum, *Register*, I, 691.

5. Heth arrived at Jefferson Barracks in August 1848. Letter, Henry Heth to the Adjutant General, 12 August 1848, subject: Receipt of Commission. Adjutant General Letters Received Book, 1848 (Supplement), No. 24, National Archives.

6. Hancock married Almira Russell, daughter of a St. Louis merchant, on 24 January 1850. Francis A. Walker, *General Hancock* (New York: D. Appleton and Co., 1897), 21-22.

7. The Fort Atkinson referred to here was located in what is now Winnashiek County, Iowa. Heth was later stationed at another Fort

Atkinson on the Arkansas River. *Rand McNally Commercial Atlas,* Plate 161.

8. Thomas D. Alexander, a member of the Class of 1830, received brevets at Contreras and Churubusco. After long frontier service he became Lieutenant Governor of the Soldiers' Home, serving from May 1858 until his retirement in October 1863. Cullum, *Register,* I, 461.

9. Charles Henry Smith, a Virginian, served as Assistant Surgeon, U.S. army from December 1847 to April 1861. Subsequently, he was a Confederate medical officer. Heitman, *Historical Register,* I, 895.

10. A. N. McLaren was Assistant Surgeon, U.S. Army with the 6th Infantry. Richard W. Johnston, *A Soldier's Reminiscences in Peace and War* (Philadelphia, J. B. Lippincott, 1886), 41.

11. William Henry Harrison Taylor, a great grandson of Benjamin Harrison of "Berkeley," married Anna Tuthill Harrison in 1836. Reginald B. Henry, *Genoalogies of the Families of the Presidents* (Rutland, Vt.: Charles Tuttle Co., 1935), 166, 171, 188.

12. Anderson D. Nelson, Class of 1841, served with the 6th Infantry in Mexico and on the frontier. During the Civil War he was a mustering and disbursing officer in Minnesota, and an inspector general in the Departments of Arkansas and Louisiana. Cullum, *Register,* II, 104.

13. Charles T. Baker graduated from West Point in 1842. He served with the 6th Infantry until he resigned in December 1851. Baker did not participate in the Civil War. Ibid., 148.

14. George W. Lay, a Virginian, was also a member of the Class of 1842. He won brevets at Monterey, Contreras, and Churubusco. After the Mexican War he served as aide to Twiggs and later to Scott. Lay resigned in March 1861 and entered the Confederate army. Until June 1862 he was an inspector general in the Army of Northern Virginia. Subsequently, he served under Beauregard at Charleston, commanded the Conscript Bureau in Richmond, and was an inspector general in the field. Eliot, *West Point in the Confederacy,* 371.

15. The troops killed 22 civilians in this riot which was touched off by partisans of Edwin Forrest. It occurred during William C. McCready's performance at the Astor Opera House in 1849. *Encyclopaedia Britannica,* XIV, 598.

Chapter IX

1. Nathaniel Chapman, a Virginian, went to Philadelphia at the age of 17 and studied at the University of Pennsylvania. According to his biographer, Chapman, before he attained the age of 30 "stood in the first rank of his profession in America." *National Encyclopaedia of American Biography,* III, 294.

2. Richard E. Cunningham was the husband of Virginia Heth. Beverly Stockton and Fanny Cadwallader were Heth's youngest brother and sister. Ida J. Lee, "The Heth Family," *Virginia Magazine of History and Biography,* XLII, 280.

3. Julian Harrison was the second son of Randolph Harrison of Elk Hill, Goochland County. Lavinia Heth was his first wife. *Virginia Magazine of History and Biography,* XXXVIII, 88-89.

4. John Young Mason served twice as Secretary of the Navy. He also was Attorney General of the United States and Chairman of the House committee on foreign affairs. Mason returned to Richmond in 1846, becoming president of the James River and Kanawha Company. He was Minister to France from October 1853 until his death in 1859. *Dictionary of American Biography,* XII, 369.

5. Heth spent January and February 1850 in Richmond. Letter, Henry Heth to the Adjutant General, 1 January 1850, sub: Lieutenant Heth reports; and Letter, Henry Heth to the Adjutant General, 5 March 1850, subject: Lieutenant Henry Heth reports for duty. Adjutant General Letters Received Book, 1850, No. 26, National Archives.

6. Heth did not succumb to Fannie Mason, but as mentioned in the Introduction, he did propose to a Richmond girl at this time. Letter, Henry Heth to Elizabeth Heth, 6 January 1850, VIH M55 2H4 72a 40, Virginia Historical Society.

Chapter X

1. Heth reported on 18 March 1850. Letter, Henry Heth to the Adjutant General, 18 March 1850, subject: Lieutenant Henry Heth reports for duty. Ibid.

2. Prior to returning to the West Heth made a trip to Florida with a draft of recruits. This is covered in the Introduction. Report

Henry Heth to the Adjutant General, 24 May 1850, Adjutant General's Office Letters Received Book, 1850, No. 26, National Archives.

3. Ewell at this time was a brevet captain in the 1st Dragoons. He was en route to New Mexico. Cullum, *Register,* II, 41.

4. Buford, also a brevet captain, was a member of the same organization and headed for New Mexico too. During the Civil War Buford served in the Confederate Cavalry under Hardee and Bedford Forrest. Eliot, *West Point in the Confederacy,* 309-10.

5. Pleasanton at this time was a First Lieutenant, 2d Dragoons. During the Civil War he received brevets at Sharpsburg, Gettysburg and in the Campaign against Price in Missouri. Cullum, *Register,* II, 196-97.

6. Jonas P. Holliday was a brevet second lieutenant in the 2d Dragoons. During the early part of the Civil War Holliday served as a colonel in the 1st Vermont Cavalry. He died in April 1862. Ibid., 425.

7. Bingham, a classmate of Holliday's, both graduating in 1850, was also en route to New Mexico. He apparently joined the Confederate army in the Civil War, but his war record is unknown. Eliot, *West Point in the Confederacy*; 301; and Cullum, *Register,* II, 428.

8. The original Woodpecker was a dark chestnut Kentucky stallion, famous as a 20 mile pacer. Frank Forester, *Horse and Horsemastership* (New York: Stringer and Townshend, 1857), 11, 95, 219.

9. Fort Atkinson was built in 1850 and abandoned in 1853. The fort consisted of a single sod building. Soldiers called it "Fort Soddy" and "Fort Sodom." The post was located in the vicinity of present day Dodge City, Kansas. George B. Grinnell, *The Fighting Cheyennes* (New York: Charles Scribner's Sons, 1915), 108, 116.

10. Edwin Vose Sumner, a long-time dragoon, had served in the Black Hawk and Mexican Wars, winning two brevets in the latter. He served on the frontier and participated in several Indian fights. During the Civil War Sumner initially commanded the Department of the Pacific. Later he joined the Army of the Potomac and commanded the Right Grand Division at Fredericksburg. Boatner, *Civil War Dictionary,* 818.

11. Majors required his men to pledge: "While I am in the employ of A. Majors, I agree not to use profane language, not to get drunk, not to gamble, not to treat animals cruelly and not to do anything

that is incompatible with the conduct of a gentleman." *Dictionary of American Biography*, XII, 214-15.

12. Edmund A. Ogden had served in the Black Hawk, Florida, and Mexican Wars. He served at Fort Leavenworth from 1849-1852. Ogden died in August 1855. Cullum, *Register*, I, 486-87.

13. Actually, Majors began hauling freight from Independence to Santa Fe in August 1848. In 1855 he, William H. Russel and William B. Waddell formed their partnership. One of their more glamorous enterprises was the short lived "Pony Express." *Dictionary of American Biography*, XII, 214-15.

14. Johnston commanded the Department of Utah from August 1857-November 1860. During the Civil War he was a Confederate. Johnston was killed at Shiloh 6 April 1862. Cullum, *Register*, I, 368.

15. Albert L. Magilton, Class of 1846, won brevets at Contreras and Churubusco. After serving on the frontier for several years he resigned in December 1857. During the Civil War, Magilton saw action in Virginia as a Colonel, 4th Pennsylvania Reserve Volunteers. Ibid., II, 269-70.

16. Alexander Byrdie Dyer, a Virginian was brevetted at Santa Cruz de Rosales during the Mexican War. He remained with the Union in the Civil War becoming Chief of Ordnance, U.S. army. He served in this capacity until 1874. Cullum, *Register*, 665.

17. Neither the Masons, nor Randolph Harrison Dyer can be identified.

18. Longworthy cannot be identified.

19. William Hoffman served with the 6th Infantry during the Black Hawk and Mexican Wars. He won brevets at Contreras, Churubusco, and Molino del Rey. Until the Civil War Hoffman served on the frontier. During the war he served as Commissary General of Prisoners. Cullum, *Register*, I, 433.

20. Tohausen (Little Mountain) later turned hostile. In 1859 he resisted Bent's efforts at effecting a treaty and led the Kiowa against the whites during the Civil War. Grinnell, *The Fighting Cheyennes*, 92, 118.

21. These Indians cannot be identified.

Chapter XI

1. Probably this was Philip R. Thompson, Class of 1835, who

was cashiered in 1855 for appearing as a witness at a court martial while drunk. Cullum, *Register*, I, 616.

2. As mentioned in the Introduction, another version of this incident is that two civilians, William Bent and Thomas Fitzpatrick, averted the massacre. Grinnell, *The Fighting Cheyennes*, 109.

3. John Heth was born on 6 June 1833. He was sutler at Fort Atkinson and later at Fort Kearney. *Book of Nancy Vanderhoof*, 85; and Grinnell, *The Fighting Cheyennes*, 110.

4. Robert H. Chilton, Class of 1837, later served in the Confederate Adjutant General's Office and as Lee's Chief of Staff. Chilton signed the famous lost order of the Sharpsburg campaign. Eliot, *West Point in the Confederacy*, 315.

5. This action occurred on 3 March 1851. List of Campaigns, Henry Heth, Heth Papers, 5071, University of Virginia.

6. Casey cannot be identified.

7. Heth reported an incident of this nature which occurred during the summer of 1851. Letter, Henry Heth to the Adjutant General, 4 September 1851, Adjutant General's Office Letters Received Book, 1851, 341H1851, National Archives.

Chapter XII

1. Robert Johnston, a Virginian, served under Magruder during the Civil War and later commanded the Confederate Cavalry at Yorktown. Eliot, *West Point in the Confederacy*, 365.

2. Grattan, an irresponsible hothead, provoked a fight with the Brule, Oglala, and Minneconjou Sioux in the summer of 1854 about nine miles east of Fort Laramie. The following year Harney led a punitive expedition against the Sioux. Grinnell, *The Fighting Cheyennes*, 100, 103-5.

3. Lovell was transferred to Fort Hamilton, New York, in the fall of 1851. Cullum, *Register*, II, 122.

4. John Baptist Lamy was born in France. In 1848 the Pope transferred ecclesiastical jurisdiction of New Mexico to the United States and named Lamy vicar apostolic to New Mexico. The nuns were Sisters of Loretto from Kentucky. *Dictionary of American Biography*, X, 566-67.

Chapter XIII

1. Frederick Grant was born 30 May 1850. Lewis, *Captain Sam Grant*, 291.

2. Grant bought the "Chicote mare" for $250 in 1849. The ice course was on the River Rouge near Dearborn. Ibid., 280.

3. Thomas Fitzpatrick was agent for the Upper Platte Agency. In the summer of 1851 he had negotiated a treaty with most of the larger plains tribes at Horse Creek, 35 miles west of Fort Laramie. Grinnell, *The Fighting Cheyennes*, 96.

4. In the Whig convention of 1852 Botts cast the only Southern vote for Winfield Scott on the first ballot. *Dictionary of American Biography*, II, 472.

5. Shirley was the girlhood home of Anne Carter, Robert E. Lee's mother. It is about 18 miles from Richmond. Frances A. Christian and Susan W. Massie, *Homes and Gardens in Old Virginia* (Richmond: Garret and Massie, 1950), 210-11.

6. Heth reported Fitzpatrick's distribution of supplies and the threat to the garrisons in Texas early in November 1852. Letter, Henry Heth to the Adjutant General, 6 November, 1852, subject: Indian Relations. Adjutant General's Office Letters Sent Book, 1852, 481H 1855, National Archives.

7. Probably this was Thomas K. Jackson, a South Carolinian. He served as an escort officer for trains going to Texas and the Southwest from 1849 to 1851. Cullum, *Register*, II, 359.

Chapter XIV

1. Crooked Creek begins about 10 miles south of Fort Atkinson and flows south into the Cimmaron. *Commercial Atlas*, 171.

2. Aquila Talbot Ridgeley, a Marylander, was Assistant Surgeon, U.S. Army from June 1851 to June 1861. Heitman, *Historical Register*, I, 830.

3. Fort Riley is approximately 300 miles northeast of Fort Atkinson and 102 miles southwest of Fort Leavenworth. Rand McNally, *Commercial Atlas*, 171.

4. Henry W. Wharton, an Alabaman, joined the 6th Infantry as a second lieutenant in 1837. During the Civil War he served as

Colonel, 2d Delaware Infantry until his retirement in 1863. Heitman, *Historical Register*, I, 1022.

5. Edward J. Steptoe, Class of 1837, was actually leading the 9th Infantry to Washington Territory. Cullum, *Register*, I, 689.

6. William Scott Ketchum, Class of 1834, served in the 6th Infantry until June 1860. During the Civil War he served initially as Acting Inspector General, Department of the Missouri. From November 1862 until he retired in 1870 Ketchum served on various War Department auditing boards. He died in Baltimore on 28 June 1871. Cullum, *Register*, I, 583-85.

7. Heth testified during the trial at Annapolis in the fall of 1871. Heth Papers, 5071, University of Virginia.

8. Heth assumed command at Fort Kearny on 20 June 1854. Letter, Henry Heth to the Adjutant General, 20 June 1854, subject: Asumption of Command, Army Commands, Fort Kearny Letters Sent Book, 1848-1855, National Archives.

9. Richard Henry Alexander was an Assistant Surgeon, U.S. Army from 2 December 1853 to March 1865. Heitman, *Historical Register*, I, 156.

10. Fort Laramie is now Laramie, Wyoming; Fort Kearny is in present-day Nebraska. *Times Atlas*, V, Plate 108.

11. The order was issued on 24 November 1854; there was a delay of several months pending Wharton's arrival. Report, Commanding Officer, Jefferson Barracks to the Adjutant General, 4 November 1854, subject: Appointment of Regimental Quartermaster, Adjutant General Letters Received Book, 1854, No. 30, National Archives.

12. Cooke, a Virginian, and J. E. B. Stuart's father-in-law, served many years in the pre-Civil War cavalry. In 1854 and 1855 he commanded Fort Leavenworth. During the Civil War he commanded a Cavalry Division in the Army of the Potomac. Cullum, *Register*, I, 398.

13. Heth was the first man in his class to make captain. In fact, after his promotion on 3 March 1855 only 16 members of the preceding class ranked him. Cullum, *Register*, II, 249-343.

14. Samuel Cooper was Adjutant General, U.S. Army from 15 July 1852 to 7 March 1861. Although a New Yorker he joined the Confederacy and served as Adjutant and Inspector General throughout the war. Eliot, *West Point in the Confederacy*, 318.

15. Grimsley cannot be identified.

16. Nathan Augustus Monroe Dudley was appointed First Lieutenant, 10th Infantry, on 3 March 1855. During the Civil War he served as a Colonel, 30th Mass. Infantry, and won a brevet to brigadier in the volunteers. Heitman, *Historical Register,* I, 386.

17. Deshler, an Alabaman, graduated from West Point in 1854. He joined the 10th Infantry as a second lieutenant on 3 March also. Deshler served on frontier duty until 1861. As a Confederate he served under Holmes at Goldsboro and later under Bragg in Tennessee. Eliot, *West Point in the Confederacy,* 327.

18. The command left Fort Leavenworth on 5 August 1855. J. P. Dunn, Jr., *Massacres of the Mountains: A History of the Indian Wars of the Far West 1815-1875.* (New York: Archer House, 1958), 206.

19. Stewart Van Vliet, a New Yorker, had been Captain, Assistant Quartermaster, since June 1847. During the Civil War he served as Chief Quartermaster, Army of the Potomac. Van Vliet was brevetted Major General, U.S. Army in March 1865. Cullum, *Register,* II, 31.

20. Joseph Tesson was a long-time trapper employed as a guide for the expedition. Grinnell, *The Fighting Cheyennes,* 104.

Chapter XV

1. The Harney expedition reached the camp at Ash Hollow on 2 September. Julius C. Morton, *History of Nebraska* (Lincoln: Jacob North & Co., 1907), II, 150-51.

2. Albion P. Howe commanded Company G., 4th Artillery; Heth commanded Company E, 10th Infantry. Harney's official report states that Howe did not take part in the pursuit. *Ibid.*

3. Marshal S. Howe, Class of 1827, served with the dragoons up to the Civil War. During the war he was a colonel in the 3rd U.S. Cavalry. Heitman, *Historical Register,* I, 547-48.

4. Wirz was tried and executed in November 1865. Boatner, *Civil War Dictionary,* 941-42.

5. Edward McK. Hudson was a First Lieutenant, 4th Artillery, at this time. During the Civil War he was aide to McClellan. Cullum, *Register,* II, 388.

6. Aaron B. Hardcastle, a Marylander, joined the 6th Infantry as a second lieutenant in June 1855 and served until 1861. During the Civil War he was a colonel in the 33rd and 34th Mississippi

Volunteers. Heitman, *Historical Register,* I, 499. Tutt cannot be identified.

7. This was probably Sir Henry Hardinge, Viscount Hardinge of
Lahore. He served under Wellington, later saw service in India, and
finally rose to be master general of the ordnance. Leslie Stephens and
Sidney Lee (eds.) *The Dictionary of National Biography,* (London:
Oxford University Press, 1950), VIII, 1227.

8. Heth submitted his report in June 1856. It was forwarded to
the Adjutant General and the Chief of Ordnance. Letter, Henry Heth
to Captain Pleacannon, Adjutant, 10th Infantry, 10 June 1856, subject:
Report on system of target practice. Adjutant General Letters Received
Book, 1856, No. 32, National Archives.

9. The distance from Fort Pierre on the west bank of the Missouri
in South Dakota to Fort Snelling on the outskirts of Minneapolis is
approximately 360 miles. *Times Atlas,* V, Plate 108.

10. Sanders cannot be identified.

11. Edward R. S. Canby served at various frontier posts in the
mid- and southwest until the Civil War. During the war he saw service
in the New Mexico and Trans-Mississippi Departments as a Brevet
Major General, U.S. Volunteers. Cullum, *Register,* II, 18-19.

12. Charles F. Smith became Lieutenant Colonel, 10th Infantry,
in March 1855 and remained with the regiment until 1861. During
the Civil War he fought at Fort Donelson as a Major General, U.S.
Volunteers. Smith died in April 1862. Cullum, *Register,* I, 354-55.

13. Lavinia married Fitzallen Deas, an officer in the U.S. and
later the Confederate Navy. *William and Mary Quarterly* (new series),
VII, 195.

14. Harriet C., "Teny," Selden was the daughter of Miles Cary
Selden and Harriet Heth, sister of John Heth. Douglas Vanderhoof,
Book of Nancy Selden Vanderhoof, 12-13.

15. Edward D. Blake, a South Carolinian, was a first Lieutenant,
8th Infantry, at this time. During the Civil War he served as a staff
officer under Polk and E. Kirby Smith. After June 1863 he was chief
of the conscription bureau in Nashville. Eliot, *West Point in the Confederacy,* 362.

16. John C. Kelton, a Pennsylvanian, was a First Lieutenant, 6th
Infantry, at this time. During the Civil War he served as an adjutant
general, becoming Assistant Adjutant General, U.S. army, in July
1862. Kelton won a brevet as brigadier general in March 1865. Cullum, *Register,* II, 459-60.

17. Johnston was a First Lieutenant, 1st Dragoons. In the Civil War he commanded the 2d Confederate Cavalry. Eliot, *West Point in the Confederacy*, 365.

18. Pegram was a First Lieutenant, 2d Dragoons. During the early part of the Civil War he served under Bragg but joined the Army of Northern Virginia in August 1863. Pegram fell at Hatcher's Run in February 1865. Ibid., 406-7.

19. Heth requested duty in Washington in May 1857. Letter, Henry Heth to the Adjutant General, 15 May 1857, subject: Request for duty. Adjutant General Letters Received Book, 1857, No. 33, National Archives.

20. The board convened on 17 August 1857; Lieutenant Colonel B. L. Beall, 1st Dragoons, was president. The report of this board stated: "the board are (sic) of the unanimous opinion that the breech-loading rifle submitted by A. E. Burnside is best suited for the military service." Ben-Perley Poore, *The Life and Public Services of A. E. Burnside* (Providence: J. A. & R. A. Reid, 1882), 83-85.

21. Burnside resigned on 2 October 1853, Cullum, *Register*, II, 320.

22. McClellan was then president of the Illinois Central. Burnside took a job as a cashier in the Railroad Land Office on 27 April 1858. Poore, *A. E. Burnside*, 88.

23. Heth is in error. See note 8.

24. Heth submitted his system to the Adjutant General on 8 February 1858. Floyd approved it for use in the field on 1 March. Letter, Henry Heth to the Adjutant General, 8 February 1858, subject: System of target practice, with 1st Indorsement by Secretary of War, 1 March 1858. Adjutant General's Office Files, Record Group 94 (37H), National Archives.

25. Louis H. Marshall, a nephew of Robert E. Lee, was at this time a First Lieutenant, 10th Infantry. During the Civil War he remained with the Union, serving as Pope's aide from 1861 to 1865. Cullum, *Register*, II, 399; and Douglas S. Freeman, *Lee's Lieutenants* (New York: Charles Scribner's Sons, 1943), II, 21.

26. Johnston arrived in Salt Lake City in the spring of 1858. John K. Herr and Edward S. Wallace, *The Story of the U.S. Cavalry, 1775-1942* (Boston: Little, Brown & Co., 1953), 84.

27. Hector MacLean, the outraged husband, killed Parley Parker Pratt on 13 May 1857 near Fort Gibson, Arkansas. Hubert H. Ban-

croft, *The History of Utah* (San Francisco: The History Co., 1890), 546.

28. Captain Fancher's train of immigrant Texans reached Salt Lake City in August 1857. From there they took the southern route through Provo, Fillmore, and Cedar City. Dunn, *Massacres of the Mountains*, 253.

29. The train made camp at Mountain Meadows on 3 September. *Ibid.*, 225.

30. Lee's command consisted of a band of Pah-Utes and some Mormons disguised as Indians. Ibid., 257.

31. The actual date may have been any time from the 10-12 September. Ibid., 263.

32. Lee was finally convicted in 1876. Two previous attempts to bring him to justice in 1859 and 1875 failed. He was executed at Mountain Meadows at the site of the massacre on 23 March 1877. *Dictionary of American Biography*, XI, 115.

Chapter XVI

1. John Cradlebaugh became a justice in the Utah Territory in June 1857. His jurisdiction included the southern counties of Utah. Cradlebaugh conducted an investigation of the Mountain Meadow Massacre. Hubert L. Bancroft, *History of Utah* (San Francisco: The History Co., 1890), 500, 539-40.

2. Provo is located near the western base of the Wasatch Mountains. Ibid., 310.

3. Heth reported this incident through channels in March 1859. Letter, Henry Heth to Commanding Officer, Utah Department, 28 March 1859, subject: Record Group Attack by mob. Adjutant General Letters Received Book, 1859, No. 35, National Archives.

4. Gabriel R. Paul joined the 7th Infantry after graduating from West Point in 1837. He won a brevet at Chapultepec. During the Civil War Paul served in New Mexico and later with the Army of the Potomac as a Brigadier General, U.S. Volunteers. Cullum, *Register*, I, 575.

5. Orson Pratt, a native of Hartford, New York, was a younger brother of Parley P. Pratt, Orson became an apostle in April 1835. *National Cyclopaedia of American Biography*, XVI, 17.

6. Orson Hyde became an apostle in February 1835. In August 1850 Hyde, along with Brigham Young and Heber C. Kimball, laid out the city of Ogden. He became a probate judge in Utah in 1855. Bancroft, *History of Utah,* 111, 307.

7. Kimball, a Vermonter, became a Mormon in April 1832. He was named a member of the Council of Twelve in February 1835. Kimball went to Europe in 1837 and while in England preached the first Mormon discourse ever heard in England. *National Cyclopaedia of American Biography,* XVI, 17.

8. D. W. Patten, popularly known as "Captain Fearnot," organized the Danites in 1837. They were a secret terrorist society. Bancroft, *History of Utah,* 124-25.

9. While Heth exaggerates Brigham Young's power and personal wealth and ignores the positive accomplishments of the Mormons in Utah, his accounts of the Mountain Meadows Massacre, the Danites, and the organization of "Deseret," the Mormon theocracy, are accurate. Bancroft, *History of Utah,* III, 124-25, 539-40; Dunn, *Massacres of the Mountains,* 257-69; and *Britannica,* XIII, 760.

10. Alfred Cummings accepted the appointment as Governor of the Utah Territory in June 1857. He attempted to mediate between the Mormons and the military authorities. Ibid., 500, 526-27.

11. Probably this was Sir Richard Francis Burton, an officer of the Indian Army. He made the pilgrimage to Mecca in 1833 disguised as a Pathan. In 1854 Burton and Captain J. H. Speke explored the Somaliland. During this expedition Burton made a journey to Harrar, the capital, alone, becoming the first white man to enter it. In 1858 Burton and Speke explored Tanganyika. Speke and James A. Grant traced the Nile to its source in 1860; Burton, however, did not accompany them. *Encyclopaedia Britannica,* IV, 446-47; and X, 633.

12. Neither won. This championship fight took place in England on 17 April 1860. John Camel Heenan, the American contender, and Tom Sayers, the English champion, fought for 42 rounds. Since the referee left before the end of the fight, neither man was declared the winner, and both received belts. Henry Downes Miles, *Pugilistica, The History of British Boxing* (Edinburgh: John Grant, 1906), III, 422.

13. Heth left Camp Floyd on 9 October 1860. Letter, Henry Heth to the Adjutant General, 26 November 1860, subject: Request for extension of leave. Adjutant General Records, Record Group 94 (289H), National Archives.

14. Edward B. Alexander, was Colonel, 10th Infantry from 3

March 1855 until I May 1863. During the Civil War he served as Assistant Provost Marshal General, Superintendent of Recruiting, and Chief Mustering and Dispersing Officer for Missouri. Cullum, *Register*, I, 317.

15. George H. Crossman remained quartermaster general for the Utah Department until September 1860. During the Civil War he served as a quartermaster in Philadelphia and later as Chief Quartermaster, Department of the East. Ibid., 315-16.

16. John Dunovant enlisted in Company B of the Palmetto Regiment, South Carolina Volunteers, in December 1847. He became a captain in the 10th Infantry in March 1855. During the Civil War Dunovant rose to be a brigadier general. He was killed at Vaughn Road, Virginia on 10 October 1864. Heitman, *Historical Register*, 389.

17. Heth resigned on 17 April 1861. Special Order 199, 27 April 1861 announced his separation from the U.S. Army. Letter, Henry Heth to the Adjutant General, 17 April 1861, subject: Resignation. Adjutant General Records, Record Group 94 (189H), National Archives.

18. Robert J. Garnett was a member of the 9th Infantry at this time. He resigned from the U.S. Army on 30 April 1861. Garnett was killed at Carrick's Ford, West Virginia on 13 July 1861. Eliot, *West Point in the Confederacy*, 343.

19. Edwin J. Harvey was then a First Lieutenant, 9th Infantry. He resigned from the U.S. Army on 15 March 1861. Throughout the Civil War Harvey served as an inspector general. Heitman, *Historical Register*, I, 508.

20. Heth received an appointment as Major of Infantry, Confederate State Army on 27 April 1861, with date of rank, 16 March 1861. Register of Appointments, Confederate States Army. Confederate Archives, Chapt. I, No. 88, National Archives.

21. William Booth Taliaferro, former Major, 9th Infantry, and commander of the militia during John Brown's raid on Harper's Ferry, led the expedition to Norfolk in April 1861. Warner, *Generals in Grey*, 297.

22. Floyd had been Governor of Virginia from 1848-1852. He served as Buchanan's Secretary of War from 1857 to 29 December 1860. Floyd became a Confederate brigadier on 23 May 1861. Ibid., 90.

23. Wise was elected to Congress in 1833. He served as Minister

to Brazil from 1844-1847 and as Governor of Virginia from 1856 to 1860. Wise became a Confederate brigadier on 5 June 1861. Ibid., 341-42.

Chapter XVII

1. General Order 33, Headquarters Virginia Forces, 31 May 1861 assigned Heth to Floyd's command. *War of the Rebellion A Compilation of the Official Records of the Union and Confederate Armies,* LI, 121. (cited hereafter as *O.R.*)

2. Colonel John W. Lowe, 12th Ohio Regiment, attacked Wise at Scary Creek near Charleston, West Virginia, on 17 July 1861. Ned Bradford (ed.), *Battles and Leaders of the Civil War,* (New York: The Century Co., 1914), I, 139.

3. They met on 6 August. Douglas S. Freeman, *Robert E. Lee* (New York: Charles Scribner's Sons, 1934), I, 581.

4. Floyd's command moved to Carnifix Ferry on 21 August 1861. *O.R.,* LI, 243.

5. This mountain is in Fayette County, West Virginia, approximately 30 miles northwest of Lewisburg. Rand McNally, *Commercial Atlas,* 465.

6. This regiment actually was the 7th Ohio. Erastus B. Tyler, a New York Businessman, assumed command in April 1861. Later he became a brigadier of U.S. Volunteers. Boatner, *Civil War Dictionary,* 855.

7. Floyd and Heth routed Tyler at Cross Lanes on 26 August. *Battles and Leaders,* I, 143.

8. William S. Rosecrans, then in command of the Department of the Ohio, marched south from Clarksburg, West Virginia on 8 September. Freeman, *R. E. Lee,* I, 584-85.

9. Hawk's Nest is about 12 miles southwest of Carnifix Ferry.

10. Rosecrans launched his assault on Carnifix Ferry in the afternoon of 10 September. Ibid.

11. Floyd withdrew to the south bank on the night of 10-11 September. *Battles and Leaders,* I, 145.

12. Jacob D. Cox at this time commanded the "Brigade of the Kanawha." Later he commanded the IX Corps at Sharpsburg and the 3rd Division, XXIII Corps, in the Franklin, Nashville, and North Carolina Campaigns. Boatner, *Civil War Dictionary,* 205-6.

13. The council took place on 16 September. Freeman, *R. E. Lee,* I, 585.

14. Floyd's headquarters was at Meadow Bluff, Greenbrier County, 16 miles west of Lewisburg. Muddy Creek is several miles southeast of Meadow Bluff. Freeman, *R. E. Lee,* I, 586; and Rand McNally *Commercial Atlas,* 405.

15. Lee arrived at Meadow Bluff on 21 September. Freeman, *R. E. Lee,* I, 587.

16. Daniel, some-time editor of *The Richmond Examiner,* was more adept with the pen than the sword. He softened the severity of camp life by carrying around two slaves and an elaborate set of equipage. In the summer of 1862 Daniel was wounded in the right arm, enabling him to declare himself incapacitated for further field service. *Dictionary of American Biography,* V, 67.

17. Cotton Hill is in Fayette County approximately 18 miles northwest of Sewell Mountain. Rand McNally, *Commercial Atlas,* 465.

18. Heth and the other brigade commanders recommended to Floyd that they evacuate the Cotton Hill position on 4 November; Floyd, however, refused to consider it. *O.R.* LI, 368-371.

19. The pursuit from Cotton Hill to Raleigh County, Virginia occurred from 12 to 16 November 1861. Cullum, *Register,* I, 661.

20. Heth apparently is in error. Neither Cullum, the *Rebellion Records,* nor Boatner indicates that Benham was court-martialed for this action. Benham was arrested, relieved of command, and reduced for his failure at Secessionville in June 1862. Boatner, *Civil War Dictionary,* 58-59.

Chapter XVIII

1. Heth reported to Richmond in November 1861. Return, 45th Virginia Regiment, 31 November 1861. Confederate Records 19076, 45-1-5-5. Virginia State Library Archives.

2. Sterling "Pop" Price had been a brigadier in the Mexican War. He served under McCulloch in the Wilson's Creek Campaign, August to November 1861. Price became a major general on 6 March 1862. Boatner, *Civil War Dictionary,* 699.

3. Ben McCulloch, a former Texas Ranger and Indian fighter, had served at San Jacinto and in the Mexican War. As a colonel of Texas state troops he received Twigg's surrender in 1861. McCulloch

commanded the Confederate forces at Wilson's Creek and was killed at Pea Ridge on 7 March 1862. Warner, *Generals in Grey,* 200.

4. The disputes regarding Heth's appointment occurred in early December 1861. *O.R.,* VIII, 701; and LIII, 761-62.

5. Heth made brigadier on 6 January 1862 and assumed command at Lewisburg on 6 February. Register of Appointments, Confederate States Army, January 6-12, 1862. Confederate Archives, No. 86; and General Order No. 1, District of Lewisburg, 6 February 1862, National Archives.

6. Johnston, a classmate of R. E. Lee, was appointed General, Confederate State Army, on 31 August 1861. Samuel Cooper, Albert Sidney Johnston, and R. E. Lee ranked him. Johnston wrote his famous letter on 12 September, and Davis replied on the 14th. Hudson Strode, *Jefferson Davis Confederate President* (New York: Harcourt Brace Co., 1955), II, 156-57.

7. Heth is mistaken. Varina Anne Jefferson Davis, "Winnie," was born on 27 June 1864. *Dictionary of American Biography*, V, 145.

8. Finney had formerly served as assistant adjutant general under Heth in the Army of Kanawha. *O.R.,* LI, 369.

9. Miles Selden was "Teny's" brother. Vanderhoof, *Book of Nancy Selden Vanderhoof,* 13.

10. Stockton Heth was Henry's youngest brother. Ibid., 82.

11. The battle took place on 10 May. *O.R.,* XII, 491.

12. Hayes visited Richmond in the fall of 1877. Hamilton J. Eckenrode, *Rutherford B. Hayes Statesman of Reunion* (New York: Dodd Mead Co., 1930), 259.

13. David M. Key, a Tenneesean and former Confederate, was a member of Hayes' first cabinet. *Dictionary of American Biography*, VIII, 447.

14. Hayes was colonel of the 23rd Ohio at this time. He became a brevet major general in March 1865. Ibid.

15. Crook's 44th Ohio Volunteers routed Heth on 23 May 1862. *O.R.,* XII, 804.

16. Heth arrived in Chatanooga on 1 July 1862. *O.R.,* XVI, 717.

17. George Washington Morgan, a Mexican War veteran, commanded the 7th Division, Army of Ohio, at this time. Boatner, *Civil War Dictionary,* 565-66.

18. Jefferson Columbus Davis led the 3rd U.S. Division at Pea Ridge. He shot William "Bull" Nelson on 29 September 1862 after

an argument. Nelson was in command of the Army of Kentucky at the time of his death. Boatner, *Civil War Dictionary*, 227, 586.

19. Preston Smith was then in temporary command of Cleburne's Division. Joseph Howard Parks, *General Edmund Kirby Smith C. S. A.* (Baton Rouge: Louisiana State University Press, 1954), 213-16.

20. The Battle of Richmond took place on 30 August 1862. The actual Federal losses were: 206 killed, 844 wounded, 4303 captured or missing. Ibid.

21. Kirby Smith entered Lexington on 2 September. Ibid.

22. Heth started on 6 September. *O.R.*, XVI, 933.

23. Kirby Smith issued the order on 10 September. Ibid., 807.

24. Braxton Bragg commanded the Army of the Tennessee at this time. He and Buell fought an inconclusive battle at Perryville on 8 October. Don C. Seitz, *Braxton Bragg General of the Confederacy* (Columbia, S.C.: The State Co., 1924), 192-200.

25. Don Carlos Buell commanded the Army of the Ohio at this time. He resigned from the service in June 1864, following the investigation of his campaign in Tennessee and Kentucky. Cullum, *Register*, II, 96-7.

26. Bragg notified Kirby Smith of his decision not to interfere with Buell's movements on 21 September. Parks, *Edmund Kirby Smith*, 229.

27. Kirby Smith reached Mount Sterling on 25 September. Ibid., 233.

28. Richard Hawes' inaugural ceremony was interrupted on 1 October by Buell's troops approaching from Louisville. Ibid., 233.

29. On the morning of 9 October Bragg fell back toward Harrodsburg where Kirby Smith joined him on the 10th. Bragg initially agreed with Kirby Smith's recommendation that they fight Buell at Harrodsburg, but later he changed his mind and began to withdraw on the morning of 11 October. Ibid., 237-38.

Chapter XIX

1. Special Order No. 14, Adjutant and Inspector General's Office, 17 January transferred Heth to the Army of Northern Virginia. *O.R.*, XX, 499.

2. Kirby Smith commanded a brigade at Manassas. He was shot from the saddle on 21 July. Parks, *Edmund Kirby Smith*, 132-35.

3. Moss Neck is about 10 miles southeast of Fredericksburg. William W. Hassler, *A. P. Hill, Lee's Forgotten General* (Richmond: Garrett and Massie, 1957), 125.

4. The V, XI, and XII Corps began the march to Kelly's Ford on 27 April. The II Corps marched toward Banks' Ford on the same day. The crossings began on 28 April. John Bigelow, *The Campaign of Chancellorsville* (New Haven: Yale University Press, 1910), 173-74, 183.

5. The II Corps moved at 11 A.M. 1 May, Robert Emmett Rodes, VMI, Class of 1848, leading the advance. Raleigh Edward Colston, also Class of 1848, VMI, brought up the rear with Trimble's Division. Freeman, *Lee's Lieutenants*, II, 531-35; and Warner, *Generals in Grey*, 58-59; 263.

6. Troops of O. O. Howard's XI Corps detected Jackson's move, but neither Hooker nor Howard believed they were in danger. Boatner, *Civil War Dictionary*, 137.

7. Heth refers to Jackson's deployment which began at 3 P.M., 2 May. Freeman, *Lee's Lieutenants*, II, 555-57.

8. Rodes attacked at 5:15 P.M. Ibid., 558.

9. As pointed out in the Introduction, this statement is in error. Lane's brigade did become engaged. Hassler, *A. P. Hill,* 137.

10. Melzi Chancellor's is also referred to as Dowdall's Tavern. Ibid., 560n.

11. Catherine Furnace is about two and a half miles southwest of Chancellorsville. Martin Schenck, *Up Came Hill* (Harrisburg: The Stackpole Co., 1958), 247.

12. A shell fragment or minie ball grazed the calves of Hill's legs, temporarily paralyzing him. Hassler, *A. P. Hill,* 139.

13. On the morning of 3 May the Light Division was in two lines across the Plank Road west of Chancellorsville. Archer was on the extreme right of the first line with his front refused as Heth describes. Samuel McGowan's Brigade was on Archer's left. James H. Lane's Brigade was between McGowan and the Plank Road. Dorsey Pender's Brigade was on Lane's left, north of the Plank Road, Heth's Brigade, commanded by Colonel J. N. Brockenbrough, formed the second line; it was deployed across the road. Bigelow, *Chancellorsville,* 346-47.

14. Heth refers to Archer's seizure of Hazel Grove, a key terrain feature about a mile southwest of Chancellorsville. Schenck, *Up Came Hill,* 255.

15. The new battalion organization of the Confederate artillery was a significant factor. "Never in the annals of the Army of Northern Virginia had so great a concentration of guns been effected so quickly or with comparable ease." Freeman, *Lee's Lieutenants*, II, 589, 591-92.

16. Hancock commanded the II Corps at Chancellorsville. Cullum, *Register,* II, 210.

17. This is not altogether accurate. Jackson's Corps, now under J. E. B. Stuart, still had heavy fighting to do before securing Chancellorsville on the morning of 3 May. Freeman, *Lee's Lieutenants,* II, 644.

18. The last of Hooker's troops withdrew during the night of 5 May. Ibid., 644.

19. Ewell was promoted to lieutenant general on 23 May and given command of Jackson's Corps. Hill was appointed on 24 May and assigned to command the new III Corps. Ibid., 696-99.

20. Heth made major general on 24 May 1863. Register of Appointments, Confederate States Army, Chap. I, File No. 86, Confederate Archives, National Archives.

21. The division was organized on 30 May 1863. J. J. Pettigrew's 1st Brigade consisted of the 11th, 26th, 47th, and 52nd North Carolina Regiments. J. M. Brockenbrough's 2nd Brigade included the 40th, 47th, 55th, and 22nd Virginia Regiments. J. A. Archer commanded the 3rd Brigade consisting of the 5th and 13th Alabama Regiments, and the 1st, 7th, and 14th Tennessee. J . R. Davis's 4th Brigade was composed of the 2nd, 11th, and 42nd Mississippi, and the 55th North Carolina. *O.R.,* XXV, 840; and XXVII, 288, 289.

22. Rodes of Ewell's Corps crossed the Potomac on 14 June. Hill's Corps forded the Potomac at Shepherdstown on 25 June. Freeman, *Lee's Lieutenants,* III, 27; and Hassler, *A. P. Hill,* 149.

23. Cashtown is northwest of Gettysburg. Freeman, *Lee's Lieutenants,* III, 77.

24. Archer led the van along the Chambersburg Pike. Davis's, Pettigrew's, and Brockenbrough's Brigades followed in that order. Ibid., 78.

25. Willoughby Run is about a mile and a half from Gettysburg. Ibid., 80.

26. John Buford commanded the Cavalry Division, Army of the Potomac, at this time. Cullum, *Register,* II, 353.

27. These were troops of the "Iron Brigade" of John J. Reynold's I Corps. Freeman, *Lee's Lieutenants,* III, 80; and *O.R.* XXVII, 243-57.

28. George Gordon Meade became commander of the Army of the Potomac on 28 June 1863. Cullum, *Register,* I, 602.

29. William F. Fox, *Regimental Losses in the American Civil War* (Albany: Brandow Printing Co., 1899).

30. Colonel H. K. Burgwyn, commander of the 26th North Carolina, was killed on 1 July. Colonel John R. Lane replaced him. Walter Clark (ed.), *Histories of the Several Regiments and Battalions from North Carolina in the Great War 1861-65* (5 Vols. Goldsboro, N.C.: Nash Bros., 1901) II, 335.

31. LaFayette Guild was Medical Director, Army of Northern Virginia. *O.R.* (Ser. 2), IV, 798.

32. Captain Joseph J. Young was Quartermaster, 26th North Carolina, at Gettysburg. *Histories of North Carolina Regiments,* V, 600.

33. Thomas A. Smyth, an Irishman, commanded the 2d Brigade of Alexander Hay's 3rd Division. Hancock commanded II Corps until wounded on 3 July. William Hays succeeded him. Boatner, *Civil War Dictionary,* 189, 389, 777.

34. Captain Romulus M. Tuttle commanded Company F, 26th N.C. *Histories of the North Carolina Regiments,* V, 599.

35. This was Captain Francis W. Bird. Ibid., 131.

36. At Gettysburg the 26th NC lost 708 killed, wounded and missing. Fox, *Regimental Losses,* 569.

37. Two of Heth's brigades, Brockenbrough's under the command of Robert M. Mayo and Joseph R. Davis's formed the left flank elements of the assault force. They fell back without orders. Freeman, *Lee's Lieutenants,* III, 160.

38. Longstreet said: "That your division, with bloody noses after its severe fight on the 1st, was put in to do a great part in the assault of the 3rd was a grievous error. The opinion expressed on the field that day that not less than thirty thousand fresh troops supported by the other corps could make a successful assault on the field of the 3rd is justified by the events and doubly shows that your division should not have been ordered as a part of the column to march a mile under concentrated fire and carry a position held by veterans four times our number, very strongly posted." Letter, Longstreet to Heth,

14 February 1897, Heth Papers, MC 3H480, Confederate Museum, Richmond.

39. Heth's Division lost 420 killed, 2116 wounded, and 1534 missing during the period, 1-3 July inclusive. Report of Casualties in the Battle of Gettysburg, MC 3H480, Confederate Museum, Richmond.

40. Heth covered the rear during the crossing at Falling Waters from the night of 13-14 July until noon of 15. Freeman, *Lee's Lieutenants,* III, 167.

41. The skirmish at Falling Waters occurred on 14 July. *O.R.* XXVII, 639-42.

42. Heth, as indicated in the Introduction, also suffered a subsequent cavalry attack. Altogether he lost two guns and about 5,000 stragglers before returning to Virginia. Freeman, *Lee's Lieutenants,* III, 167.

43. This was the Federal III Corps crossing at Broad Run. *O.R.* XXIX, 919.

44. The Orange and Alexandria Railroad ran northeast from Culpeper through Bristoe Station. Freeman, *Lee's Lieutenants,* III, 240.

45. Warren's II Corps was concealed in the railroad cut. Ibid., 244.

46. Heth attacked with Cooke's and Kirkland's Brigades astride the Greenwich Road. Ibid.

47. Heth lost an aggregate of 1361 men and a battery of McIntosh's Battalion which was supporting the attack. *O.R.* XXIX, 430-32, 433. Freeman, *Lee's Lieutenants,* III, 270.

48. Mine Run crosses the Old Turnpike about 12 miles northeast of Orange Court House.

49. Warren had originally recommended an attack. Ibid., 273.

50. Warren, then commanding V Corps, was relieved by Sheridan who charged him with dilatory leadership at Five Forks. The court exonerated Warren, but its findings were not made public until 1881. Boatner, *Civil War Dictionary,* 891-92.

Chapter XX

1. Grant crossed the Rapidan at Germanna and Ely's Fords about

10 miles northwest of Fredericksburg. Freeman, *Lee's Lieutenants,* III, 347.

2. Ewell marched northeast along the Old Turnpike leading from Orange to Fredericksburg. Hill marched parallel along the Orange Plank Road. Longstreet initially marched northwest along Brock's Bridge Road. At its intersection with the Orange Plank Road he turned right and marched northeast. Ibid., 346.

3. These were patrols of the 5th New York and 3rd Pennsylvania Cavalry. Ibid., 351.

4. The Confederates deployed at about 1 o'clock, 5 May. Ibid.

5. This was George Washington Getty's 2nd Division, VI Corps. *O.R.,* XXXVI, 677.

6. Getty's report of 13 October states: "Their lines outflanked the division, and though forced back some distance in the center, they held in the main their ground, and repulsed every attack." Ibid.

7. John M. Jones's brigade, Johnston's Division, made contact at about 11 A.M. Ibid., 349.

8. Freeman relates the same incident, maintaining that Hill's disability was possibly psychosomatic. *Lee's Lieutenants,* III, 353-54.

9. At 5 A.M. the 3rd and 4th Divisions of Hancock's II Corps and the 2d Division of Sedgewick's VI Corps attacked. Ibid., 355.

10. Heth's and Wilcox's regiments broke and ran. Ibid.

11. Freeman relates this conversation using Heth's *Memoirs* as a basis. Ibid., 398.

12. This is also known as the "Mule Shoe." Ibid., 410.

13. This was George Hume "Maryland" Steuart. Ibid.

14. Freeman also recounts this conversation. Ibid., 398.

15. Heth's division was driven twice before the enemy fell back across the Po. Also, as pointed out in the Introduction, the Federals withdrew under orders from higher headquarters. Ibid., 392-93.

16. The North Anna is 23 miles north of Richmond. Ibid., 496.

17. The skirmish at Bethesda Church occurred on 2 June 1864. Burnside commanded the IX Corps and Warren the V. Boatner, *Civil War Dictionary,* 163.

18. The III Corps crossed on the night of 17 June. Freeman, *Lee's Lieutenants,* III, 535.

19. This was W. F. "Baldy" Smith, commander of the Federal XVIII Corps, Benjamin F. "Beast" Butler's Army of the James. Boatner, *Civil War Dictionary,* 109, 775.

20. Actually Wise's brigade was also present, and Hoke's leading

brigade arrived on the night of the 15th. Possibly, Heth is confusing this action with that of the 9th when a force of old men, freeman, young boys, and convicts staved off a Federal attack on Petersburg. *Lee's Lieutenants*, III, 518, 528-29.

Chapter XXI

1. This was in the vicinity of Globe Tavern south of Petersburg. Freeman, *Lee's Lieutenants*, III, 588.

2. Heth refers to Mahone who commanded the flanking force. This account, as stated in the Introduction, conflicts with that of Orlando B. Willcox, the Union brigadier who received the assault. He states: "Mahone, who was best acquainted with the woods, burst in on Ayres's right and swept down on Crawford in column of fours, carrying off Crawford's skirmishers, and seizing parts of the main line, and compelling Ayres's right and Crawford's line to fall back." Hassler, A. P. Hill's biographer substantiates Willcox's version which is certainly more in keeping with Mahone's aggressiveness than Heth's story. Possibly, Heth succumbed to understandable jealousy of his fellow division commander. *Battles and Leaders*, IV, 568; and Hassler, *A. P. Hill*, 216-17.

3. Mahone made this attack, delivered, according to Freeman, "furiously but in vain" Freeman, *Lee's Lieutenants*, III, 589.

4. This was probably Major Ben Ficklen who served with John Wilkinson aboard the *Robert E. Lee*. Robert Carse, *Blockade: The Civil War at Sea* (New York: Rhinehart and Co., 1958), 125, 126.

5. The anecdote concerning Heth's wife and the horse together with the gap in the line is also set forth in Freeman, *R. E. Lee*, III, 530; and John B. Gordon, *Reminiscences of the Civil War* (New York: Charles Scribner's Sons, 1903), 379-80.

6. William Johnson Pegram, an artillerist, was John Pegram's younger brother. Freeman, *Lee's Lieutenants*, III, xliv.

7. Hancock's II Corps attempted to cut the Weldon Railroad at Reams Station approximately five miles south of Petersburg. Heth and Cadmus Wilcox of A. P. Hill's III Corps, Army of Northerm Virginia, attacked from the south while Wade Hampton's dismounted troopers assaulted the Federal left flank. Pegram's eight guns were so placed that they could enfilade the Federal flank and rear at close range. Wilcox made the initial assault and failed. At about 5 P.M. after Pegram's

guns had further softened the Federal position Heth led Lane's, Cooke's, and MacRae's brigades in a successful assault on the Federal right. The Unionists were routed. Heth personally placed the standard of the 26th N.C. on the Federal breastworks. Hancock lost 2,742 men, 12 stand of colors, and nine field pieces. Hassler, *A. P. Hill,* 226-27; and Boatner, *Civil War Dictionary,* 683.

8. Sheridan with three cavalry divisions participated along with the II and V Federal Corps. The battle began on 30 March. Pickett suffered a costly defeat. Freeman, *Lee's Lieutenants,* III, 662-71.

9. Horatio G. Wright's VI Corps had shattered Heth's lines at 4:40 A.M. A. P. Hill was killed while en route to Heth's position. Ibid., 678-80.

Chapter XXII

1. Irvin McDowell was adjutant general of the 6th Military Department at that time. Cullum *Register,* I, 711.

2. Braxton Bragg was then a captain in the 3rd Artillery, Ibid., 663.

3. John "Hindquarters" Pope commanded the Department of the Missouri from 27 June 1865 to 6 August 1866. Ibid., II, 126.

4. On 3 June 1862 Pope telegraphed Halleck: "The roads for miles are full of stragglers from the enemy, who are coming in in squads. Not less than 10,000 are scattered about, who will come in in a day or two." On 4 June Halleck, on the strength of this optimistic forecast wired Stanton that Pope had captured thousands of prisoners and that thousands more were throwing down their arms. In short, both had dreams which did not materialize. Kenneth P. Williams, *Lincoln Finds a General* (New York: The MacMillan Co., 1952), 419-20.

5. In May 1866 Heth leased a portion of Norwood, his father-in-law's farm. Letter, Burnside to Heth, 22 May 1866, Heth Papers, 5071, University of Virginia.

6. George Sykes, commander of Sykes's "Regulars" during the war, was in charge of the District of the Rio Grande and Fort Brown, Texas, from December 1877-10 April 1881. Cullum, *Register,* II, 140-41.

7. John C. Bates, Charles Oscar Bradley, Thomas William Lord, William Henry Hamner, John B. Rodman, and John F. Huston were

all junior officers in the 20th Infantry during Sykes's tenure. Heitman, *Historical Register,* I, 199, 238, 496, 642, 841, 559.

8. Bates made brigadier on 4 May 1898. Heitman, *Historical Register,* I, 199.

9. William R. Maize joined the 20th as a second lieutenant in April 1870. Ibid., 685.

10. John Sherman, Secretary of the Treasury, attempted to win the Republican nomination in 1880. *Dictionary of American Biography,* XVII, 84-67.

11. Georgetown is on Winyah Bay near the coast. It is 55 miles northeast of Charleston. The Pee Dee and Waccamaw Rivers empty into the bay near Georgetown. Rand McNally, *Commercial Atlas,* 391.

12. L. Q. C. Lamar appointed Heth on 26 June 1885. Indian Office Executive Appointment Register, 199, National Resources Records Division, National Archives.

13. Heth resigned in June 1889. Bureau of Indian Affairs, 16987, National Resources Division, National Archives.

14. Heth assisted in the 11th Indian Census of 1890. He began work on 22 May. Bureau of Indian Affairs, National Resources Records Division, National Archives.

15. Francis A. Walker, *History of the Second Army Corps In The Army Of The Potomac* (New York: Charles Scribner's Sons, 1886), 598-99.

16. Ibid., 602.

Chapter XXIII

1. Rockbridge Baths and Springs are about ten miles north of Lexington in Rockbridge County. Rand McNally, *Commercial Atlas,* 445.

2. Agnes was Robert E. Lee's oldest daughter. *Dictionary of American Biography,* II, 121.

3. Heth was a special agent for the Washington Life Insurance Company at this time. *Richmond City Directory,* 1877-78, Virginia State Library, Richmond.

4. John G. Parke had commanded the 3rd Division at Sharpsburg. Later he was Burnside's chief of staff and subsequently commanded IX Corps in the Army of the Tennessee. Boatner, *Civil War Dictionary*, 619.

5. Before the Civil War Sherman had been superintendent of a military school in Alexandria, Louisiana. Ibid., 750.

6. John Randolph Tucker, a Confederate naval officer, commanded the *Patrick Henry*, the wooden fleet at Drewry's Bluff, and the Confederate ironclad *Chicora*. Ibid., 851.

7. This could be either Matt Whitaker Ransom or his younger brother Robert. Both were North Carolinians and generals in the Army of Northern Virginia. Ibid., 253-54.

8. This is probably John B. Gordon; however, it could be George Washington Gordon, one of Hood's brigadiers. Warner, *Generals in Grey*, 109, 110.

9. Beverly H. Robertson was Jackson's former cavalry commander and a bitter critic of J. E. B. Stuart. Ibid., 259.

10. Charles W. Field as a brigadier participated in the Seven Days, Cedar Mountain, and Second Manassas. Later he commanded Hood's old division. Ibid., 87-88.

11. Richard Taylor, Zachary's son, went to England in May 1873 and visited the future Edward VII and his wife Alexandra. *Dictionary of American Biography*, XVIII; 340 and *Enclyclopedia Britannica*, VIII, 10.

12. Frederick William of Prussia married Princess Victoria, the daughter of Victoria and Albert. *Encyclopaedia Britannica*, XXIII, 620.

13. This was probably Field Marshall Garnet Joseph Wolseley. Ibid., 700.

14. Apparently Heth refers to Upper Canada College founded by Sir John Colborne, lieutenant governor of Upper Canada, in 1837. *Encyclopedia of Canada*, ed. Stewart Wallace (Toronto: University Associates of Canada, 1937), VI, 220.

15. Goldwin Smith, a fellow of University College, a strong pro-union man in the Civil War, migrated to the United States in 1868 and taught history at Cornell until he moved to Canada in 1871. *Encyclopaedia Britannica*, XX, 831.

16. This is not true. Napoleon III was strongly pro-Southern; however, he did not dare to intervene because of the refusal of the British to cooperate and the hostility of the French people toward the Con-

federacy. Smith in *The United States Political History 1792-1871* discusses the various attitudes toward intervention, but he does not state that Napoleon was on the verge of intervening in 1865. To the contrary, Smith, Owsley and Randall maintain that by that date he had abandoned any idea of aiding the Confederacy.

Frank L. Owsley, *King Colton Diplomacy: Foreign Relations of the Confederate States of America* (Chicago: University of Chicago Press, 1931) 562-78; Goldwin Smith, *The United States Political History 1792-1871* (New York: Macmillan Co., 1893); and J. G. Randall, *The Civil War and Reconstruction,* (New York: D. C. Heath Co., 1937), 646-57.

17. Gordon W. McCabe was William Pegram's adjutant. Freeman, *Lee's Lieutenants,* III, 672-74.

Chapter XXIV

1. Grinell maintains that Cheyenne women were noted for their virtue and the Arapahoes for the reverse. George B. Grinnell, *The Cheyenne Indians: Their History and Way of Life* (New Haven: Yale University Press, 1924), I, 156.

2. This quotation is from the "Treaty With the Tribes Of Middle Oregon" negotiated in 1885 by Joel Palmer, superintendent of Indian Affairs of Oregon Territory. Charles J. Kappler (ed.), *Indian Affairs Laws and Treaties,* (Washington: Government Printing Office, 1904), II, 715.

3. This is an extract from the supplementary treaty negotiated by I. W. Perit Huntington, superintendent of Indian Affairs for Oregon Territory on 15 November 1865, Article 3 of Huntington's treaty provides that Indians leaving the reservation must have written passes. Ibid., 908.

4. Gessner cannot be identified.

5. Old Bark, also known as Ugly Face and Feathered Bear, led the Cheyennes in the 1850's. Grinnell, *The Fighting Cheyennes,* 97n.

6. Heth probably means Old Whirlwind, Feathered Bear's son-in-law, who joined Feathered Bear in a fight with the Sac and Fox in 1854. Ibid., 97.

7. The first volume was published in July 1881. *O.R.,* Serial 120, "General Index and Corrections," x.

8. The final work, Ser. 3, III, was published on 23 June 1900 after Heth's death. Ibid., v.

9. John C. Kelton, Assistant Adjutant General, U.S. army at the time, recommended Heth. He received the appointment and served until October 1894. Letter, John C. Kelton to the Quartermaster General, 14 February 1891, subject: Recommendation of Henry Heth Office of the Quartermaster General Document File, 8586, Record Group 92, National Archives and letter, Henry Heth to the Quartermaster General, 29 October 1894, subject: Enclosure of maps and records. Office of the Quartermaster General Document File, 10048, Record Group 92. National Archives.

10. Robert N. Scott took charge of the work in December 1877. *O.R.*, Serial 120, viii.

11. Henry M. Lazelle succeeded at Scott's death on 5 March 1887. Lazelle served until 2 March 1889. Ibid., xii, xxi.

12. George W. Davis replaced George B. Davis on 1 July 1895 as president of the board. Ibid., xiv.

13. The preface to Serial 120, "General Index and Corrections" states: "the name most closely associated with the work from its inception to its completion is that of Joseph W. Kirkley." Ibid., xxi.

14. Wright, Harvie, Cadmus M. Wilcox, Charles W. Field, Lunsford Lomax, Jed Hotchkiss, and Heth were the former Confederates who assisted in the compilation. Ibid., xi.

15. Van Vliet served many years as a quartermaster officer, retiring in 1881. Wright retired as Chief of Engineers, U.S. Army, in 1884. Flagler commanded Frankford Arsenal in the 1890's. Parke was superintendent of the Military Academy, and Baird was Inspector-General, U.S. Army, at the time Heth wrote the memoirs. Cullum, *Register*, II, 31, 64, 372, 378, 815.

16. Drum served as an adjutant-general throughout the Civil War and afterwards. He retired from the U.S. Army in 1899. Heitman, *Historical Register*, I, 384.

17. Kelton was Adjutant General, U.S. Army, at the time Heth wrote his memoirs Williams was serving as an Assistant Adjutant-General, U.S. Army; Ruggles was Adjutant-General, Department of Texas; MacFeely was Commissary General of Subsistence; Morgan was an Assistant Commissary General of Subsistence; Perry was Assistant Quartermaster General, Department of the Pacific; Wilcox was Governor of the Soldiers' Home, Washington; and Mason was

teaching school in Chester, Pa. Cullum, *Register*, II, 311, 313, 450, 454, 460, 585, 624.

18. Burns died in 1892, Gibbon in 1896. Boatner, *Civil War Dictionary*, 107.

19. See Heth's chapters on West Point.

20. Edward McK. Hudson retired in 1870 after long service as an inspector general. Cullum, *Register*, II, 388. "Old Rucker" probably refers to Daniel Henry Rucker mentioned earlier in the same paragraph. Rucker saw long service as a quartermaster officer until he retired as a brigadier general in 1882. Heitman, *Historical Register*, I, 849.

Chapter XXV

1. The effort to determine Heth's occupation while in Raleigh was fruitless: however, he mentions Col. James L. Corley, then in the insurance business: Furthermore, Heth took up the same business on his return to Richmond. It therefore seems probable that he was an insurance agent in Raleigh.

2. The Battles, Hoggs, Blunts, Heywoods, Barringer, Simons, and Mason cannot be identified precisely. After the war Hoke became an iron mine developer and a director of the Richmond and Danville Railroad. Cox practiced law, participated in state politics, served in Congress, and was appointed Secretary of the U.S. Senate in 1892. Samuel Ashe (ed.), *Biographical History of North Carolina From Colonial Times to the Present*. (2 Vols., Greensboro, N.C.: Charles L. Van Noppen, 1905), I, 321, 226-34.

3. Cooke's Brigade consisted of the 1st, 27th, 46th, 48th, and 55th North Carolina Regiments while McRae's was composed of the 11th, 26th, 44th, 47th, and 52nd Regiments from the same state. *O.R.*, XLVI, 1272.

4. Mrs. Abby Horne House, "Aunt Abby the Irrepressible," was a native of Franklin County, N.C. After Appomattox she walked back to Greensboro and is reputed to have cooked the last meal Jefferson Davis ate in North Carolina. Archibald Henderson, *North Carolina The Old North State and the New* (Chicago: Lewis Publishing Co., 1941), II, 289.

5. Robert Mitchell Saunders served as minister plenipotentiary to Spain from 1846 to 1850. *Biographical History of North Carolina*, III, 393.

6. Johnson commanded the 1st Maryland Regiment (Confederate) at First Manassas during Jackson's Valley Campaign. Johnson was responsible for the burning of Chambersburg, Pennsylvania. He died in Amelia County on 5 October 1903. Warner, *Generals in Grey*, 156-57.

7. Corley had been Chief Quartermaster, Army of Northern Virginia, since June 1862. After the war he was an insurance agent in Raleigh, North Carolina and Norfolk. He died in March 1882. Eliot, *West Point in the Confederacy*, 318.

8. Heth, Carter, and B. C. Gray visited Hays in July 1877. Richmond, *The State* (newspaper), 21 July 1877, 1.

9. Joseph E. Johnston was chief marshal. Heth was his principal assistant during the ceremony on 26 October 1875. John Esten Cooke, *Stonewall Jackson A Military Biography* (New York: D. Appleton and Co., 1876), 574.

10. The Hill monument was unveiled on 31 May 1892. *The Richmond Dispatch*, 31 May 1892, 1.

11. Davis was buried at Hollywood on 31 May 1893. Heth was an honorary pall bearer as well as commander of visiting troops. *The New York Times*, 1 July 1893, 5.

12. Kemper was governor from 1873-1877. Lyon G. Tyler (ed.), *Encyclopedia of Virginia Biography*, (New York: Lewis Historical Publishing Co., 1915), III, 4.

13. After the Civil War Anderson was president of the Tredegar Iron Works. His son Archer served on the executive committee of the Virginia Historical Society for many years. Eliot, *West Point in the Confederacy*, 290; and *Virginia Magazine of History and Biography*, X, xvi.

14. John Montague is probably J. H. Montague, president of the Merchants and Planters Bank. Palmer, A. P. Hill's chief of staff, was a Richmond banker after the war. Uncle George was probably George S. Palmer, a commission merchant. Minor organized the historical department of the Society of Alumni, University of Virginia; after the war he practiced law in Richmond. Haxall was a flour miller. Willie Trigg is probably William R. Trigg, clerk. Paige, a cousin of Robert E. Lee, practiced law in Richmond after the war. Since there are fifteen listings for Wise in the *Richmond City Directory*,

1870-71, it is impossible to make a precise identification. *Richmond City Directory, 1870-71,* 12, 120, 157. Ibid., *1874-75,* 114. *Encyclopedia of Virginia Biography,* I, 336. Ibid., III, 208, 317, 371-2.

15. Cullen was Longstreet's medical director; he practiced in Richmond after the war. Chamberlain was a grocer and liquor dealer. Aubin L. Boulware was a director of the Southern Railroad and the president of two Richmond banks. McCaw taught at the Medical College of Virginia. Williams, a lawyer, also served as president of the Westmoreland Club and headed R. E. Lee Camp No. 1, Confederate Veterans. Daniel was a district attorney in Washington, D.C. Randolph Barksdale was a physician; his brother George served as Vice-Consul to Uruguay. Branch was a banker and a commission merchant. Cranz was a liquor dealer. Mr. Ott was probably William Ott, bookkeeper for the First National Bank of Virginia. Dooley was a lawyer and a rail and construction magnate. There were too many Peytons and Wellfords to permit precise identification. Cary was associated with Heth in the Piedmont Life Insurance Company from 1869 to 1871. Tyler, *History and Genealogy Magazine,* X, 63, 65. *Richmond City Directory 1870-71,* 19, 31, 38, 119. *Encyclopedia of Virginia Biography,* I, 482. Ibid., III, 171, 241, 246, 258, 261, 292. *William and Mary Quarterly,* (1st Ser.), XIII, 173.

16. Charles Minnegerode, D.D., was Rector of St. Paul's in Richmond until 1894. *The Church Almanac of 1888* (New York: Charles Pott Co., 1888); 86; and *Journal of the Special Council of the Protestant Episcopal Church in Virginia, 1894* (Richmond: Wm. E. Jones, 1894), 3.

17. This could be either George Peterkin or his father Joshua. Both were Rectors of St. James Episcopal Church in Richmond. *Encyclopedia of Virginia Biography,* III, 335.

18. This may have been Reverend M. D. Hoge, pastor of the Second Presbyterian Church. *Richmond City Directory, 1870-71,* 80.

19. This was probably James M. M. Davis, Class of 1868, University of Virginia, a great-great-grandnephew of Jefferson. He practiced law in Richmond after the Civil War. *Students of the University of Virginia* (Baltimore: Charles Harvey and Co., 1878), (no page number).

20. William L. "Buck" Royall was a lawyer. Watkins was a clerk. *Richmond City Directory, 1871-72,* 22, 144.

21. Heth was president of the Westmoreland Club when it was founded in March 1877. *The Constitution and By-laws of the West-*

moreland Club of Richmond Virginia (Richmond: Bell Book and Stationery Co., 1909), 2.

22. This was possibly George Byrd Harrison, M.D., a Richmond physician. Harrison died in July 1898. *Virginia Magazine of History and Biography,* XXXVII, 81.

23. McKim had been an aide to George Steuart during the Civil War. McKim wrote *Westmoreland County, Va., 1653-1912 and The Soul of Lee.* Ibid., XX, 448; XXVI, 437; and XXX, 96.

Bibliography

Books

Alexander, E.P. *Military Memoirs of a Confederate*. New York: Charles Scribner's Sons, 1912.

American History Atlas. Maplewood, N. J.: C.S. Hammond, 1953.

Ashe, Samuel A. (ed.) *Biographical History of North Carolina From Colonial Times to the Present*. 5 Vols. Greensboro, N.C.: Charles L. Van Noppen, 1905.

Ayres, Anne. *The Life and Work of William Augustus Muhlenberg*. New York: Anson D. Randolph and Co., 1883.

Bache, Richard Meade. *Life of General George Gordon Meade, Commander of the Army of the Potomac*. Philadelphia: Henry T. Coates Co., 1897.

Bancroft, Hubert H. *History of Utah*. San Francisco: The History Co., 1890.

Bandel, Eugene. *Frontier Life in the Army, 1854-1861*. Glendale, Cal.: The Arthur H. Clark Co., 1932.

Bartholomew, John (ed.) *The Times Atlas of the World*. London: The Times Publishing Co., 1957.

Basso, Hamilton. *Beauregard The Great Creole*. New York: Charles Scribner's Sons, 1933.

Bigelow, John W., Jr. *The Campaign of Chancellorsville*. New Haven: Yale University Press, 1910.

Bill, Alfred H. *Rehearsal for Conflict: The War With Mexico, 1846-1848*. New York: Alfred A. Knopf, 1947.

Boatner, Mark M. *The Civil War Dictionary*. New York: David McKay Co., 1959.

Bradford, Ned (ed.) *Battles and Leaders of the Civil War*. 4 Vols. New York: The Century Co., 1914.

Caldwell, J.F.J. *The History of a Brigade of South Carolinians Known First as Gregg's and Subsequently as McGowan's Brigade*. Marietta, Ga.: Continental Book Co., 1951.

Carse, Robert. *Blockade: The Civil War at Sea*. New York: Rhinehart Co., 1958.

Catton, Bruce. *Glory Road*. Garden City, N.Y.: Doubleday and Co., 1954.

The Centennial of the United States Military Academy at West Point New York, 1802-1902. 2 Vols. Washington: Government Printing Office, 1904.

Christian, Frances A. and Susan W. Massie, *Homes and Gardens in Old Virginia*. Richmond: Garrett and Massie, 1950.

The Church Almanac of 1888. New York: Charles Pott Co., 1888.

Clark, Walter (ed.) *Histories of the Several Regiments and Battalions from North Carolina in the Great War, 1861-65*. 5 Vols. Goldsboro, N.C.: Nash Bros., 1901.

Cockrell, Monroe F. and Bell Irvin Wiley (eds.) *Gunner With Stonewall: Reminiscences of William Thomas Poague*. Jackson, Tenn. McCowat-Mercer Press, Inc., 1957.

Cooke, John Esten. *Stonewall Jackson: A Military Biography*. New York: D. Appleton and Co., 1876.

Cox, Jacob D. *Military Reminiscences of The Civil War*. 2 Vols. New York: Charles Scribner's Sons, 1900.

Cullum George W. *Biographical Register of the Officers and Graduates of the United States Military Academy at West Point, New York*. 3 Vols. New York: James Miller, 1868.

Davis, Jefferson. *The Rise and Fall of the Confederate Government*. 2 Vols. New York: D. Appleton and Co., 1881.

Dowdey, Clifford. *Lee*. Boston: Little, Brown and Co., 1965.

Duffus, H.L. *The Santa Fe Trail*. New York: Longmans, Green Co., 1930.

Dunaway, Wayland F. *Reminiscences of a Rebel*. New York: Neale Publishing Co., 1913.

Dunn, J. P. *Massacres of the Mountains: A History of the Indian Wars of the Far West, 1815-1875*. New York: Archer House, Inc., 1958.

Eckenrode, Hamilton J. *Rutherford B. Hayes, Statesman of Reunion*. New York: Dodd Meade and Co., 1930.

Eliot, Ellsworth, Jr. *West Point in the Confederacy*. New York: C. D. Baker Co., 1941.

Elliott, Charles W. *Winfield Scott the Soldier and the Man*. New York: The MacMillan Co., 1937.

Evans, Clement A. (ed.) *Confederate Military History*. 13 Vols. Atlanta: Confederate Publishing Co., 1899.

The Family of Armistead of Virginia. Boston: David Clapp and Sons, 1899.

Flournoy, H.W. (ed.) *Calendar of Virginia State Papers and other Manuscripts*. 11 Vols. Richmond: (no publisher), 1893.

Forester, Frank. *Horse and Horsemastership*. 2 Vols. New York: Stringer and Townshend, 1857.

Forman, Sidney. West Point: *A History of the United States Military Academy*. New York: Columbia University Press, 1950.

Fox, William F. *Regimental Losses in the American Civil War*. Albany: Albany Publishing Co., 1893.

Freeman, Douglas Southall. *Lee's Lieutenants*. 3 Vols. New York: Charles Scribner's Sons, 1949.

——————. *Robert E. Lee*. 4 Vols. New York: Charles Scribner's Sons, 1934.

Fuller, John F.C. *The Generalship of Ulysses S. Grant*. London: John Murray, 1929.

Furniss, Norman F. *The Mormon Conflict, 1850-1859*. New Haven: Yale University Press, 1960.

Ganoe, William A. *The History of the United States Army*. (Revised). Ashton, Md.: Eric Lundberg, 1964.

Goodrich, Frederick E. *The Life and Public Services of Winfield Scott Hancock*. Boston: Lee and Shepard, 1880.

Gordon, John B. *Reminiscences of the Civil War*. New York: Charles Scribner's Sons, 1903.

Grant, Ulysses S. *Personal Memoirs*. 2 Vols. New York: Charles L. Webster, 1885.

Grinnell, George B. *The Cheyenne Indians*. 2 Vols. New Haven: Yale University Press, 1924.

——————. *The Fighting Cheyennes*. New York: Charles Scribner's Sons, 1915.

Hafen, Leroy R. and W. J. Ghent. *Broken Hand: The Life Story of Thomas Fitzpatrick*. Denver: The Old West Publishing Co., 1931.

Hamersly, T.H.S. *Complete Regular Army Register of the United States For One Hundred Years (1779-1879)*. Washington: T.H.S. Hamersly, 1880.

Harman, George D. *Sixty Years of Indian Affairs: Political, Economic, and Diplomatic, 1789-1850*. Chapel Hill: University of North Carolina Press, 1941.

Hassler, William W. *A.P. Hill: Lee's Forgotten General*. Richmond: Garrett and Massie, 1957.

Heatwolfe, Cornelius J. *A History of Education in Virginia*. New York: The MacMillan Co., 1916.

Heitman, Francis B. *Historical Register and Dictionary of the United States Army*. 2 Vols. Washington: Government Printing Office, 1903.

Henderson, Archibald. *North Carolina: The Old North State and the New*. 2 Vols. Chicago: Lewis Publishing Co., 1941.

Henderson, G.F.R. *Stonewall Jackson*. New York: Longmans, Green, and Co., 1949.

Henry, Reginald B. *Genealogies of the Families of the Presidents*. Rutland, Vt.: The Tuttle Co., 1935.

Herr, John K. and Edward S. Wallace. *The Story of the U.S. Cavalry, 1775-1942*. Boston: Little, Brown and Co., 1953.

History of the Second Corps in the Army of the Potomac. New York: Charles Scribner's Sons, 1886.

Johnson, Richard W. *Reminiscences in Peace and War*. Philadelphia: J.D. Lippincott Co., 1886.

Johnson, R.V. and C.C. Buel (eds.) *Battles and Leaders of The Civil War*. 4 Vols. New York: The Century Co., 1914.

Johnston, Charles H.L. *Famous Scouts*. Boston: L.C. Page Co., 1910.

Journal of the Special Council of the Protestant Episcopal Church in Virginia, 1894. Richmond: W.E. Jones, 1904.

Kappler, Charles J. (ed.) *Indian Affairs, Laws and Treaties*. 2 Vols. Washington: Government Printing Office, 1904.

Kennedy, Mary Selden. *The Seldens of Virginia and Allied Families*. Frank Allaben Genealogical Co., 1911.

Lavender, David. *Bent's Fort*. Garden City, N.Y.: Doubleday and Co., 1954.

Lee, Fitzhugh. *General Lee*. Great Commanders Series, Vol. IV. New York: D. Appleton, 1894.

Lewis, Lloyd. *Captain Sam Grant*. Boston: Little, Brown and Co., 1950.

Livermore, Thomas L. *Numbers and Losses In The Civil War In America, 1861-1865*. 2nd ed. Boston: Houghton-Mifflin, 1901.

Lonn, Ella. *Desertion During The Civil War*. Gloucester, Mass.: Peter Smith, 1966.

Maury, Dabney H. *Recollections of a Virginian in the Mexican, Indian, and Civil Wars*. New York: Charles Scribner's Sons, 1894.

Miers, Earl Schenck and Richard A. Brown (eds.) *Gettysburg*. New Brunswick: John Grant, 1906.

Mitchell, Joseph B. *Decisive Battles of the Civil War*. New York: Fawcett World Library, 1965.

Morrison, Alfred J. *The Beginnings of Public Education in Virginia, 1776-1860*. Richmond: State Board of Education, 1917.

Morton, Julius C. *Illustrated History of Nebraska*. Lincoln, Neb.: Jacob North and Co., 1906.

Napier, William F.P. *History of the War in the Peninsula And in the South of France From A.D. 1807 to A.D. 1814*. 3 Vols. New York: Redfield Co., 1856.

The National Cyclopaedia of American Biography. 20 Vols. New York: James T. White Co., 1904.

Official Register of the United States. Washington: Government Printing Office, 1903.

Parks, Joseph H. *General Edmund Kirby Smith, C.S.A.* Baton Rouge: Louisiana State University Press, 1954.

Phisterer, Frederick. *Statistical Record of the Armies of The United States*. Supplementary Vol. Campaigns of the Civil War. New York: Charles Scribner's Sons, 1887.

Pickett, LaSalle Corbell. *Pickett and His Men*. Philadelphia: J.B. Lippincott Co., 1913.

Poore, Ben-Perley. *The Life and Public Services of Ambrose E. Burnside*. Providence, R.I.: J.A. and R.A. Reid, 1882.

Porter, Horace. *Campaigning With Grant*. New York: The Century Co., 1906.

Pratt, Fletcher. *A Short History of The Civil War*. New York: Bantam, 1968.

Rand McNally Commercial Atlas. 91st ed. New York: Rand-McNally and Co., 1960.

Reavis, L.U. *The Life and Military Service of General William Selby Harney*. St. Louis: Bryan, Brand and Co., 1878.

Register of Graduates and Former Cadets, United States Military Academy, 1949 and 1963 issues. West Point: West Point Alumni Foundation.

Robinson, Doane, *A History of the Dakota or Sioux Indians*. Minneapolis: Ross and Haines, Inc., 1956.

Schenck, Martin. *Up Came Hill*. Harrisburg, Pa.: The Stackpole Co., 1958.

Seitz, Don C. *Braxton Bragg, General of the Confederacy*. Columbia, S.C.: The State Co., 1924.

Selden, Edna Mae. *Selden and Kindred of Virginia*. Richmond: Virginia Stationery Co., 1941.

Seymour, Flora Warren. *Indian Agents of the Old Frontier*. New York: D. Appleton-Century Co., 1941.

Smith, Justin H. *The War With Mexico*. 2 Vols. New York: The MacMillan Co., 1919.

Strode, Hudson. *Jefferson Davis: American Patriot, 1808-1861*. New York: Harcourt, Brace, 1955.

————. *Jefferson Davis: Confederate President*. New York: Harcourt, Brace, 1959.

Strong, George S. *Cadet Life at West Point*. Boston: T.O.H.P. Burnham Co., 1862.

Students of the University of Virginia. Baltimore: Charles Harvey Co., 1878.

Tebbel, John and Keith Hennison. *The American Indian Wars*. New York: Bonanza, 1950.

Thomason, John W. *JEB Stuart*. New York: Charles Scribner's Sons, 1948.

Tyler, Lyon G. (ed.). *Encyclopedia of Virginia Biography*. New York: Lewis Historical Publishing Co., 1915.

Utley, Robert M. *Frontiersmen in Blue: The United States Army and The Indian, 1848-1865*. Macmillan Wars of the United States. New York: Macmillan Co., 1967.

Vandiver, Frank. *Mighty Stonewall*. New York: McGraw-Hill Co., 1957.

Walker, Francis A. *General Hancock*. New York: D. Appleton Co., 1897.

Warner, Ezra B. *Generals in Grey*. Baton Rouge: Louisiana State University Press, 1955.

Weigley, Russell F. *History of The United States Army*. Macmillan Wars of the United States. New York: The Macmillan Co., 1967.

Welch, Spencer G. *A Confederate Surgeon's Letters To His Wife*. Marietta, Ga.: Continental Book Co., 1954.

Wheeler-Bennett, John W. *A Wreath to Clio, Studies in British, German, and American Affairs*. London: St. Martin's Press, 1967.

White, Leonard D. *The Jacksonians, A Study in Administrative History, 1828-1861*. New York: Free Press, 1954.

Williams, Kenneth P. *Lincoln Finds a General*. New York: The Macmillan Co., 1952.

Williams, T. Harry, *P.G.T. Beauregard: Napoleon in Grey*. Baton Rouge: Louisiana State University Press, 1955.

Wright, Marcus J. *General Officers of the Confederate Army*. New York: Neale Publishing Co., 1911.

Young, Otis E. *The West of Philip St. George Cook*. Western Frontiersman Series, Vol. V. Glendale, Cal.: Arthur H. Clark, 1955.

Younger, Edward (ed.) *Inside the Confederate Government: The Diary of Robert Garlick Hill Kean*. New York: Oxford University Press, 1957.

Manuscripts

Annual Reunion, U.S. Military Academy, 12 June 1900. U.S. Military Academy Archives.

Adjutant's Letter Book, Nos. 1 and 2, U.S. Military Academy Archives.

Ayres, Romeyn B. MSS. U.S. Military Academy Archives.

Boitnott, John W. "Secondary Education in Virginia," unpublished PH.D. dissertation. University of Virginia, 1935.

"Circumstances of Parents of Cadets, 1842-1879." U.S. Military Academy Archives.

"Descriptive List of New Cadets, 1833 to 1868." U.S. Military Academy Archives.

Forty-Fifth Virginia Regiment of Volunteers, Rosters for 1861. Confederate Records, 19076 45-1-1-4. Virginia State Library.

Gibson, Horatio G. "History of the Class of 1847, USMA." U.S. Military Academy Archives.

Heth, Henry Papers. Fourteen letters, 1863-1892; five battle reports, 1863-1865; three U.S. Army commissions; diaries (Miles Selden) 14 March 1869-23 April 1873; and Bill, U.S. Senate, 45th Cong., 2nd. Sess., 14 March 1878. University of Virginia.

Heth, Henry, MSS. Eight letters, 1847-1853. Virginia Historical Society.

Interior Branch, Social and Economic Records Division, Bureau of Indian Affairs. Record Group 75, National Archives.

Lee, Robert E., MSS. Headquarters Papers, 1855-78. Virginia Historical Society.

McClellan, Henry Brainerd, MSS. Letter, 27 March 1875, and five newspaper clippings, September-December 1877, *Weekly Times* (Philadelphia). Virginia Historical Society.

Morrison, James L., Jr. "The United States Military Academy, 1833-1866: Years of Progress and Turmoil," unpublished Ph.D. dissertation, Columbia University, 1970.

Post Orders, Nos. 2 and 3, U.S. Military Academy, U.S. Military Academy Archives.

"Register of Delinquencies, 1843-1847." U.S. Military Academy Archives.

"Staff Records," III and IV. U.S. Military Academy Archives.

"Superintendent's Letter Book," No. 1-1/2 (Part II). U.S. Military Academy Archives.

U.S. Office of Indian Affairs. Index of Letters Received, Vols. E-K, H-L. Record Group 75, National Archives.

U.S. War Department, Adjutant General's Office File. Record Group 94, 1848-1861. National Archives.

U.S. War Department, Adjutant General's Office, Letters Received Books, XXVI-XXXV, 1850-1859. National Archives.

U.S. War Department, Adjutant General's Office, Letters Sent Book, XXIX-XXXVII, 1854-1861. National Archives.

U.S. War Department, Adjutant General's Office, Military Academy File, 152-42. National Archives.

U.S. War Department, Antietam Board, Record Group 92, 10028. National Archives.

U.S. War Department, Army Commands Letters Sent, Fort Kearny, 1844-1855, Record Group 98. National Archives.

U.S. War Department, Confederate Archives, Record Group 109. National Archives.

U.S. War Department. Mexican Dependents, File 12452, 1893-1908. National Archives.

U.S. War Department, Quartermaster General's File, 10048, 1894. National Archives.

Vanderhoof, Douglas, "The Book of Nancy Selden Vanderhoof," unpublished private book, property of Mrs. Douglas Vanderhoof, Richmond, Virginia.

Articles

Brock, Robert A. "Orderly Book of Major William Heth of the Third Virginia Regiment," *Collections of the Virginia Historical Society,* XI (1892), 320-21.

Devitt, Edward I. "Georgetown College in the Early Days," *Records of the Columbia Historical Society,* XII (1909), 21-37.

Drumm, Stella M. "Alexander Majors," *Dictionary of American Biography,* XII, 214-15.

Gunn, Sidney. "Samuel Ward," *Dictionary of American Biography,* XIX, 340-41.

Heth, Henry. "The Gettysburg Campaign - Official Reports," *Southern Historical Society Papers,* VI (December 1878), 258-61.

——————. "Report of the Affair at Falling Waters," *Southern Historical Society Papers,* VII (April 1879), 196-99.

Lee, Ida J. "The Heth Family," *Virginia Magazine of History and Biography,* XLII (July 1934), 273-82.

Mackey, Franklin H. and Charles C. Ivey, "Heth's Obituary," *Confederate Veteran,* VII, No. 12 (1899), 569.

Morrison, James L., Jr. "The Memoirs of Henry Heth, Part I." *Civil War History,* VIII, No. 1 (March 1962), 5-24.

——————. "The Memoirs of Henry Heth, Part II." *Civil War History,* VIII, No. 3 (September 1962), 300-25.

——————. "The Struggle Between Sectionalism and Nationalism at Ante-Bellum West Point, 1830-1861." *Civil War History,* XIX, No. 2 (June 1973), 138-48.

Mosby, John S. "Heth Intended to Cover His Error," *Southern Historical Society Papers,* XXXVII (December 1909), 369-74.

Nevins, Allan, "Rutherford Birchard Hayes," *Dictionary of American Biography*, VIII, 446-51.

Nichols, Jeannette P. "John Sherman," *Dictionary of American Biography*, XVII, 84-8.

Owsley, Frank Lawrence. "William Selby Harney," *Dictionary of American Biography*, VIII, 280-81.

Pearson, C.C. "John Moncure Daniel," *Dictionary of American Biography*, V, 67-69.

Shuster, George N. "John Baptist Lamy," *Dictionary of American Biography*, X, 566-67.

Stephenson, Martha T. "Varina Anne Jefferson Davis," *Dictionary of American Biography*, V, 145-46.

Stephenson, Wendell H. "Richard Taylor," *Dictionary of American Biography*, XVIII, 340-41.

Swift, Eben. "The Military Education of Robert E. Lee," *Virginia Magazine of History and Biography*, XXXV (April 1927), 97-160.

Tyler, Lyon G. "The Armistead Family," *William and Mary College Quarterly Historical Magazine*, VI, (April 1898), 226-34.

Weir, Jeanne Elizabeth, "John Minor Botts," *Dictionary of American Biography*, II, 472-3.

Young, Kimball. "John Doyle Lee," *Dictionary of American Biography*, XI, 114-15.

Newspapers

The New York Times, 1 July 1893.
The Richmond Dispatch, 18 July 1877, 21 August 1877, 29 May 1892, 31 May 1892, 27-28 September 1899.
The Richmond State, 21 July 1877.
The Roanoke Times, 23 May 1960.
The Washington Post, 30 September 1899.
(Washington) *The Evening Star*, 27 September 1899.

Published Letters and Public Documents

Dowdey, Clifford (ed.) *The Wartime Papers of R.E. Lee*. Boston: Little, Brown and Co., 1965.

Freeman, Douglas Southall (ed.). *Lee's Confidential Dispatches to Davis*. New York: G.P. Putnam's Sons, 1915.

General Assembly of Virginia, "Heth Manufacturing Company." *An*

act to incorporate the Heth Manufacturing Company, passed 24 Feb-
ruary 1836.

Official Register of the United States: Containing a List of Officers
and Employees in the Civil, Military and Naval Service on the First
of July, 1883. Washington: Government Printing Office, 1883.

Rowland, Dunbar (ed.). *Jefferson Davis Constitutionalist: His Papers,*
Letters, and Speeches. 10 Vols. Jackson, Miss.: Mississippi Department of Archives and History, 1923.

U.S. Army, Adjutant General. *Official Army Registers, 1847-1861.*

U.S. Commissioner of Indian Affairs. *Fifty-Sixth Annual Report,*
1887. Washington: Government Printing Office, 1887.

U.S. Commissioner of Indian Affairs. *Fifty-Seventh Annual Report,*
1888. Washington: Government Printing Office, 1888.

U.S. Treasury Department, Customs Bureau. Special Agents, Reports
and Correspondence, 1865-1915. Record Group 36, National
Archives.

U.S. Treasury Department. General Records of the Treasury Department, Special Agents and Inspectors Applications. Record Group
56, National Archives.

U.S. War Department. *Annual Reports of the Secretary of War,* 1847-
1861, 1881-1884, 1892.

Virginia Business Directory and Gazetteer and Richmond City Direc-
tory, 1877-1878. Richmond, Chataigne and Gillis, 1877.

War of the Rebellion: A Compilation of the Official Records of the
Union and Confederate Armies. Ser. I, II, and IV. Washington:
Government Printing Office, 1880-1901.

Index

293

Dooly, James, 233
Dooly, Mrs. James, 233
Drewry's Bluff, lii
Drum, R. C., 227
Dublin Depot, xxxix, 159
Ducks, 116, 203
Dudley, N. A. M., 125
Dunovant, John, 149
Dyer, Alexander, 89
Dyer, Henry, 97
Dyer, Randolph Harrison (Harry),
    89–90, 95, 109, 117, 125

Early, Jubal, 1, li, 188–89
Elk Wood (brother-in-law's estate),
    80
Evans, George F., 18
Ewell, Richard, xxii, li, 54, 81, 89,
    172, 174, 182, 183, 187, 189

Falling Waters, xlviii, xlix, lx, 178
Ficklin (Ficklen), Ben, 192–93
Field, Charles W., 210
Finney, Randolph H., 163
Fitzpatrick, Thomas, xxvii, xxviii,
    113, 114
Five Forks, Battle of, 180, 195,
    196
Flagler, D. W., 227
"Flirt" (greyhound), 98
Floyd, Camp, xxxiv, 142, 144,
    146, 147, 148, 149
Floyd, John B., xxxiii, xxxvi–
    xxxvii, 138, 151–59, 160–62
Floyd's Mountain, xxxix
"Fly" (greyhound), 98
Forrest, Edwin, 73
Forrest, Nathan Bedford, xli, lvii
Forts, see names of forts
Fox, William F., 175
Frankfort, Kentucky, 167
Fredericksburg, Virginia, xlv, 182
Freeman, Douglas, lix
Fry, James B., 18

Gaines's Mill, lviii–lix
Galena, Illinois, 210
Garcia, Isabella, 60
Garnett, Robert, 149
Gauley Bridge, 152, 153, 155,
    156
Gauley River, xxxvi, 153, 154,
    156
Georgetown, South Carolina, lxiii,
    205
Georgetown College, xvi, 12
Gessner (Indian Agent), 220
Getty, George Washington, 183
Gettysburg, Battle of, xxxii, xlvi–
    xlvii, xlix, lxii, 56, 173–78,
    181, 195
Gibbon, John, 18, 227
Giles Courthouse, xxxix, 163, 164
Globe Tavern, lii
Gordon, General, 210, 215
Governor's Island, xxvi, 81, 125,
    205
Granger, Captain, 51
Grant, James A., 148
Grant, Ulysses S., xxv, li, lii, liii,
    liv, 18, 62, 111–12, 113, 160,
    181–82, 184, 185, 186, 188,
    189, 190–92, 194, 196–97,
    198–99, 209, 210
Grant, Mrs. Ulysses S., 111, 113–
    14
Grasshoppers, 121
Grattan party, xxxi, 107, 121–22,
    123, 127
Gray, B. C., 231
Great Southern Railway, lxiii
Gregg's Cavalry, lv
Griffin, Charles, 18
Grimsley, ____ , 125
Grymes, Alfred, 39
Grymes, Athenais, 40, 47, 48
Grymes, Edgar, 39
Grymes, John Randolph, 39, 40
Grymes, Mrs. John Randolph, 39, 40